withdrawn

2.99

Rebuilding Community

Also by John Pierson

DICTIONARY OF SOCIAL WORK (*co-author with Martin Thomas*)

Rebuilding Community

Policy and Practice in Urban Regeneration

Edited by

John Pierson
Senior Lecturer
Institute of Social Work and Applied Social Studies
Staffordshire University

and

Joan Smith
Director
Housing and Community Research Unit
Staffordshire University

Consultant Editor: Jo Campling

First published 2001 by
PALGRAVE
Houndmills, Basingstoke, Hampshire RG21 6XS and
175 Fifth Avenue, New York, N. Y. 10010
Companies and representatives throughout the world

PALGRAVE is the new global academic imprint of
St. Martin's Press LLC Scholarly and Reference Division and
Palgrave Publishers Ltd (formerly Macmillan Press Ltd).

ISBN 0–333–74765–8

This book is printed on paper suitable for recycling and
made from fully managed and sustained forest sources.

A catalogue record for this book is available
from the British Library.

Library of Congress Cataloging-in-Publication Data
Rebuilding community : policy and practice in urban regeneration /
edited by John Pierson and Joan Smith.
     p. cm.
  Includes bibliographical references and index.
  ISBN 0–333–74765–8
  1. Urban renewal. 2. Urban renewal—Citizen participation.
  3. Urban policy. 4. Community organization. I. Pierson, John, 1944–
  II. Smith, Joan (Joan M.)
  HT175 .R423 2001
  307.3′416—dc21
                                                        2001021627

10   9   8   7   6   5   4   3   2
10   09   08   07   06   05   04   03   02

Printed in Great Britain by Antony Rowe Ltd, Chippenham, Wiltshire

For Rita Pierson and in memory of Frank C. Pierson
For Ivy Smith and in memory of Reginald Smith

Contents

List of Tables

List of Contributors

Irene Bruegel Co-Director, Local Economy Policy Unit, South Bank University, London

James P. Connell, Director, Institute of Research and Evaluation in Education, Philadelphia

Gary Craig, Professor of Social Justice, University of Hull

Julien Damon, Head of Research, Caisse Nationale des Allocation Familiales, Paris

Karen Fulbright-Anderson, Research Officer, Aspen Roundtable for Comprehensive Initiatives

Anne C. Kubisch, Director, Aspen Roundtable for Comprehensive Community Initiatives

Keith Lawrence, Research Officer, Aspen Roundtable for Comprehensive Community Initiatives, New York City

Chris Miller, Senior Lecturer, University of West of England, Bristol

Peter North, Research Assistant, Local Economy Unit, South Bank University, London

Sarah Pearson, Research Associate, Sheffield Hallam University

Frank C. Pierson, Lead Organizer, South West Industrial Areas Foundation, Tucson, Arizona

John Pierson, Senior Lecturer, Institute of Social Work and Applied Social Studies, Staffordshire University

Joan Smith, Director, Housing and Community Research Unit, Staffordshire University

Rebecca Stone, Research Officer, Chapin Hall Centre for Children, University of Chicago, Chicago

Mercer L. Sullivan, Associate Professor, Rutgers University at Newark

Acknowledgements

The editors would like to thank both the Lipman Miliband Trust and the Staffordshire University Research Initiative for grants that enabled the work on this volume to be completed. They would also like to thank the Local Economy and Policy Unit at South Bank University for hosting a seminar in Autumn 1998 that brought the contributors of this volume together to discuss issues and perspectives. In particular they wish to thank Jo Campling for her considerable help and advice in the preparation of this volume.

John Pierson is extremely grateful to Harold Richman, Joan Wynn and other colleagues at the Chapin Hall Center for Children and Families, University of Chicago, for providing an opportunity in the autumn of 1996 to study the range of comprehensive community initiatives underway in the United States.

1
Introduction

John Pierson and Joan Smith

The concentration of poor people in highly defined urban areas across the developed nations of northern Europe and the United States has given rise to unprecedented levels of academic, governmental and philanthropic attention. Concerns over high rates of crime have fused with fears over the future of the family; fears over environmental degradation and decaying empty properties overlap with decline in educational standards; the sense of loss of 'community' points also toward the political disenfranchisement of citizens. The social devastation that has emerged in some urban areas is taken as the most conspicuous sign of the growing gap between rich and poor. The unspoken query is whether these extremes in wealth can be absorbed or whether national societies will fracture beyond repair as poor urban districts are cut adrift from prosperity.

The search for area-based solutions to urban poverty has thus far produced more questions than answers. Important new concepts such as social capital and social networks have become the focus (and hope) of recent endeavor, both scholarly and in the field, and in turn the subject of intense debate. The field is also extending its range to embrace matters such as the relationship between school and community, the intricacies of effective local job training schemes, community safety and the virtues of mixed income tenancies. Perhaps most importantly the accumulated experience of urban programs, from the 1960s on, have themselves been engulfed by secular trends such as popular support for welfare reform, disenchantment with party politics, experimentation with regionalism, and globalization. For European researchers in particular, the collapse of the state socialist alternative to market capitalism still presents something of an intellectual trauma with the realization that whatever solutions are eventually found, they will emerge in a market-dominated society.

This volume examines the range of new initiatives in community building that are responding to new trends and pressures. Two powerful drivers of the field stand out. One is popular pressure for inclusion, recognition and participation. The other is the growing realization that urban poverty is a complex, inter linked phenomenon that requires a 'comprehensive' or holistic response. It is not easy to reconcile the two. Building a program that recognizes the complexity of urban problems, needing expertise and resources, and at the same time creates pathways of influence for local citizens is an intricate task.

The volume seeks to facilitate international discussion on these points. Its themes are located at the crossroads where the nature of comprehensiveness and the ramifications of popular participation intersect. It brings together a number of contributors from the UK, France and the US. By drawing on together their respective experiences it is hoped to create unexpected links and generate a wider field of possible solutions. The international exchange of ideas, particularly between northern Europe and the US, remains a vital stimulus for future policy and this volume communicates some of the excitement of this important transaction. Within a shared commitment to alleviate the social devastation caused by extreme urban poverty each author proposes, discusses and evaluates programs that bring social justice in our cities a step nearer.

Converging experience

Three new and powerful factors are shaping a common set of experiences. As a consequence a wide but single field of policy and practice in community building is emerging with common themes and common areas of promise.

The first of these is the rise of what Richard Freeman (1999) has called 'the new inequality', which resulted from the social dislocation as industrial economies restructured. Throughout the 1970s and 1980s urban centers in both Britain and the US lost large numbers of manufacturing jobs through plant closures. This proved traumatic for cities dominated by a single industry, whether cars for Detroit and Birmingham (UK), or steel in Sheffield and Pittsburg. In the ten years from 1981 Birmingham lost 70,000 manufacturing jobs while Detroit lost 43,000. But the loss of manufacturing jobs also occurred across the board. London, between 1981 and 1996, lost 212,000 jobs; Philadelphia lost some 100,000. Three quarters of a million male jobs were lost in the UK between 1981 and 1991 (Turok 1999; Office of City Controller of Philadelphia 1999).

The polarized society which emerged from this restructuring has been well documented by Freeman among many in the US and by Power (1997) and others in the UK who charted the social effects of the low-wage, low-skill service economy existing alongside a high-wage, high-skill knowledge economy.

The widespread concern with 'ghettoization' of certain urban areas – the manifest compression of great numbers of citizens, living in poverty, without access to services or employment, and fearful of their surroundings – stretches from the US to Britain and France. The work of William Julius Wilson (1987, 1996) influenced the work of the Social Exclusion Unit in the UK and similar thinking on social exclusion in France (Power 1997). Wilson argued that the 'concentration effects' of geographically contained poverty are distinctive: residents are not only poor, they are without jobs and lose awareness of work discipline. Other trends escalate such as rates of drug-related crime, teenage pregnancy and families headed by lone mothers. This establishes an environment in which employed role models leave and schools underperform. The relative helplessness of young unskilled males when faced with a complex, service-oriented labor market reduces their attraction as partners.

In the UK Anne Power, influenced by Wilson's work, has documented a similar process. She has identified a number of push-pull factors that led to the abandonment of inner city neighborhoods in Europe. Poor services, particularly education, accelerated physical decay, and aggressive, disruptive behavior on the part of some tenants deterred would-be tenants from living on social housing estates. A rapid shift in social balance occurred with the arrival of families and individuals in extreme need for whom the social housing estates were a last resort (Power and Mumford 1999).

A second factor was the dismantling of public housing systems in the 1980s as a consequence of aggressive market policies by central government. The right-to-buy policies introduced in the early 1980s by the Conservative government in Britain, which gave tenants of local authority housing the right to purchase their homes at well-below market rates, wrought certain well-documented changes. Within a short space of time public housing became a residual service where once it had enjoyed significantly mixed tenancies. In the US the 'new federalism' of the Reagan administration combined with drastic cuts in federal monies to cities and the evisceration of the Department of Housing and Urban Development also produced dramatic effects. Public housing projects across the country became characterized by high density, separation from the rest of the city, admission of the very lowest income households and poor property management.

A third factor in common arose when political power began to decentralize in the interplay between federal arrangements and devolution in the 1980s and 1990s. New regional and metropolitan developments were at work in both the US and Europe. In the US power and authority devolved to the states through financial transfers under the Personal Responsibility and Work Opportunity Reconciliation Act while regionalism in Europe and devolution in the UK has reshaped the lines of political authority there. This new federalism shifts power and resources to local and regional units and has combined with widespread implementation of market discipline throughout public services (Hugg 1998).

As a result of these three factors the ecology within which area-based community building programs now take place is very different from that of the past. It is characterized by post-industrial and global modes of production, flexible organizational networks and social polarization between areas, households and individuals. On both sides of the Atlantic there has been a resurgence of oppositional social movements embedded in a range of concerns that touch on local communities. Across many countries protest movements seek to soften the effects of world trade agreements, corporate autonomy, anti-trade union legislation, and financial exclusion. The global protests at the meeting of the World Trade Organization in Seattle in December 1999, provide only the most arresting example of this phenomenon.

The perspective of this volume places less emphasis on the idea of opposition between an 'American model', with its supposed emphasis on the primacy of the untrammeled market, and a 'European model' with its presumed emphasis on public spending and government intervention. Rather, while acknowledging national differences of approach, it find links and commonality as a generator for more effective programs. To categorize any one policy initiative as idiomatic of a particular national model of urban regeneration lacking relevance elsewhere ignores the convergence of thinking taking place in the field. Take the example of the American Community Reinvestment Act (CRA). The CRA compels banks in the US to lend a certain proportion of their assets to borrowers in the local community; indeed banks are monitored precisely on these grounds. Is this simply a component of an 'American model' or a useful tool which would be effective at reversing the trend in the UK where banks are cutting all ties to locality?

There are many areas where programs are beginning to move in parallel. These include training and workforce development schemes, establishing financial intermediaries, and 'housing plus' programs which link community development activities to social housing providers.

This not to deny the relative differences in the capitalisms of Europe and the US or to pretend that there is no further debate required over whether a 'social' or 'economic' model of community building is adopted, but to affirm that these differences are diminishing. The forces of convergence provide powerful reasons to exchange both the middle-range theories behind community-building initiatives and the experience of specific practices.

Area-based urban poverty has become both a global and local, rather than purely a national, matter; responsive programs will have to find the level where they can work most effectively. Citizens are looking for two forms of public authority: small units that can respond to their needs in a way they can control, and regional units that are big enough to have an impact on the direction of economic life. Many experiments are taking place through the rise of small, local units of governance to deal with practical issues at neighborhood level. Thus, across both the UK and the US a rough dialectic seems at work. The aggressive market solutions proposed for the economy and social policy in the 1980s and early 1990s have produced a broad awareness of the limits of the market and a quiet but perceptible drumbeat from the people has arisen for alternative solutions. Globalization has not drowned out this voice (Dionne 1998). Paul Osterman captures this new popular mood: 'In the end people do not want their lives governed by impersonal and atomistic forces, and they eventually seek to limit the scope and power of those forces. Sometimes the market may have the upper hand, and other times it is in retreat. However, in no circumstances is the triumph of the market complete or permanent, nor should we expect or desire it to be' (1999: 8).

The field of area-based programs that this volume considers is predicated on an awareness of the limits of market solutions. An interchange of new concepts, research findings and ground-level initiatives is taking place across borders, regions, municipalities – extending upwards to federal arrangements and downwards to neighbourhoods. In developed countries governmental authority is both devolving and fusing back together. Public urban issues are not responding to the traditional boundaries of government, while matters such as environmental degradation, education and transport dominate public concern.

Common themes

Three major themes stand out in the chapters ahead. First is the way in which programs respond to the interlinked nature of the problems of poor urban neighborhoods, such as crime, weak labor markets, poor education and crumbling housing. Americans use the word comprehensive, Europeans tend to use 'holistic' but the point is the same. In promoting comprehensive programs instructive experiences are emerging on both sides of the Atlantic, from the Ford Foundation's Neighborhood and Family Initiative to the New Deal for Communities in the UK. The second theme concerns the way programs respond to popular pressure for inclusion, recognition and participation in program development and implementation. The real level of influence that local citizens may have and the processes for encouraging greater levels of participation, often confound the interests of other stakeholders, particularly funders and service professionals, and present a number of dilemmas as well as opportunities for creative forms of governance.

Third is the necessity for politics. The nature of power and the importance of clarifying interests are examined and debated throughout the volume. People feel outmaneuvered by the dominance of the market and globalization, recognizing that although it is a great wealth generator it is unjust in social impact. As a consequence citizens are looking to re-establish democratic controls to provide greater security. 'All politics is local,' said Tip O'Neil, the former speaker of the US House of Representatives. This is now understood in a radical way from Hispanic neighborhoods in southwest US to communities in Northern Ireland and London where a more dispersed politics and a reinvigorated civil society are taking shape.

The volume opens by examining the most important developments in community building in the US in the last decade. These examine different approaches – comprehensive community initiatives, the 'more than housing' strategy adopted by some community development corporations, and the work of broad-base organizations which focus first on developing local citizens' political capacity to act. These chapters are interlaced with debates over the role of services in neighborhood revitalization, the nature of political power and how comprehensive programs for low-income neighborhoods confront the dilemmas thrown up by grassroots participation.

What is distinctive in the US is the way funding from philanthropic sources, independent of government initiatives, have enabled a range of community regeneration approaches to develop within different communities. In chapter 2 Kubisch and Stone explain the concept of comprehensive community initiatives that grew out of the realization that the problems facing the urban poor are interrelated and therefore that responses in the field also have to address this interrelationship of problems. While funded through large philanthropic foundations (on a scale not found in Europe) these initiatives are often service-oriented and place considerable emphasis on local representation on collaborative boards. These characteristics make comprehensive community initiatives, or CCIs, an innovative, well-evaluated approach that is a repository of valuable experience. They discuss a number of issues that CCIs have uncovered in the course of their community building. These include the challenge to develop a sufficiently broad view of the neighborhood's problems, the optimum size of collaborative partnerships, and the degree of staff and technical assistance required to assist initiatives in implementation.

But CCIs have gaps in their experience not least in relation to African Americans and ethnic minorities. In chapter 3 Lawrence examines the absence of race in comprehensive urban initiatives. He argues powerfully that this historical neglect has meant that programs, concerned as they are with social justice outcomes, have failed to grapple with the structural imperatives that have generated racial segregation and impoverishment. He particularly focuses on the ideological limitations of community revitalization, noting that these derive from the same set of moral assumptions that have always ignored the root problem of racial inequality. White political privilege, he argues, is a legacy of the pre-civil rights order, and ensures the continuity of traditional value preferences in political economy. Lawrence calls for a redefinition of comprehensiveness based on what he terms 'structural racism'. Although drawing on his involvement with initiatives in the US the wide-ranging agenda that he sets out makes a significant contribution to the international debate on how area regeneration programs should tackle racism.

Community development corporations have provided a means by which low-income communities were able to leverage funds for capital investment, primarily in low-cost housing in the US. They have elicited some interest in the UK in the past (Twelvetrees 1989) but before they had moved beyond their role in providing housing for low-income families. In the last ten years they have developed work in strengthening neighborhood social fabric by paying attention to issues such as community safety. This 'more than housing' strategy offers a compelling story for community development in the UK, for example in housing associations as they explore a similar path in 'housing plus'.

Sullivan in chapter 4 examines the rise of CDCs and how some of them have moved beyond their initial role in housing construction to a strategy that tackles other aspects of neighborhood life such as residents' sense of security in order to make good that initial investment.

Using their roots in the local community some CDCs began to pay attention to building social capital. Sullivan draws out the strengths and weaknesses of this work. His chapter also considers the vital role that national intermediaries, such as the Local Initiative Support Corporation, have played in facilitating the community building efforts of CDCs.

Evaluating comprehensive community initiatives is a complex task, not least because they have multiple objectives and aim to address a number of interrelated social problems associated with low-income areas – whether poor educational attainment, community safety or neighborhood relationships. Such initiatives also often draw on a range of social science theory. Thus there are a number of variables with which any evaluation has to grapple. Because of this experimental design becomes impractical. In chapter 5, drawing on their nationally recognized work for the Aspen Round Table for Comprehensive Community Initiatives Kubisch, Connell and Fulbright-Anderson succinctly lay out both the difficulties in evaluating initiatives using experimental constructs and the promising means of meeting this challenge through articulating a program's 'theory of change'. The theory of change requires the major stakeholders in a comprehensive community initiative to articulate how they think that the change they are intending to effect will come about. As a new round of evaluative activity is about to begin in the UK there is a growing familiarity with the theory of change approach as a critical component of evaluative activity (Traynor et al. 1998).

The revival of a local politics as a prerequisite for sustainable community rebuilding is explored in chapter 6. Frank Pierson, a lead organizer with the Southwest Industrial Areas Foundation in the US, explains both the development of the work of the IAF and its focus on the necessity of building local political power first. 'Power before program' simply means that unless independent local political capacity exists, any revitalization program, no matter how dedicated to 'resident participation', will fail local residents. For Saul Alinsky, who founded the IAF in the 1940s, government programs by definition could not empower local citizens; they had to develop their own independent political base. The IAF has widened its strategy in recent years, moving beyond the combative legacy of its founder.

For all its emphasis on building an independent power base, it becomes clear in Pierson's account that this is only achieved through patient one-to-one work: listening to people's stories, developing the capacity of local leaders, finding commonality in diversity. Understanding and interpreting the nature of power in the course of building a broad-based organisation may entail conflict with a party, group or official in one phase and then working with them as allies in the next. There is a world of difference between *mobilizing capacity*, which by its nature is temporary, and *political capacity* capable of sustained intervention.

In chapter 7 Pearson and Craig pick up the themes of local participation and influence within the UK context. In particular they focus on the range of anti-poverty strategies that many local authorities have constructed in order to limit the damage inflicted on their communities during the triumph of neoliberal belief in the efficacy of the free market in the 1980s. They find important political energy within local government ready to adopt such strategies. From this experience they raise questions in relation to the definitions of 'community', the targeting of particular communities for additional funding (leading to the exclusion of others, equally poor, living in communities next door) and examine the 'representativeness' of local partnership structures. Their contribution is to demonstrate the positive role that local government can play in alleviating area-based poverty if pursued with ingenuity and determination.

In chapters 8 and 9 Miller from the UK and Damon from France provide critiques of two quite different national traditions of urban revitalization. Miller describes the genesis of these programs in the UK. He notes the historic emphasis on top-down initiatives and the partial attempts by central government to encourage local participation and partnership. His chapter sets in context the new emphasis on a 'holistic' approach to community rebuilding and provides a critique of urban governance of the 'Third Way' as exemplified by the New Deal for Communities program recently inaugurated in the UK.

The experience in France has differed from that of the UK and the US in certain important respects. It offers perhaps the clearest model of large-scale state intervention. Damon presents both an overview of French programs for urban regeneration and evaluates the 'targeting' of particular areas in the latest phase of urban policy, *'la politique de ville'*. In the course of his chapter he offers a substantial discussion of how the pressing circumstance of urban social exclusion can conflict with and override previous national consensus and ideology. For French political theory the idea of targeting raises particularly difficult political questions given the historic commitment of the state to the formal equality of citizens' rights. Despite this the French government has intervened on a scale which contrasts with central government programs in the US and the UK. The experience in France suggests a greater national concern over the loss of social cohesion and the willingness of political elites to use state mechanisms to repair that damage.

In chapter 10 North and Bruegel discuss the lessons that learned from the experiences of community activism, which has rejected government-proffered community partnerships. They review the price that community groups pay for joining such partnerships. Drawing attention to the role of 'community' in the theories of New Labour, which they argue has replaced the old attachment to 'class', they discuss the flaws of communitarian and Third Way thinking. They then turn to examples of alternative forms of community rebuilding organizations that are oppositional and reject partnership arrangements. These include the setting up of Local Exchanges, the anti-roads movement and local opposition to community re-planning.

Joan Smith's important insight in chapter 11 is to show how the Labour government, elected in the United Kingdom in 1997, has subtly based its program for low-income neighborhoods on communitarian social thinking, wrapped up in the language of social exclusion. In the course of her discussion she discloses the controlling, inequality-perpetuating language of communitarianism at the heart of New Labour's two flagship programs for low-income neighborhoods – the New Deal for Communities and the Crime and Disorder Act 1998. Smith's argument leads her to examine elements of communitarian discourse and the allied concept of 'social capital' which, within a rhetoric of apparent inclusiveness, pins responsibility for raising the level of well-being and prosperity in poor urban neighborhoods onto those neighborhoods themselves. 'Third Way' social governance achieves this through exerting explicit controls over nuisance neighbors and young men's behavior and bearing down heavily on parental obligation to control their children's behavior. To find an effective counter-perspective Smith turns to feminist concepts of organizing. This, she maintains, is the only perspective that is capable of detecting and opposing mythical universalisms and the falseness of the dichotomy between a public and private sphere of action.

John Pierson concludes the volume by outlining three themes, evident on both sides of the Atlantic, that are set to dominate community rebuilding in the twenty-first century. The first is the debate between the 'social' and 'economic' models for community rebuilding – often identified as the poles of European and American policy and the degree to which market imperatives should be incorporated in initiatives. The second is the effectiveness of strategies for participation within national programs, and the importance of local urban regimes to sustainable success. Third is the necessity of placing 'power' – the capacity to get things done – at the center of initiatives. By linking the work of the

Citizens Organizing Foundation in the United Kingdom and the IAF in the US he notes the growing emphasis on creating a vigorous public sphere in which local citizens find voice and create the channels through which to express it.

The contributors to this book, in developing and amplifying area-based anti-poverty policy, have moved well beyond the small-area fixture of neighbourhood revitalisation programs. In doing so they convey the widening arc of influence and resource mobilization that now has to be pressed into service for effective practice. Community has been defined simply by Ferguson and Dickens (1999: 4) as 'residents of a geographic neighbourhood or multi-neighbourhood area – no matter how they relate to each other'. Nor do they regard community in a restrictive sense. In particular they avoid the notion of 'coziness', of densely related populations enjoying strong personal relationships, what Sampson calls 'community lost' (Sampson 1999: 245).

Yet it is also evident that 'community' – a bounded space in which citizens live across a period of time – does matter. Poor neighborhoods matter as localities. Both America and European experience demonstrates that in this sense the notion of 'community' is central to our respective futures.

References

Dionne, E. (1998) *They Only Look Dead* (New York: Simon and Schuster)

Ferguson, R. and Dickens, W. (1999) Introduction in R. Ferguson and W. Dickens, *Urban Problems and Community Development* (Washington, DC: Brookings Institution)

Fraser, N. (1998) Social Justice in the Age of Identity Politics: Redistribution, Recognition and Participation, *The Tanner Lectures on Human Values* 19, 1–67

Freeman, R. (1999) *The New Inequality. Creating Solutions for Poor America* (Boston: The Beacon Press)

Hugg, P. (1998) Transnational Convergence: European Union and American Federalism, *Cornell International Law Journal* 32: 1, 43–108

Office of City Controller of Philadelphia (1999) *Philadelphia. A New Urban Direction* (Philadelphia: St. Joseph's University Press)

Osterman, P. (1999) *Securing Prosperity The American Labor Market: How it Has Changed and What to Do about it* (Princeton, NJ: Princeton University Press)

Perri 6 (1997) *Holistic Government* (London: Demos)

Power, A. (1997) *Estates on the Edge: The Social Consequences of Housing in Northern Europe* (London: Macmillan – now Palgrave)

Power, A. and Mumford, K. (1999) *The Slow Death of Great Cities? Urban Abandonment or Urban Renaissance* (York: Joseph Rowntree Foundation)

Sampson, R. (1999) What 'Community' Supplies, in R. Ferguson and W. Dickens, *Urban Problems and Community Development* (Washington, DC: Brookings Institution)

Stokes, P. and Knight, B. (1998) *Civil Society and Public Policy* (Birmingham: Foundation for Civil Society)

Traynor, T., Smith, K. and Hughes, M. (1998) *Still Challenging Disadvantages* (Ilford: Barnardos)

Twelvetrees, A. (1989) *Organising for Neighbourhood Development: A Comparative Study of Community Development Corporations and Citizen Power Organisations* (Aldershot: Avebury)

Turok, I. and Edge, N. (1999) *The Jobs Gap in Britain's Cities Employment Loss and Labour Market Consequences* (Bristol: Policy Press)

Turok, I. (1999) Employment in British Cities, *Radical Statistics* 71, 3–9

Wilson, W. (1987) *The Truly Disadvantaged* (Chicago: University of Chicago Press)

Wilson, W. (1996) *When Work Disappears. The World of the New Urban Poor* (New York: Knopf)

2
Comprehensive Community Initiatives: The American Experience

Anne C. Kubisch and Rebecca Stone

In the late 1980s a broad set of initiatives was launched which placed 'community' at the heart of anti-poverty policy in poor urban neighborhoods. These efforts were loosely grouped under the generic name of 'comprehensive community initiatives' or CCIs. The 'new' thinking that informs CCIs emerged from the lessons learned from both the successes and failures of nearly a century of economic support and social services for the poor. Indeed, their very designation sought to distinguish them from the older, more prevalent community development corporation which in certain cities at least shared the same community building agenda.

Financed chiefly by liberal private foundations, CCIs are typically sited in poor, urban communities of color, which have suffered high levels of physical and economic decline, social isolation and political disempowerment. Their programs use a set of guiding concepts – comprehensiveness, coordination, collaboration and community participation (Kubisch et al. 1997). Their holistic approaches seek to revitalize neighborhoods by combining strategies of community organization, rehabilitating infrastructure, expanding local economic potential, reforming social service delivery and strengthening informal social networks. These mechanisms are thought to correlate with healthy human development, increased civic engagement and well-functioning neighborhoods.

Though different in their programmatic emphases, their institutional settings and even their theories of how change occurs, CCIs have much in common with each other. In particular, each has struggled with a set of 'tensions' embedded in their principles and design and with a series of challenges to implementation (Kubisch et al. 1997; Stone 1996). Chief among these is mediating the enduring rivalry between physical and economic development on the one hand, and a focus on individual and human development on the other. But there are other challenges such as reforming the traditional power relationship between funders and recipient organizations in order to give greater voice and control to community residents. Perhaps most daunting of all is incorporating awareness of both the history and current realities of racism in the US that have helped to create and sustain the impoverished conditions that CCIs hope to ameliorate.

CCIs have also advanced a larger movement devoted to integrating the concept of 'community building' into the political mainstream. This guiding principle of CCIs emphasizes that sustained positive change in individual and community well-being is best achieved through a participatory and just process that promotes individual leadership, associational ties and institutional capacity. Helped along by the widespread embrace of this principle among leading foundations in current anti-poverty efforts, community building may prove to be CCIs' most enduring contribution to American social policy.

This chapter describes how CCIs have developed in the US, explains some of the persistent issues that confound them, and points out the areas needing more rigorous probing in order to assess the progress and potential of current initiatives and any future incarnations of their core ideas.

Investing in communities to improve residents' well-being

In the US, the history of community-based initiatives to improve poor urban neighborhoods and the lives of their residents dates from the settlement houses of the late nineteenth century. In the twentieth century, neighborhood-focused efforts included the fight against juvenile delinquency in the 1950s, the Ford Foundation's Gray Areas program, the War on Poverty in the 1960s and the community development corporation movement from the 1970s (see chapter 4 in this volume). Over this same period, opposing ideologies have moved in and out of favor in policy discussions and research in the anti-poverty field. Taken together, these opposing ideologies reveal the dominant tensions that exist in the theory and practice of contemporary community building.

- *People versus place*: Should interventions be designed to target a particular category of individuals or should they be aimed at improving neighborhood conditions for *all* residents?

- *Public versus private*: Should social and economic development in poor neighborhoods rely primarily on initiatives and resources from the governmental sector or from the private sector (broadly defined to include corporate, religious, voluntary, or philanthropic actors)?
- *Top-down versus bottom-up*: Is reform best driven by leadership from those in positions of political, economic or intellectual power or by leaders within the targeted community?
- *Deficit-oriented versus asset-oriented*: Should interventions be designed to 'fix' identifiable problems or to reinforce and build upon the strengths and assets of an individual or community?
- *Categorical versus comprehensive*: Should interventions be tailored and focused on the specific needs of specific target groups or should they try to address multiple problems simultaneously?

Key actors in the anti-poverty field are trying to bridge these divides. Rather than choosing between 'opposing' approaches, a new synthesis aims to bring the best elements from each together in an effort to make significant improvements in individual and community well-being. This hybrid approach is being tested in a variety of initiatives commonly referred to as comprehensive, community-building initiatives, or CCIs.

CCIs were first introduced in the late 1980s when certain liberal foundations – Ford, MacArthur and the Rockefeller Foundations among them – launched a number of ambitious multi-year neighborhood-focused initiatives to improve the lives of individuals and families as well as their neighborhoods, by working comprehensively across social, economic and physical sectors. They aimed to develop capacity in distressed neighborhoods by concentrating political and financial resources on those neighborhoods. They sought to achieve this by bringing to bear the most up-to-date knowledge and experience about poverty alleviation, by employing flexible and collaborative institutional arrangements, and, perhaps most importantly, by using and promoting 'community building' – individual and community empowerment and enhanced social capital – to advance and sustain community gains.

At the individual and family level, CCIs seek to improve the quality of life of poor children and their families. Much of what CCIs actually do is targeted at individuals through, for example, employment training and job placement, services provision and reform, cultural and social support, youth activities and leadership development. CCIs generally aim to expand the quantity and to improve the quality of services and activities in those domains and to add a preventive, human-development orientation to them. At the neighborhood level, CCIs are concerned with the accessibility and quality of social supports, economic opportunity and physical infrastructure, and with the safety of the local environment. CCIs also are concerned with improving the quality of collective life through strengthening personal networks, and enhancing social capital and a 'sense of community'.

Broadly defined, up to 100 CCIs have been created over the past 15 year. Most have been created by and received funding from private foundations, although there are a number of federal, state and locally sponsored initiatives. Examples of some of the best known initiatives include the following:

- *The Neighborhood and Family Initiative (NFI)*: A four-site initiative (Hartford, Detroit, Memphis and Milwaukee) launched in 1990 by the Ford Foundation and now in its last round of funding. Local community foundations in each city were designated as site managers and received initial grants of $1 million for a three-year period. Each local foundation established a group to define the problems facing the target neighborhood and planned how NFI funds should be passed on to local projects and programs. Funds have been used for a range of activities including development of new businesses, housing construction, social services and community organizing to bridge the separation between human services and physical regeneration of the locality. NFI projects have also placed great emphasis on mobilizing broad local participation and developing local leaderships in implementation. Currently several of the sites have spun off new neighborhood organizations that will continue to carry out the work of the NFI.

- *Community Building in Partnership*: Launched in 1990 in Sandtown-Winchester, one of the most distressed neighborhoods in Baltimore, MD, through the leadership of The Enterprise Foundation and in partnership with the City of Baltimore. The initiative is now operated by an independent corporation, CPB, Inc., and staffed by outside professionals as well as neighborhood residents. It has a comprehensive revitalization agenda for the neighborhood and has had recognized success in building and rehabilitating housing, promoting reform in the local public schools and increasing the availability of health services for residents.

- *The Comprehensive Community Revitalization Program*: Established in 1992 by a consortium of 13 philanthropies, led by the Surdna Foundation. The consortium provided $9 million in flexible funding over a six-year period to enhance the work of four long-standing community development corporations (CDCs) in an impoverished area of the south Bronx, New York. The CDCs joined together to develop a neighborhood-wide development plan, expanding their traditional work in housing development to include economic development, social services, cultural and recreational activities, and community organizing. CCRP aimed to enhance the CDCs' capacity to act as intermediaries for their neighborhoods in securing resources and services from city agencies and from the non-profit and private sectors. The foundation funding was used to plan, build institutional capacity, provide seed funding and to leverage more than $45 million in new public sector funding for the neighborhood. In terms of results CCRP has achieved considerable national attention through its success in an urban area which for decades had served as the epitome of inner city devastation.

- *The Making Connections initiative*: Launched in 1999, Making Connections is the most ambitions of the foundation community building initiatives. Comprising a major shift in the grant-making portfolio of the Annie E. Casey Foundation, the NT/FD commits the Foundation to devote half of its resources to neighborhood revitalization on behalf of children and families. According to the Foundation, 'This effort seeks to build on and unify our grant making on behalf of disadvantaged children and families, intertwining the best that we and others have learned from the fields of family support, economic development, system reform, and community building. The basic conviction behind this work is that it is possible to improve outcomes for children by strengthening their families. For far too many kids, however, it is unrealistic to do so without changing the conditions in which they and their families live' (Annie E. Casey Foundation 1999).

The size and visibility of the CCIs have generated interest and activity in supporting fields. Many individuals and institutions now provide technical assistance to CCIs, evaluate and carry out research to increase understanding of CCI work, or serve as clearing houses to share knowledge among CCIs and to disseminate information about them to a broader policy audience. Many of these roles have been developed at the behest of the foundations sponsoring the CCIs.

CCIs have also sparked the foundations themselves to modify their own role in the change process. In particular, foundations have explored two new areas of operations: strengthening local 'intermediaries' such as CDCs, local collaborative boards, or community foundations in an attempt to bolster local technical, institutional or financial assets; and changing the nature of their own role as a 'partner' in local community initiatives, taking a collaborative and more politically strategic role in the CCI experience. Different foundations have had varying levels of success in making these new approaches work, and each objective has brought with it a set of challenges to the implementation of CCIs that command time and attention (Brown and Garg 1997; Stone and Butler 2000).

The roots of comprehensive community-building initiatives in research, program and policy

The origins of CCIs can be traced through three distinct pathways. New directions in social science research, conclusions drawn from program experience and trends in the policy environment converged to allow the principles and strategies that underlie CCIs – most notably comprehensiveness and community building – to come forward. These principles are increasingly guiding a wide array of publicly and privately sponsored initiatives in education, health, child and youth development, crime prevention, substance abuse, prevention of child abuse and neglect and welfare reform. Thus, while CCIs may represent the 'purest' application of comprehensiveness and community building, they are by no means the exclusive expression of those principles.

Recent research influences on community initiatives

In the last 30 years, researchers have increased their efforts to understand why children and families in poor urban neighborhoods experience disproportionately greater social and economic problems than their middle-class counterparts. Developmental and community psychologists, economists, sociologists, historians, anthropologists and political scientists have all turned their attention to the causes of these problems. From this an important theme has emerged: to identify the *interrelationships* that link poverty with poor physical and mental health, crime, crumbling infrastructure, low business activity, racism and weak social and cultural institutions in American cities. A critical dimension of this work has focused specifically on the interaction between individual outcomes and the conditions of the surrounding environment, and a growing body of research is attempting to describe and analyze this phenomenon.

With regard to early child development, for example, many scholars followed Bronfenbrenner's (1977, 1979) early lead and have worked to define the importance of 'context' on a child's well-being, including family dynamics, child care and educational circumstances, neighborhood attributes and socio-cultural practices. In the past 20 years, research has begun to demonstrate how children are influenced by the resources and risks in their neighborhoods, including institutional supports, presence or absence of affluent residents, neighborhood stability and density of social networks. (See Brooks-Gunn, Duncan and Aber 1997, for an excellent compilation of literature in this domain.) These factors intersect with individual attributes to produce healthy or unhealthy outcomes for children as they develop.

In the last decade or so, the field of youth development also has begun to demonstrate the critical relationship between contextual and individual factors for young people in the 13–24 year age range. To become economically self-sufficient adults with healthy relationships and good citizenship practices, youths need to learn how to be productive and how to navigate in a complex world (Connell, Aber and Walker 1995). But those developmental processes are influenced by such factors as the physical and demographic characteristics of neighborhoods (Briggs 1996; Sampson and Morenoff 1997), the structure of economic opportunities (Wilson 1996), the actions and attitudes of individuals with whom children establish key relationships, and the institutional capacities and resources in the neighborhood (Wynn et al. 1994).

An even more recent line of research that has helped fuel interest in the community–individual relationship focuses on the importance of 'social capital' in promoting and maintaining the overall health of a community and its residents. In the context of comprehensive, community-building initiatives, social capital is defined quite broadly as the relationships among individuals and institutions and the 'sense of community' that are created among neighborhood residents through, for example, social networks, informal associations in a neighborhood, civic activities and so on. The theoretical work and research in this domain was spurred by sociologists (Wellman and Leighton 1979; Coleman 1990; Castells 1996), but has been popularized by the publications of political scientist Robert Putnam (1993, 1995) linking social capital to good governance and other types of civic action. In general, this perspective attempts to analyze the attributes of healthy communities from a social perspective and to link them to healthy individual behavior and outcomes. (For a thorough and clear review of this literature, see Sampson and Morenoff 1997).

Over the last few years, initiative funders and designers have referred increasingly to the research on social capital as theoretical justification for the 'community-building' dimension of CCIs. The research resonated with their intuitive sense that anomie had replaced a sense of community in distressed inner cities, leaving individuals isolated from both mainstream structures or networks and from their immediate surroundings and neighbors. Work that focuses on strengthening social networks, building ties across groups, developing civic capacity and promoting community efficacy can all find some rationale in the recent academic work on social capital. Yet, as will be discussed below, this research is still young and it does not yet indicate a causal connection between community-building principles and other desired outcomes for individuals and neighborhoods.

Recent programmatic influences on community initiatives

Running parallel to the research on the interrelationships among various dimensions of individual and community circumstances has been a trend toward more 'comprehensiveness' in the design of social programs. Evidence has been accumulating from program experience over 30 years that even highly focused service strategies for individuals have inherent limitations and cannot be expected, on their own, to achieve *sustained* improvements in individual and community well-being in poor urban neighborhoods in the United States. This lesson emerges from many programmatic directions.

We have learned a great deal from Head Start, one of the most successful and best-studied programs for young children living in poor communities in the United States. An enriched development program for children aged 3 to 5 years, Head Start has been credited with successfully advancing social and cognitive development among children living in extremely disadvantaged, high-risk families and neighborhoods. Those who participate in Head Start often make major developmental gains and enter school better equipped than children who do not participate in the program. According to the longitudinal study of the pilot program in the 1960s, those children also go on to exhibit fewer problem outcomes such as teen pregnancy, dropping out of high school and criminal behavior than their non-participating peers at age 19 (Berrueta-Clement et al. 1984). On the other hand, Head Start children still have higher teen pregnancy rates, drop-out rates and arrest rates than the national average. Two years of enriched education at ages 3 and 4, however powerful, do not inoculate children for life nor eliminate the long-term disadvantage they face when they grow up in distressed families and communities.

A similar lesson comes from those who have been engaged in the physical revitalization of low-income urban neighborhoods. During the 1970s and 1980s, substantially backed by national philanthropies such as the Ford Foundation, community development corporations (CDCs) became the largest producers of low-income housing in the country, changing the face of many physically blighted communities. Despite this impressive record, most of the neighborhoods in which CDCs are active are poor today, with aging and sometimes poorly kept housing, and their residents continue to experience a range of social and economic problems. CDCs, as a result, are seeking ways to complement their focus on housing development with work that strengthens the social fabric of neighborhoods such as community security (see Sullivan this volume).

Recent policy influences on community initiatives

The core theme of the policy debate around poor individuals and neighborhoods for the better part of the twentieth century focused on the role and responsibility of government in supporting individuals in need. Because the foundations of the American political system are based on the premise of limited government, any public sector intervention must be strongly justified both morally and economically, not just at its inception but on an ongoing basis.

The debate is further shaped by an enduring ideological dispute between behavioralists and structuralists on the causes of poverty and appropriate remedies. Behavioralists generally ascribe undesirable outcomes, such as unintended teen pregnancy, unemployment or criminal behavior, to individual-level characteristics, including intelligence, values, attitudes and motivation. Their policy prescriptions have tended to focus on changing individuals through skills development, attitude change, reduction of their dependency on public assistance and incentives to change their behavior. Structuralists, on the other hand, have focused on how changes in the macroeconomy, racist practices in housing and employment, lack of investment in the public school system and so on have had a disproportionately negative impact on the poor, people of color and low-skilled workers. Their policy prescriptions focus more on contextual factors, such as working toward more equitable regulatory, tax or investment policies at the national level or, at the local level, seeking to revitalize communities (economically, politically and socially) that are most hurt by these macroeconomic forces.

The structuralist-behavioralist divide is particularly acute in discussions of race in America. Recent research has begun to uncover the complicated influences of race in creating and perpetuating urban distress and confounding attempts to alleviate it. Both William Julius Wilson's (1987) arguments about the creation of an economic underclass and the race-focused analyses of residential and economic segregation (Massey and Denton 1993) helped elevate race as a necessary, if insufficient, lens through which to analyze urban poverty. Thus it effectively replaced the question of *whether* race matters with *how* it matters (O'Connor 1999).

Behavioralists argue that because there are no longer laws that deliberately limit minority advancement in the US, persistent minority disadvantage, especially African-American disadvantage, must be explained by problems within the community itself (the 'cultural' inferiority argument). According to this perspective, it is not a public responsibility to resolve social inequities; rather it is a problem that the minority community itself must tackle. The structuralist perspective, on the other hand, points out racist practices that persist in discriminatory zoning, mortgage red-lining and other minority 'containment' strategies that manifest themselves in continued under-investment in neighborhoods of color. Further, structuralists identify the numerous ways in which racism is embedded in American culture and systems, even when it may have been formally erased through civil rights legislation and protections. For example, political scientists point to the influence of racism on black social cohesion, political action and civic participation (Dawson 1998; Thompson 1998) that are critical to the policy change process.

CCI initiatives map quite well onto the current neoliberal policy environment by accommodating and responding to its manifold ambivalent streaks. For example, CCIs emerge out of concern for structural and environmental factors causing poverty, but not exclusively: they also focus on changing individual behavior. CCIs promote social welfare programs and an enlarged safety net for those most in need, but not exclusively: they also place primary emphasis on job placement, entrepreneurship and business development. CCIs depend on public sector programs, but not exclusively: they require the collaboration of philanthropy, voluntary organizations, the private sector and neighborhood residents. CCIs are founded on the notion that community empowerment will be key to the success of their revitalization strategies, but not exclusively: they recognize the importance of the political, financial and technical resources of institutions and individuals in traditional positions of power. And, finally, CCIs take into account the history and continued effects of structural racism in this country, but not exclusively: they ask communities themselves to recognize and take responsibility for the problems – and the assets – of their residents.

Interestingly, while CCIs may appear to be ideologically acceptable to all sides of the political landscape, leadership for this new form of community revitalization has not come from the public sector. This is largely explained by the substantial influence of the American private philanthropic sector. In the United States, when government-sponsored program practice seems to fall behind either social scientific or conventional wisdom, the private philanthropic sector typically steps in to promote innovation in social policy and programming. And because the philanthropic sector is quite substantial in the US, this foundation sponsorship can set the stage for the more cumbersome shift in government thinking and spending. This is precisely what happened in the case of CCIs.

An agenda for research, practice and policy

A number of pressing issues require further attention in future research and debates on implementation on comprehensive initiatives.

How to promote individual and community change

Having made the argument that CCIs grew, in part, out of new directions in social science research about key factors relating to individual and community well-being, there are still too many holes in what is actually known about determinants of change. Specifically, although we have made progress in developing richer information about the *correlates* of individual and community success, we are still sorely lacking in information about *causes* of individual and community success defined in a way that can guide policy and program design. So, for example, while the research suggests that poverty is generally the result of problems on multiple social and economic fronts, we still have little evidence that simultaneous attention to individual and community needs across a comprehensive spectrum of program areas will have a 'synergistic' effect that will achieve significant positive outcomes in distressed neighborhoods.

The critical questions revolve around how, when, why and under what conditions change occurs. The challenge is to lay out in a much more sophisticated and detailed manner than is currently available the paths that individuals, communities and programs need to follow to achieve desired outcomes. The focus needs to be on developing two distinct but interrelated pathways.

The first is the more straightforward: organizing social science research, program experience, community knowledge and policy history into systematic and nuanced 'theories of change' at the individual, institutional and community levels that can then guide policy and program decisions. (See Kubisch, Connell and Fulbright-Anderson this volume, for a discussion of theories of change and their importance to planning and evaluation.) The aim would be to identify desired longer-term outcomes and then link them back through well-known precursors of those outcomes to programmatic intervention. Take, for example, the work by Gambone (1999) identifying the pathways to positive change that have been distilled in the youth development field. Successful outcomes in cognitive, social, physical, emotional and moral development are dependent upon the presence in young people's lives of supportive relationships, challenging and interesting learning experiences, meaningful involvement and membership, and a safe environment. These, in turn, are dependent on a set of specific developmental supports and opportunities that experts in the field have identified through research and practice. In some fields of endeavor, more is known about these pathways of change than in others and this information needs to be sorted and catalogued across the many outcomes sought by CCIs.

The second pathway is more problematic because it is less linear: it encompasses the conditions and capacities at the individual, neighborhood or organizational level to ensure that policies and program are implemented effectively. These paths include creating political power, building social capital, developing effective local leadership and strengthening local institutions. These latter paths need to be better understood, both theoretically and empirically, and – in particular – need to incorporate qualities of local culture that make individual strategies appropriate or not for a given neighborhood.

Without sufficient investment in defining these pathways, stakeholders will have no clear sense of where to intervene and how to assess progress. All stakeholders, particularly politicians and funders, have always been impatient for outcomes that suggest residents' lives have improved in meaningful ways. They want to have quantifiable answers to difficult questions: does the program reduce poverty rates, reduce unemployment, decrease the incidence of babies with low birth weight, prevent child abuse or teen pregnancy, decrease drop-out and crime rates, improve the stock of affordable housing? These kinds of outcomes, however, are difficult to achieve, especially quickly. Without sufficient investment in defining the pathways of change, policy-makers and funders will be able to judge an initiative only by whether it results in the ultimate outcomes – leaving them no options for redirection in mid-course and little incentive to stay the bumpy course to change. Similarly, by not attending to the likelihood that one set of changes will lead to the next in a given community, residents and local practitioners have no basis for belief in a 'new' approach and no way to assess whether, once it has begun, anything is going according to plan.

The state of the knowledge base about social capital is a relevant case in point. The growing number of studies correlating social capital with desirable outcomes is helping to motivate the community-building emphasis of many current policies and programs in the US. But we still have only a preliminary understanding of the links between social capital and some of those outcomes. Robert Sampson and his colleagues have done excellent work linking social capital to incidence of crime. They discovered that what they refer to as 'collective efficacy' – the informal mechanisms by which local residents achieve public order – depends in large measure on conditions of mutual trust and solidarity among neighbors (see Sampson et al. 1997). Others have focused on positive correlations with good government (Putnam 1993), civic engagement of youth and young adults (Youniss, McLellan and Yates 1997), employment (Granovetter 1973; 1995), housing (Keyes 1999) and even health (Kawachi et al. 1997; James, Schulz and van Olphen 1999). As the scientific community is quick to note, however, correlation does not equal causation.

In CCIs, community building can be thought of as the term used to describe the development of social capital. Community building is generally defined as strengthening the capacity of residents, neighborhood associations and neighborhood organizations to work toward sustained change in conditions. Early outcomes are defined as, for example: a more organized and mobilized community; a wider and more diverse leadership base in the neighborhood; a widely shared vision for the community and a strategic plan for achieving the vision (a broadly accepted, compelling and specific theory of change); strengthened informal associations among neighborhood residents; more and better functioning community institutions; healthy interracial or cross-cultural dynamics; and intergenerational involvement in revitalization.

These elements are now front and center in community revitalization strategies and, indeed, may be the most enduring legacy of the CCI era. Two sets of questions, however, need answering. First, are the investments in community building actually leading to enhanced social capital and civic engagement? What community building activities (or combination of them) specifically effect sustained increases in social capital? Can we establish when or how an initiative might reach a critical mass of these sorts of activities?

Second, does enhanced social capital lead to improved outcomes in priority policy areas such as health, income and crime as the theory predicts? If yes, what are the pathways through which this occurs and what are appropriate points of intervention?

Community building as a concept, tool and objective has usefulness because it has broad appeal for the mainstream as well as for more marginalized groups. For the mainstream, it appeals to a populist image of family and community for which many are (perhaps unrealistically) nostalgic. For communities of faith it allows attention and respect for spirituality and spiritual community, as well as for the rich tradition of churches and other places of worship as community centers and providers of service to the poor. For liberals, it echoes the democratic values of local voice, social justice and economic and racial equity. And for conservatives, it offers the prospect of the poor taking responsibility for solving their problems. Thus, despite little evidence of its actual value for driving civic participation, reversing decline, or promoting prosperity, community building has enormous momentum. Researchers and practitioners must be rigorous in their analysis of how it plays out over time.

Improving practice by linking the theoretical to the operational

While there exists a general consensus around *what* CCIs should do – undertake a comprehensive and integrated array of social, economic and physical revitalization activities – there is a great deal of uncertainty about *how* to put such programs into place. Program comprehensiveness requires institutional flexibility and a breadth of capacities. Community building demands that residents participate meaningfully in initiative governance, and that the institutional base of the CCI be responsive to community needs on an ongoing basis through outreach and mobilization. Trying to realize these principles while implementing and managing a CCI on a day-to-day basis turns out to be more difficult than many planners and funders anticipated. As one observer stated, 'we're building the plane as we're flying it.'

Few organizations enter a CCI process with the capacity to carry out such ambitious efforts. To begin with, the last two decades of government anti-poverty policy nurtured organizational specialization and narrowness by funding single problem-focused interventions instead of more flexible and comprehensive treatments of social ills. To a large extent, public funding streams still reinforce this programmatic tunnel vision. As a result, all CCIs have had to embark on some form of institutional capacity building in the early stages of the initiative. A wide variety of strategies have been needed and employed, each depending on the makeup of the governance structure for the initiative as well as other factors such as local political rivalries, public agencies' involvement in planning, and so on. The kinds of capacities that need to be developed, and some of the pitfalls encountered to date – sometimes referred to in the field as the 'process-product tension' (Kubisch et al. 1997) – include the following:

- *Broad-based community planning*: Almost all CCIs begin with a participatory and comprehensive community planning process. Where CCIs have been led by long-standing neighborhood institutions – notably CDCs as in the south Bronx or multi-service agencies – the first challenge for these organizations has been how to develop a broader view of the neighborhood's problems and assets beyond their established programmatic perspective. Chaskin, Joseph and Chipenda-Dansokho (1997) found that in one major, multi-site initiative, political and operational barriers led the sites to undertake several parallel activities rather than a comprehensive and integrated set of programs.
- *Collaboration*: Most CCIs, even those based within a single organization, must reach out and develop partnerships with other institutions in the neighborhood. There has been considerable experience with launching and managing collaborative governance structures, notably in the social services, that is being applied to CCIs (Blank Melaville, and Asayeh 1993; Amherst Wilder Foundation 1999). But collaboratives are often unwieldy, politicized and lethargic and, for the most part, CCIs have not yet resolved many of the challenges associated with making them work effectively (Chaskin and Joseph 1995; Pitt, Brown and Hirota 1999). As one group of early observers of the field noted, collaboration is 'an unnatural act among non-consenting adults' (Levitan, Mangum and Pines 1989).
- *Staffing and technical assistance*: Expertise in areas such as community organizing, political negotiation, planning and facilitation is often more highly valued than more technical skills in the implementation of a CCI. Since no formal training exists in these areas, experience is often the only route to expertise. Therefore, leadership and management capacity in the field are growing in 'real time', which may be one of the greatest constraints on the progress of CCIs.
- *Evaluation*: Most evaluations focus on measuring ultimate outcomes. Because these types of outcomes in CCIs are perpetually distant, CCI evaluators have sought alternative strategies and, too often, have resorted simply to documenting the process of implementation. Unfortunately, many of these 'process evaluations' are unhelpful because they favor anecdotal description over critical analysis, documenting the inputs – who was involved in a collaboration, how many units of service were provided or how many participants enrolled in the program – without linking them to results. Documenting whether

and how a policy or program was implemented and how it produced outcomes can be done with rigor, but it requires some work. Policymakers and program directors need a broad range of tools to find out how, why and whether a policy or program produces outcomes.

Improving our understanding of the big picture: relating CCIs to the social and political context

A disturbing concern for many in the CCI field is that the level of investment in CCIs – defined beyond financial investment to include political, institutional and technical investments – is paltry when viewed against their grand promise of 'neighborhood transformation'. All stakeholders in the field are guilty of overpromising. In order to attract funding, initiative directors and heads of local organizations commit themselves to achieving significant changes in broad social indicators, even if they know their CCI is unlikely, by itself, to transform their neighborhood, especially in the short run. Foundations and other sponsors participate actively in the creation of these myths because they need to distinguish their work as 'significant' among their philanthropic peers and in the public eye.

What is clear is that the rhetoric of the CCI agenda outpaces what is practical and achievable given the historical and structural constraints on poor neighborhoods. As the historian Alice O'Connor (1999) and policy analyst Robert Halpern (1995) have both emphasized, urban community development initiatives were 'swimming against the tide' (O'Connor 1999), for most of the twentieth century. All initiatives have operated within a macro-policy framework that were working against their objectives: the decline of the inner city, for example, has been accelerated through the subsidies of major highways, suburban business development and home mortgage tax deductions. All urban initiatives combined are unable to compete with the enormous scale of such subsidies. O'Connor (1999) underscores that *only* changes in this policy context will allow neighborhood initiatives to fulfill their promise.

The convergence of poverty with race throughout American history also makes it clear that these structural issues need to be better understood and brought to the fore in this field. Given the prominence of race in American life and the considerable attention paid to it by social scientists it is remarkable how little the practice of community regeneration has investigated issues of race and power.

The omission of race, language, culture, gender and class runs throughout the CCI field. As the chapter by Lawrence in this volume suggests there are different revitalization pathways (or theories of change) suggested by 'race-neutral' explanations of community decline and those that are 'race-conscious'. Given the concentration of efforts in communities of color, one might reasonably assume that CCIs have grappled with this important dichotomy. In the case of most CCIs, however, the theories of change have been developed with reference to the tensions described in the opening section of this chapter, between people and place, public and private, categorical and comprehensive, and so on. Put differently, the dominant theory of change guiding CCIs is implicitly race-neutral: it finesses the question of race. At best, this is naive.

Without a theory of change that embraces the well-documented influence of racist practices in creating pockets of economic hardship, CCIs are hard-pressed to 'address' coherently issues of race or the related power of political elites. As a result, CCIs – when they have addressed race at all – have tended to focus on practical issues of inclusivity and respect, such as equal representation of different cultures in CCI governance structures, translation in mixed-language community meetings, or cultural celebrations that honor community diversity. These issues are certainly important, especially as the US ushers in the era of the 'minority majority' when people of color will outnumber Caucasians. And while CCI practices that attend to diversity in the neighborhood yield benefits in terms of local understanding and goodwill, most practitioners agree that they fall far short of the mark when it comes to changing the status quo in poor communities (Stone and Butler 2000).

Those in the field tend to explain the dearth of attention to race as a combination of widespread personal discomfort with the subject, lack of clarity regarding what 'race' means and fear of having race obscure everything else in a project. There is also the belief, chiefly ascribed to whites, though not widely voiced by them, that racism is no longer an issue (Stone and Butler 2000). Whatever the explanation, it is clear that these obstacles must be surmounted so that social policy and research on social policy can address the question of how race interweaves with poverty. Further research is needed on what are the enduring practices that reinforce color lines in what is otherwise called 'socio-economic' segregation, and how practices can incorporate this understanding into strategy as well as tactics.

CCI principles and the related research findings have infiltrated policy and program design in two principal ways: more comprehensive approaches to government-sponsored urban development and inner-city revitalization, and the philanthropic community's embrace of community building as the central element in progressive reform strategies. But while the research, practice and politics that gave us CCIs described and analyzed the interaction between individual outcomes and the conditions of the surrounding environment, it remains to be seen whether the CCI hybrid strategy or its offspring will yield more generalizable, sustainable results than have been realized in the past.

Acknowledgement

The authors are grateful to the following individuals for their helpful comments on earlier drafts: Ali Abunimah, Andrea Anderson, Prue Brown, Robert Chaskin, Selma Chipenda-Dansokho, Deborah Daro, Karen Fulbright-Anderson, Mark Joseph, Jessica Pitt, Richard Stren, Michael Weir and Jolyon Wurr.

Note

Parts of this chapter were adapted from: James P. Connell and Anne C. Kubisch (1999). Community Approaches to Improving Outcomes for Urban Children, Youth and Families: Current Trends and Future Directions', in *Does It Take a Village? Community Effects on Children, Adolescents and Families* (State College, PA: Pennsylvania State University).

References

Annie E. Casey Foundation (1999) *Making Connections: A Neighborhood Transformation/Family Development Program* (Baltimore, MD: The Annie E. Casey Foundation)

Berrueta-Clement, J., Schweinhart, L.J., Steven Barnett, W., Epstein, A.S. and Weikart, D.P. (1984) *Changed Lives: The Affects of the Perry Preschool Program on Studies through Age 19* (Ypsilanti, MI: High School Educational Research Foundation)

Blank, M., Melaville, A. and Asayesh, G. (1993) *Together We Can: A Guide for Crafting and Profamily System of Education and Human Services* (Washington, DC: US Government Printing Office)

Bobo, L.D. and Smith, R.A. (1997) 'From Jim Crow Racism to Laissez-Faire Racism: The Transformation of Racial Attitudes', in Wendy Katkin et al. (eds.), *Beyond Pluralism: The Conception of Groups and Group Identities in America* (Chicago: University of Illinois Press)

Briggs, X. (1996) 'Brown Kids in White Suburbs: Housing Mobility, Neighborhood Effects and the Social Capital of Poor Youth' (unpublished doctoral dissertation, Columbia University, New York)

Briggs, X., Mueller, E.J. and Sullivan, M.L. (1997) *From Neighborhood to Community: Evidence on the Social Effects of Community Development* (New York Community Development Research Center, Robert J. Milano Graduate School of Management and Urban Policy, New School for Social Research)

Bronfenbrenner, U. (1977) 'Toward an Experimental Ecology of Human Development', *American Psychologist* 32, 513–31

Bronfenbrenner, U. (1979) *The Ecology of Human Development: Experiments by Nature and Design* (Cambridge, Mass: Harvard University Press)

Brooks-Gunn, J., Duncan, G.J., Klebanov, P.K. and Sealand, N. (1993) 'Do Neighborhoods Influence Child and Adolescent Development?', *American Journal of Sociology* 99: 2, 353–95

Brooks-Gunn, J., Duncan, G.J. and Aber, J.L. (eds.) (1997) *Neighborhood Poverty, Volume 1: Context and Consequences for Children* (New York: Russell Sage Foundation)

Brooks-Gunn, J., Duncan, G.J. and Aber, J.L. (1997) *Neighborhood Poverty, Volume 2: Policy Implications In Studying Neighborhoods* (New York: Russell Sage Foundation)

Brown, P. and Garg, S. (1997) *Foundations and Comprehensive Community Initiatives: The Challenges of Partnership* (Chicago: The Chapin Hall Center for Children)

Bruner, C. and Parachini, L. (1997) *Building Community: Exploring New Relationships across Service Systems Reform, Community Organizing, and Community Economic Development* (Washington, DC: Institute for Educational Leadership)

Burton, L.M., Allison, K. and Obeidallah, D.A. (1995) Social Context and Adolescents Perspectives on Development among Inner-City African-American Teens, in L. Crockett and A.C. Crouter, *Pathways through Adolescence: Individual Development in Relation to Context* (Hillsdale, NJ: Lawrence Erlbaum Associates)

Case, A.C. and Katz, L.F. (1991) *The Company You Keep: The Effects of Family and Neighborhood on Disadvantaged Youths*, Working Paper 3705 (Cambridge, Mass: National Bureau of Economic Research)

Castells, M. (1996) *The Rise of the Network Society*, Volume 1 (Oxford: Blackwell)

Chaskin, R.J. and Joseph, M.L. (1995) *The Ford Foundation's Neighborhood and Family Initiative: Moving Toward Implementation: An Interim Report* (Chicago: The Chapin Hall Center for Children)

Chaskin, R.J., Joseph, M.L. and Chipenda-Dansokho, S. (1997) Implementing Comprehensive Community Development: Possibilities and Limitations, *Social Work* 42: 5, 435–43

Coleman, J.S. (1990) *Foundations of Social Theory* (Cambridge, Mass: Harvard University Press)

Connell, J.P., Aber, J.L. and Walker, G. (1995) How Do Urban Communities Affect Youth? Using Social Science Research to Inform the Design and Evaluation of Comprehensive Community Initiatives, in James P. Connell et al. (eds.), *New Approaches to Evaluating Community Initiatives: Concepts, Methods, and Contexts* (Washington, DC: Aspen Institute)

Connell, J.P. and Kubisch, A.C. (1998) Implementing a Theory of Change Evaluation in the Cleveland Community-Building Initiative: A Case Study, in Karen Fulbright, Anderson et al. (eds.), *New Approaches to Evaluating Community Initiatives: Volume 2 Theory, Measurement, and Analysis* (Washington, DC: The Aspen Institute)

Crane, J. (1991) Effects of Neighborhoods on Dropping Out of School and Teenage Childbearing, in C. Jencks and P. Peterson, *The Urban Underclass* (Washington, DC: Brookings Institution)

Dawson, M.C. (1998) An Alternative Perspective on the Theoretical and Empirical Study of Race and Community. Paper prepared for The Aspen Institute Roundtable on Comprehensive Community Initiatives, New York

Freedman, R. (1982) Economic Determinants of Geographic and Individual Variation in the Labor Market Position of Young Persons, in Richard Freeman and

David Wise, *The Youth Labor Market Problem: Its Nature, Causes, and Consequences* (Chicago: University of Chicago Press)

Furstenberg, F. and Hughes, M. (1995) Social Capital and Successful Development Among At-Risk Young, *Journal of Marriage and Family* 57 (August), 580–92

Gambone, M. (1999) *Community Action and Youth Development: What Can Be Done and How Can We Measure Progress?* Paper prepared for the Aspen Institute Roundtable on Comprehensive Community Initiatives for Children and Families, New York

Granovetter, M.S. (1973) The Strength of Weak Ties, *American Journal of Sociology* 78: 6, 1360–80

Granovetter, M.S. (1995) *Getting a Job: A Study of Contacts and Careers* (Second edition, Chicago: University of Chicago Press)

Halpern, R. (1995) *Rebuilding the Inner City: a History of Neighborhood Initiatives to Address Poverty in the United States* (New York: Columbia University Press)

Halpern, R. (1999) *Fragile Families Fragile Solutions: A History of Supportive Services For Families In Poverty* (New York: Columbia University Press)

Jackson, M.–R. and Marris, P. (1996) *Collaborative Comprehensive Community Initiatives: Overview of an Emerging Community Improvement Orientation* (Washington, DC: The Urban Institute)

James, S., Schulz, A.J. and van Olphen, J. (1999) Social Capital, Poverty, and Community Health: An Exploration of Linkages. Paper prepared for the Ford Foundation conference on *Social Capital and Poor Communities: Building and Using Social Capital to Combat Poverty* (March)

Jones-Correa, M. (1998) *Structural Shifts and Institutional Capacity: Possibilities for Ethnic Cooperation and Conflict in Urban Settings.* Paper prepared for The Aspen Institute Roundtable on Comprehensive Community Initiative, New York

Kawachi, I., Kennedy, B.P. and Lochner, K. (1997) Long Live Community: Social Capital as Public Health, *The American Prospect* 35, 56–9

Keyes, L. (1999) Housing, Social Capital and Poor Communities. Paper prepared for the Ford Foundation conference on *Social Capital and Poor Communities: Building and Using Social Capital to Combat Poverty* (March)

Kingsley, T.G., McNeely, J. and Gibson, J.O. (1997) *Community Building: Coming of Age* (Washington, DC: The Urban Institute)

Kubisch, A.C., Weiss, C.H., Schorr, L.B. and Connell, J.P. (1995) Introduction, in James P. Connell et al. (eds.), *New Approaches to Evaluating Community Initiatives: Concepts, Methods, and Contexts* (Washington, DC: The Aspen Institute)

Kubisch, A.C., Brown, P., Chaskin, R., Hirota, J., Joseph, M., Richman, H. and Roberts, M. (1997) *Voices from the Field: Learning from Comprehensive Community Initiatives* (Washington, DC: Aspen Institute)

Leiterman, M. and Stillman, J. (1993) *Building Community* (New York: Local Initiatives Support Corporation)

Levitan, S., Mangum, G.L. and Pines, M.W. (1989) *A Proper Inheritance: Investing in the Self-Sufficiency of Poor Families* (Washington, DC: George Washington University Press)

Massey, D.S. and Denton, N.A. (1993) *American Apartheid: Seregation and the Making of the Underclass* (Cambridge, Mass: Harvard University Press)

Mattessich, P.W. and Monsey, B.R. (1992) *Collaboration: What Makes it Work* (St. Paul, MN: Amherst H. Wilder Foundation)

O'Connor, A. (1995) Evaluating Comprehensive Community Initiatives: A View from History, in James P. Connell et al. (eds.), *New Approaches to Evaluating*

Community Initiatives: Concepts, Methods, and Contexts (Washington, DC: The Aspen Institute)

O'Connor, A. (1999) Swimming against the Tide: A Brief History of Federal Policy in Poor Communities, in *Urban Problems and Community Development* (Washington, DC: The Brookings Institution)

Pitcoff, W. (1997) Redefining Community Development, *Shelterforce* 19: 6, 2–14

Pitcoff, W. (1998) Redefining Community Development, Part II: Collaborating for Change, *Shelterforce* 19: 1, 2–17

Pitt, J., Brown, P. and Hirota, J. (1999) *Collaborative Approaches to Revitalizing Communities: A Review of the Neighborhood Strategies Project* (Chicago: Chapin Hall Center for Children)

Potapchuk, W.R., Crocker, J.P. and Schechter, W.H. (1997) Building Community with Social Capital, *National Civic Review* 86: 2

Putnam, R. (1993) The Prosperous Community: Social Capital and Public Life, *American Prospect* 25: 13, 26–8

Putnam, R. (1995) Bowling Alone: America's Declining Social Capital, *Journal of Democracy* 6, 65–78

Sampson, R.J. (1999) 'What Community Supplies', in *Urban Problems and Community Development* (Washington, DC: The Brookings Institution)

Sampson, R. and Morenoff, J. (1977) Ecological Perspectives on the Neighborhood Context of Urban Poverty: Past and Present in J. Brooks-Gunn, G. Duncan and L. Aber (eds), *Neighborhood Poverty*, Vol. II (New York: Russell Sage Foundation)

Sampson, R., Raudenbush, S. and Earls, F. (1997) Neighborhoods and Violent Crime: A Multilevel Study of Collective Efficacy, *Science* 277, 15 August, 918–24

Spencer, M.B. (1986) Risk and Resilience: How Black Children Cope with Stress, *Journal of Social Science* 71: 1, 22–36.

Stone, R. (ed.) (1996) *Core Issues in Comprehensive Community-Building Initiatives* (Chicago: Chapin Hall Center for Children at the University of Chicago)

Stone, R. and Butler, B. (2000) *Exploring Power and Race in ommunity Initiatives* (Chicago: Chapin Hall Center for Children)

Thompson, J.P. (1998) Untitled manuscript prepared for the Aspen Roundtable on Comprehensive Community Initiatives (New York: The Aspen Institute)

Walsh, J. (1996) *Stories of Renewal: Community Building and the Future of Urban America* (New York: The Rockefeller Foundation)

Wandersman, A., Roth, R. and Prestby, J. (1985) Keeping Community Organizations Alive, *Citizen Participation* 6: 4, 16–19

Wellman, B. and Leighton, B. (1979) Networks, Neighborhoods, and Communities: Approaches to The Study of the Community Question, *Urban Affairs Quarterly* 14, 363–90

Wilson, W.J. (1987) *The Truly Disadvantaged: The Inner City, the Underclass, and Public Policy* (Chicago: University of Chicago Press)

Wilson, W.J. (1996) *When Work Disappears: The World of the New Urban Poor* (New York: Alfred A. Knopf)

Wynn, J.R., Costello, J., Halpern, R. and Richman, H. (1994) *Children, Families, and Communities: A New Approach to Social Services* (Chicago: University of Chicago, Chapin Hall Center for Children)

Youniss, J., McLellan, J.A. and Yates, M. (1997) What We Know About Engendering Civic Identity, *The American Behavioral Scientist* 40: 5, 620–31

3
Expanding Comprehensiveness: Structural Racism and Community Building in the United States

Keith Lawrence

Since the settlement house movement of the early 1900s, government, philanthropic funders, not-for-profit local organizations and social scientists have shaped and sustained a wide variety of community revitalization initiatives across urban America.[1] Over the years, these localized initiatives undeniably have improved the lives of many poor inner-city individuals and neighborhoods. Yet, on balance, they have done little to reduce the social and economic contrasts evident in many metropolitan areas.

Metropolitan disparities are particularly obvious when race is taken into account.[2] Poverty occupies a predictable niche in larger cities and the poor are, disproportionately, individuals of color. Poor white Americans distribute fairly evenly over the metropolitan landscape, but between six and eight million people of color are concentrated in a handful of distressed inner-city neighborhoods. Of these, African Americans are the most highly represented and politically visible racial group, but many other racial minority groups and subgroups bear a disproportionate share of the urban poverty burden.

But although this association between urban poverty and racial minority status has long been a constant, the preference among America's policy planners at all levels has been to approach urban poverty from vantage points that either subsume or ignore race. In contrast, this chapter examines the ways in which race and racism contribute to the persistence of urban problems, and their impact on the effectiveness of urban poverty initiatives over the years. The main theme is that past and present local efforts to remedy urban disadvantage – that sphere of research and action called 'community revitalization' and more recently, 'community building' – have been severely undermined by racism embedded in the institutions, assumptions and practices associated with this field. More specifically, the assertion is that unchallenged assumptions about 'progress' in these endeavors contribute to permanent racial hierarchies in educational attainment, employment, income, physical well-being, and other areas vital to inner-city well-being. Moreover, remedial measures that do not challenge economic, political, cultural and ideological norms that bear directly on the fates of these neighborhoods from a racial equality standpoint may hold little promise for generating locally sustainable change.

With this outlook, a race-conscious framework for analyzing urban poverty and redefining the goals of community building is suggested. An argument is also made for the active advancement of racial equity as a planning principle and yardstick for evaluation by comprehensive community revitalization advocates.

In calling the field's attention to race, this discussion places its intellectual leaders at the center of something much larger than just urban neighborhood transformation. It assigns them a role in the ongoing challenge of American democracy itself: accession to its universalistic ideals despite its legacy of white privilege and nonwhite disadvantage. Community builders are asked to conceptualize what they do as democracy building, and not merely the repair of discrete neighborhoods and communities. Past experience strongly suggests that the latter task will continue to be futile without attention to the former, and that both are unattainable within an unchanged context of racial inequality.

Several intellectual assumptions inform the discussion that follows. One is an equalitarian notion of the American social ideal. Another important assumption reflects the belief in the transformative potential of the social and cultural 'space' outside formal politics and the economy in which people interact informally to define their cultures, identities and communities, and lead their private lives. The two biggest steps toward racial equality in the US – the civil rights revolution that swept away overt legal discrimination in the 1960s, and the abolition of slavery that preceded it a century before – were initiated by social movements within civil society. Modernization in the economic sphere, America's twentieth century rise to globalism, and other broad contextual factors undeniably played important roles as well. However, the democratic energy of local activists, reformers and protestors, was the timely and indispensable catalyst for the policy and attitudinal changes that ended those undemocratic regimes.

These and other assumptions and propositions in the chapter derive from analyses and insights in the social science literature. Some of these works are cited, but on the whole, I do not attempt to cover the theoretical and empirical terrain. Discussion of deeper issues, such as the historical role of race in American social progress and the ideologies that influence that process, is neglected in favor of more direct analysis of contemporary community building. A rich literature on racial disparity in employment, housing, education, criminal justice and other sectors critical to inner city revitalization, is also excluded for brevity.[3] To summarize its thrust in one sentence, Americans of color disproportionately experience the negative outcomes related to each of these opportunity areas.

The chapter begins with a brief review of past and present urban anti-poverty themes, highlighting their racial impacts. Next, the limiting effects of the dominant ideology of race on contemporary urban anti-poverty work are explained. Then, drawing on some recent reconsiderations of race and racism, the Chapter identifies key elements of a race-conscious lens for community building. Finally, there is an attempt to identify strategies and opportunities for inquiry and action that begin to come into view when urban distress is analyzed from a race-conscious vantage point.

Race avoidance in the urban community revitalization tradition

Historian Alice O'Connor has noted that the urban community revitalization movement in the United States could be faulted for 'its almost complete avoidance of the issue of race' (O'Connor 1996). This observation captures not only the limitations of community revitalization, but the essential problem with remedial thinking and action relating to urban poverty in general over the past 50 years. There has been ideological resistance to employing racial group equity as a central principle in designing urban anti-poverty strategies. Though racial minorities – especially blacks – made gains in the 1960s and 1970s that narrowed some opportunity gaps, the American tradition of disregard for the deeper historical legacy of race largely survived. Sociological analyses that explain this legacy and argue for historically informed social policy also have had little impact on the dominant policy consensus.

As a creature of a largely unreformed ideological and policy environment community revitalization theory and practice have also manifested serious deficiencies in their approaches to racial equity. These may not be transparent, so it is worthwhile to look briefly at how race has been treated in the major anti-poverty and urban redevelopment currents of the twentieth century, and to re-examine the dominant ideological assumptions undergirding the current policy discourse and agenda.

Race in urban redevelopment

In the detailed historical reviews of urban redevelopment and neighborhood initiatives in the US (e.g. see Halpern 1995; O'Connor 1999) several distinct phases and approaches stand out for several reasons. One of these is their treatment of race. Not surprisingly, in early periods when cities were predominantly white and black inferiority was a widely accepted axiom in American social thought, urban poverty initiatives almost completely ignored black disadvantage. Changed urban demographics and politics in later years made it impossible to ignore minority poverty completely, but, as summarized below, remedies adopted since then continue to prove inadequate.

- Early organized neighborhood-based anti-poverty initiatives emerged out of concerns about immigrant European poverty. Segregationist norms meant that black urban poverty was relegated to the margins of this emerging movement.

America's first neighborhood-based social welfare movement was partially a direct response to the chaos caused by massive European immigration into squalid big city slums at the turn of century. It also grew out of a progressive ideology that disdained the Social Darwinism of the industrial age. Progressives initiated the idea of neighborhood-based institutions as a vehicle for lifting recent immigrants into the urban mainstream, securing child labor laws, building up white labor unions and providing a range of other social services. Multipurpose neighborhood centers, or 'settlements', were developed with charitable funding to serve as sites for service delivery and tools for knitting together the diverse local community.

Like most reform efforts, the settlement house movement embodied many ideological tensions and contradictions, one of which would become a constant in neighborhood revitalization – that between the recognition of the importance of local, community-driven change and the need for social and institutional reform. Reformers recognized that many social problems were not solvable at the local level, but the settlement approach seemed a pragmatic alternative which held out some promise for strengthening and integrating neighborhoods.

Another contradiction was the settlements' promotion of social integration, but explicit exclusion of African Americans, whom most settlements simply refused to serve. (Halpern 1995: 38). Urban blacks were already being confined to their 'own' ghettos early in the century via restrictive covenants, steering, threats and violence. Settlement leaders actively contributed to maintaining the color line where they could. 'Racist realism' was the broad justification: whites did not like blacks and this social fact simply had to be acknowledged. Halpern (1995: 38–9) notes that the few attempts at African American settlements were short-lived. Lack of financial and technical support and difficulties in obtaining spaces for lease in racially changing neighborhoods, were formidable barriers.

- After the Second World War, federal urban renewal and public housing schemes continued the tradition of insensitivity to race by discounting the significance of place to black and brown identity.

The postwar period saw the beginnings of a massive migration of African Americans to the urban northeast and midwest from sharecropping and hopelessness in the rural south. As happened after the First World War, employment exclusion and other forms of discrimination continued to be serious problems for blacks despite their recent demonstrations of patriotism through military service. Federal urban renewal, public housing and highway construction programs exacerbated these difficulties by devastating black communities. In what really was slum clearance and coerced relocation, local real estate interests, planners and politicians conspired to destroy many central-city black communities, giving residents the dubious option of distant new public housing estates. As one observer notes, 'today's efforts to involve residents in public–private partnerships for neighborhood revitalization are sometimes plagued with the suspiciousness born of this era' (Coulton 1998: 16).

However, it is important to note that as the civil rights movement turned its focus to the North in the late 1950s, the dominance of planners, developers and consultants over community development was increasingly challenged from below. A wide variety of grassroots organizing efforts and nonviolent 'direct actions' – rent strikes, sit-ins, boycotts, demonstrations – brought only modest tangible returns (Halpern 1995: 88) but helped to establish 'community control' as the basic local development principle for the next two decades.

- The War on Poverty of the 1960s tested the principle of federally led, community-based change. Local organizational networks grew, along with grassroots involvement in program implementation. However, by the 1970s, federal posture toward extensive local participation, and cities in general, hardened.

Federal interest in poverty reached its peak during the 1960s, encouraged in part by the acceptance of local responsibility that seemed implicit in the vigorous grassroots movement for control of urban neighborhood development. Inspiration for the urban dimension of Lyndon Johnson's 'War on Poverty', enacted in 1964, came from two neighborhood-based demonstration programs funded by philanthropic and public institutions. These were the Gray Areas program (located in five cities) and Mobilization for Youth (in Manhattan's Lower East Side). Both fell short of their own expectations for a complex of philosophical and practical reasons, including internal tensions between a desire to remain politically neutral and a desire to work actively to alleviate poverty and inequality (Halpern 1995: 100). However, they 'signaled the end of the long era of acquiescence among inner-city neighborhoods to externally initiated reform...' (ibid.) and encouraged the federal government to develop the concept of 'community action' as the basis for its War on Poverty.

Community action sought 'maximum feasible participation' within poor communities in local education, job readiness and the accessing of social services. But to residents these could not be separated from issues of race, power and American values. Thus 'the designers of community action were unprepared for the political challenge that participants would pose to the established political regimes in locales. City officials from across the U.S. responded to the challenge by pressuring the president to limit the poor's policymaking role' (Naples 1998: 1).

An important complement to community action was the Model Cities program of the new federal Department of Housing and Urban Development (HUD). Model Cities called for new housing construction and coordinated social service delivery in 150 cities hard hit by urban renewal. Its goal was to bring to those cities 'a spacious beauty and lively promise, where men are truly free to determine how they will live' (Thomas 1997: 144). Moreover Model Cities, according to Halpern (1995: 121),

> not only was to provide for a concerted, coherent social service effort but for construction of racially and economically integrated housing that would help keep upwardly mobile blacks and whites tied to central city neighborhoods.

Reviews of Model Cities from the standpoint of race are mixed. One perspective holds that federal dominance of the program's early planning and implementation stages set back the push for community control of inner-city renewal, at the very time when these communities were savoring a degree of empowerment and demanding self-determination (ibid.). Another view contends that the program did provide unprecedented opportunity for local minority participation through its 'block grant' provisions, even though this often proved to be a messy process (Thomas 1997). But in the final analysis, Model Cities failed to sustain the commitment of the federal government during the Nixon administration, which by 1969, had begun to redefine the urban crisis as one of 'law and order.' It is hard to imagine that inner-city residents would not have viewed this hasty federal retreat with disappointment, given the devastation of many of their neighborhoods, made worse in many cases by the urban riots of the 1960s.

Ultimately, the War on Poverty was short-lived and unable to reverse urban decline and the trend toward concentrated minority poverty in inner cities. Its promises and limitations have been well explored and debated (see Katznelson 1981; Katz 1989; O'Connor forthcoming), particularly its influences on community activism. Its demise lends credence to the argument that the federal and local governments initially underestimated the political impacts of enhanced participation in poor neighborhoods of color, and once these became clear, elites redefined local empowerment in ways that served the status quo.

- The 'new federalism' of the 1980s brought social welfare funding cuts and increasing devolution of responsibility for urban problems to the states. This contributed to a revival, in the 1990s, of anti-poverty perspectives that were disconnected from social structure and history.

A major shift in the federal–state relationship in the 1980s, the continuing erosion of urban tax bases due to suburbanization, and massive urban job loss due to structural changes in the domestic economy, exacerbated central-city problems. As a result the community development sector became swamped by overlapping crises at the neighborhood level. Homelessness, service unavailability and inefficiency, deplorable housing or lack of it, inner-city isolation from job markets, drug dependency and related crime, and other problems, all grew larger in scope. Although there was an increase in the number and types of community-based organizations working in distressed areas, they were no match for the depth of devastation facing the inner city.

In response, since the mid-1980s, government, foundations and researchers have advanced a new generation of theories and strategies aimed at helping inner-city residents escape poverty. There have been welfare-to-work initiatives, poverty deconcentration or dispersal strategies, mobility strategies, self-sufficiency initiatives linked to public housing subsidies, and a variety of community-based initiatives – including federal Empowerment and Enterprise Zones – that emphasize both individual and community capacity-building.

Two important conceptual shifts accompanied these initiatives. First, the civil rights consciousness that infused community revitalization thought and practice in the mid-1960s and 1970s – that is, the sense that chronic minority group disadvantages were structural and institutional problems – began losing ground to the resurgent individualism of the 'Reagan revival'. 'Empowerment', the most potent transformative idea to emerge in almost a century of anti-poverty effort (because, properly understood, it is the antidote to systemic disadvantage), rapidly became reinterpreted in this period as simply the enhanced personal capacity to make one's way in life (see Riger 1993). Despite the rhetoric of many of its proponents, empowerment was effectively stripped of its progressive community-level connotations for the framing of social policy during the 1980s.[4]

'Comprehensiveness' effectively replaced empowerment, by the 1990s, as an organizing idea in community redevelopment. And, it was linked to the place-centered notion of 'community building'. Within this context, the comprehensive community initiative (CCI) emerged as a favored strategy. CCIs[5] target specific urban neighborhoods for service reform, physical and economic development, and community building. They are place-based programs – in single or multiple neighborhoods – committed to addressing the entire complex of issues contributing to poverty and disadvantage.

Along with an ecological perspective, CCIs stress neighborhood capacity building, conceptualized as enhancement of the non-financial assets already present in poor neighborhoods. Influential theoretical writings that use market metaphors to explain capacity introduced CCIs to exciting new concepts such as 'social capital' (see Putnam 1995). For CCIs, social capital inheres in formal and informal collaborative relationships existing within neighborhoods, and in the linkages between them and the larger systems (e.g. government, economic institutions) that have an impact on those neighborhoods. The CCI vision of enriched ties within communities ('bonding' social capital), and strengthened connections to external networks ('bridging' social capital), has led to the adoption of partnership-building, cooperation and consensus organizing as favored principles.[6] Thus comprehensive community building emphasizes the strengthening of the indigenous capacities of neighborhood residents to act individually and collectively to foster positive change (see Kubisch et al. 1997: 5). At its core is an interest in building up the social capital necessary for self-sufficiency and self-efficacy, and not in simply delivering services or building housing.

Comprehensive community initiatives and race

Interest in CCIs arose from several legitimate concerns, but racial equity was not one of them. In the largest sense it came from an awareness that providing pathways out of the inner city would not solve the poverty problem. Those individuals who could, would move up and out along those pathways, but a majority would remain stranded in their distressed neighborhoods. The realization was that, in the end, broken communities had to be fixed. And, the new climate of shrinking federal support for categorical programs made strategies emphasizing linkages across program areas all the more logical.

Besides the push of federal retrenchment in the 1980s, there was also an interest in reforming local systems for delivering social services in poor communities. As one observer states, comprehensiveness implies 'coordinated or collaborative efforts to improve local economies and infrastructure, social supports and networks within communities, and services to children and families (Stone 1996: viii)'. However by the 1990s it became clear that services alone could not lift poor neighborhoods out of poverty, and that comprehensiveness had to include a community-building component (see Annie E. Casey Foundation 1998).

But the CCI scope did not encompass taking on fundamental racial barriers to local empowerment. Partially, this was because many community builders considered the racial equity issue almost moot, since CCIs already served mostly African American and Latino neighborhoods. As communities of color were the focus of their activities, there was an implicit assumption that CCIs would quietly accomplish racial equity goals sought through confrontation in the previous decades. Moreover, the urgency of quality of life problems, the seemingly unstoppable federal retreat from redistributive strategies, and the complexities of 1960s-style grassroots activism, all seemed to call for pragmatism rather than idealism on race and poverty. Indeed, one lesson of the previous generation of anti-poverty initiatives seemed to be that overemphasis on race might scare off irreplaceable private and philanthropic funders nervous about the appearance of ideological or political bias.

CCI pragmatism prevents them from dealing with race in ways that could enable them to achieve their social goals. In their outline of the theories of change guiding CCIs, Robert Chaskin and Prudence Brown (1996: 5) list six approaches, and note that only one – 'enhancing political strength' – addresses the issue of community power and race. And, they add, few CCIs lead with a commitment to this particular strategy, though 'most of them aim to accomplish it as part of the effort' (p. 5). CCIs may be deterred from confronting race by the political and interethnic complications that would arise from a forthright treatment of race and power. Rebecca Stone, a researcher at the Chapin Hall Center for Children who studies how CCIs deal with issues of race, observes that CCIs involve multifaceted power dynamics, because they deliberately 'bring diverse players to the collaborative table with different levels of authority'.[7] Stone suggests that because of the legacy of racism in the US, race can affect these dynamics at all levels. For this reason, she contends, many CCIs would rather work around issues of race and power, rather than through them.

Funders play a major role in how CCIs address race. Although the private foundations that sponsor these initiatives advocate empowerment and community control – principles that, taken seriously, could not disregard race and power, they generally lack the inclination, or institutional flexibility, to allow CCIs to follow explicitly race-conscious paths. Similar to many community building practitioners, many funders assume that since these initiatives are immersed in poor communities of color, the collaboratives formed could not avoid addressing racial disparity issues. But as the Casey Foundation discovered with its New Futures initiative, 'handling such troubling data [showing gaps between black and white families on every front, from school achievement to infant mortality to income] required comfort with racial differences that rarely comes naturally' (Annie E. Casey Foundation 1998: 17).

Even this suggestion that what CCIs really needed was 'comfort with racial differences' understates the challenge race presents. The challenge for community building as a whole in the post-civil rights period has been to understand race as a problem of *context*, rather than just *process*. CCIs have been seeking ways to collaborate across racial and cultural lines without really taking on the responsibility of pushing for racial group empowerment. CCIs have not really explored how racial group *position* shapes community capacities in fundamental ways, and what is required to remove or counteract the society's racial hierarchy.

The discussion now turns to the deeper societal reasons why racial group position has not been at the center of urban antipoverty analysis and practice.

A race-conscious framework for urban poverty and community building

Contemporary approaches to urban poverty in the US, such as the CCI movement, reflect a historical legacy of social and ideological contradictions that severely constrain prospects for fundamental change. Three propositions are explored briefly. The first is that racial stratification has been a constant in American life despite the existence of a strong individualist creed, and the great leaps toward individual equality seen in recent US history. The second is that the ideological underpinnings of the American social contract relieve the body politic of collective responsibility for alleviating the racial group inequities caused by this stratification. And third, by operating uncritically within these ideological confines, the community building field helps perpetuate the disregard of systemic, societal solutions to inner city poverty.

Racism in contemporary America

As a first step, it is important to understand the nuances of American racism. Labels vary in the racism literature but three types of racism are frequently mentioned: individual (or face-to-face, or subjective) racism, institutionalized (or institutional) racism and structural racism.

Individual racism is the kind of overt anti-black prejudice, harassment and violence Americans associate with the periods of slavery and Jim Crow Reconstruction. This is, by far, the most widely understood meaning of racism in America. However, opinion studies today consistently find overwhelming majorities of white Americans expressing disapproval of such practices (see Bobo 1998). *Institutionalized racism* refers to the characteristics of formal political and economic structures that may cause them to generate racialized, but nevertheless widely legitimized public policy outcomes. Policy and administrative processes in public and private agencies and organizations may result in adverse outcomes for blacks and other minorities that cannot be traced to obvious racial biases in the policies or practices themselves, or to acts of individual racism by elected officials or staff in these institutions. Nevertheless these institutions maintain cultures and practices that, in the end, disregard the particular needs of disadvantaged racial groups or facilitate unequal outcomes for different racial groups.

However, the concept of institutionalized racism might be expanded to capture processes of racism embedded in the wider culture that may not be tangibly evident in institutions. More comprehensive is the idea of *structural racism*, which refers to all the enduring characteristics of American political, economic and civic life – tangible and psychological – that continually create, re-create and maintain white privilege. A structural definition allows us to see that individuals and institutions are parts of a dynamic process, greater that the sum of its parts, in which policies, institutions, individuals, attitudes and historical/social context interact to specify the boundaries of racial opportunity. Because race has played such a large role in the design of the fabric of American life, racial boundaries of varying permeability and rigidity exist in most social, political and economic settings. Legislative, attitudinal, demographic and other major societal changes since emancipation have blurred and chipped away at many of these boundaries, often making them hard to pinpoint. What betray their existence, however, are persistent disparities in racial outcomes in employment, education, wealth accumulation, health status, crime and punishment and other areas.

Note that there can be disagreement over these definitions of racism with regard to 'intentionality'. To some, only unintentional racism is 'structural.' Pincus (1996: 1), for instance, defines only the inadvertently biased policies of institutions, and the behaviors of staff implementing those policies, as 'structural discrimination'. The conceptualization of structure here suggests that intent to discriminate is not as important as the fact that Americans are unavoidably exposed to a social environment that inculcates and reinforces racist attitudes.

In a democracy, the postures of dominant public and private institutions and the official conduct of those who run them reflect a preponderance of the national will. What makes the seemingly benign cultures and practices of America's institutions produce racialized outcomes, are values, beliefs and ideas embedded in the 'common sense' of individuals within those institutions, that implicitly endorse the superiority of white culture over others (see Dominelli 1992: 165). At the core of structural racism is a majority common sense about race that is inseparable from its institutional engines. There exists a pervasive racial belief system held together by a set of core assumptions (or an ideology) relating to the characteristics of whites and non-whites as groups. This belief system includes to a set of negative stereotypes about people of color.

Laissez-faire racism

What precisely are the 'common sense' ideas that structure thinking and, ultimately, behaviors that foster racial inequity today? What is the nature of modern-day racist ideology? How does it relate to persistent minority disadvantage? The sociologist Lawrence Bobo and colleagues offer the helpful notion of 'laissez faire' racism. They observe that:

> the institutionalized racial inequalities created by the long era of slavery followed by Jim Crow racism are now popularly accepted and condoned under a modern free market or laissez-faire racist ideology. Laissez-faire racism involves persistent negative stereotyping of African Americans, a tendency to blame blacks themselves for the black–white gap in socioeconomic standing, and resistance to meaningful political efforts to ameliorate U.S. racist social conditions and institutions. (Bobo, Kleugel and Smith 1997: 16)

Laissez-faire racism involves co-optation of the values and principles of the political economic system in the service of white privilege. Prior to the 1960s, this was not as necessary because discrimination in employment, voting, housing and other key areas was socially acceptable. Slavery and the subsequent Jim Crow regime used racist laws and traditions, violence and intimidation to maintain *absolute* white privilege. Economic, social and legal (civil rights) realities in the contemporary period have encouraged manipulation of the 'American Creed' (e.g. personal responsibility, fairness, merit-based achievement) to maintain *relative* white privilege. In this way, laissez-faire racism is indistinguishable from the 'normal' influences on an individual's life chances in this society. It is much more difficult to perceive substantive racial inequity today because the 'color line' has been redrawn in invisible ink.[8] Bobo, Kluegel and smith (1997: 95) write that

> Laissez-faire racism has emerged to defend white privilege. Laissez-faire racism encompasses an ideology that blames blacks themselves for their poorer relative economic standing, seeing it as a function of perceived cultural inferiority. This analysis of the bases of laissez-faire racism underscores two central components: contemporary stereotypes of blacks held by whites, and the denial of societal (structural) responsibility for the conditions in black communities.

Ironically, the growth of the black middle class in the post-civil rights period has allowed whites who hold these attitudes to avoid confronting the problems of persistent racism. It allows them to overlook long-standing racial asymmetries that privilege whites and to justify opposition to genuine racial redress in key political, economic and social policy arenas. Calls for racial equity in labor markets, college admissions, criminal justice and other areas are deflected by a professed skepticism about compensatory government intervention, regardless of the egregious injustices of the past.

At the core of structural racism, then, is a pervasive racial belief system held together by a set of assumptions relating to the characteristics of whites and non-whites as groups.This belief system includes a set of negative stereotypes about people of color. Bobo and colleagues note that the 1990 General Social Survey found 56 percent of whites rating blacks as less intelligent, and 78 percent rating them as more likely to prefer living off welfare than whites (Bobo, Kluesel and Smith 1997: 30). Communication and media researcher Michael DelliCarpini (1998: 12) cites findings that 'significant percentages of whites still say that blacks are . . . lazy (31 percent), . . . lack discipline (60 percent), and are violent or aggressive (50 percent)'.

The immense power of these negative stereotypes is reinforced by the continuous validation of white superiority in everyday life by prevailing institutional and cultural practices. Although less uniformly than in past periods, our mainstream culture steadily showcases mostly white images of virtue, beauty, self-discipline, intelligence, heroism, family, love, civility, compassion and artistic sophistication. It is important to recognize that racial minorities themselves internalize these stereotypes because they are so commonplace, durable and 'normal.' This reality, combined with minority under-involvement in institutional decision-making, facilitates perpetuation of racialized core assumptions about whites and non-whites at the institutional level.

Racist political arrangements and the calculated exploitation of non-white labor gave structural racism its initial shape and character centuries ago. Today, a legacy of mirror image stereotyping of whites and non-whites, as much as any other factor, helps to preserve the racial hierarchy. Often, this racist conventional wisdom simply overpowers formal institutional rules or policies intended to prevent discrimination. A good contemporary example is the persistence of 'racial profiling' by law enforcement personnel, despite the institutionalization of racial sensitivity or awareness training in most big-city police departments. One striking aspect of this issue is the lack of evidence that minority police officers in those departments are significantly less likely than white counterparts to engage in this practice.

Obviously, civil rights consciousness has guided many Americans toward 'progressive' alternative ideologies about race. Nevertheless, regressive thinking is still widespread enough to permit a national acceptance of unearned white privilege and non-white disadvantage. To assert that racial discrimination is 'everywhere' may be an overstatement. But racism subtly structures so many of the daily routines of American life that whites do not need its cruder manifestations remain atop the social hierarchy. As Dominelli (1992: 165) observes:

> it is the subtle presence of racism in our normal activities, coupled with our failure to make the connections between the personal, institutional and cultural levels of racism, which make it so hard for white people to recognize its existence in their particular behavior and combat it effectively.

The ideological underpinnings of community building

Structural racism is formidable because it has evolved symbiotically with the dominant national ideology. Though not obvious at first glance, the norms, beliefs and principles of this racialized ideology undergird community building, just as they influence all other aspects of American social policy. The longstanding axiom that poor individuals and their immediate surroundings should be the principal foci of intervention on the matter of urban poverty, is perhaps the main indicator of the ascendancy of this ideology. A brief exploration of the constructs of this belief system would illuminate the normative biases inherent in current community building.

In the US, judgements about social equity derive from an amalgam of related core beliefs and values that, collectively, might be termed 'the American Creed': democracy (one person, one vote), free-market economics, pragmatism, pluralism, individualism (progress and self-sufficiency through industry and merit) and equality. Altogether the Creed instructs that, with the state acting as impartial referee, all have the opportunity to make the best of themselves in an impartial society. Democratic and pluralistic beliefs also convince Americans that their society fashions rules of fair conduct in response to the expressed interests of wide cross-sections of its members.

Equality, however, is a particularly fuzzy element of this ideology, and because equalitarian assumptions run through most of the other values and beliefs, this fuzziness lies at the root of many of America's social policy dilemmas. Americans overwhelmingly support the idea of equality of opportunity, regardless of race. They also mostly acknowledge the reality of chronic racial disparity in social opportunities and outcomes. Yet there is no clear agreement on what society needs to do (if anything) to achieve racial equity in politics, the economy and other opportunity areas. As the ongoing affirmative action debate shows, most blacks feel that racially redistributive and preferential measures are warranted to compensate for past and present discrimination. But many whites argue that such redress could only come at their expense as a racial group, and thus would be 'reverse discrimination': an unjustifiable remedy that victimizes them for the sins of their forefathers. Equality, then, translates into obligation by the state to provide no more than the most basic tools, such as voting rights or access to education and employment, for individuals to make their way in society.

But when this egalitarian ideology is applied to the political economy a major defect is revealed: it obscures the social content of institutional and individual behaviors. It assumes that social outcomes, i.e. 'winners' and 'losers', are distributed in the population purely on the basis of individual ability and talent. In so doing, it fails to reconcile individualism with some of the harsher realities of social constraint.

The ascendancy of political conservatism after the civil rights period has provided ideological cover for those who prefer to blame the disadvantaged for their plight. They can do so under the guise of 'principled conservatism', that is, by '...stress[ing] the importance of values, attitudes, habits, and styles in explaining the differences, behavior, and outcomes of groups' (Wilson 1996: xiv). In this ideological climate conservatives have been freer to infer that since racial discrimination had been outlawed, minority poverty amounted to a 'personal', 'cultural' and even 'moral' problem. Though insisting that society could not legislate 'morality' and 'personal responsibility', conservative ideologues have sought to tailor social policy in ways that remove 'perverse incentives' for welfare dependency, idleness, educational underachievement, illegitimacy, substance abuse, and so on.

This shift in the ideological balance was facilitated by a rightward intellectual realignment within liberalism as well. After civil rights many on the political left, instead of continuing to emphasize economic, political and other barriers to equal opportunity, either joined in or remained silent about the conservative reaction to minority gains. The contemporary liberal retreat from affirmative action[9] reveals how prominent liberal intellectuals (white and black) have defended the 'race-neutral' precepts of American democracy and capitalism.

During the 1980s and 1990s, some liberal social scientists provided a theoretical rationale for de-emphasizing embedded social, psychological, economic and other structures by advancing the concept of the 'urban underclass'. By far the most influential body of work in this vein comes from sociologist William Julius Wilson (1987, 1996). Wilson has described a subculture of Americans existing outside the economic and cultural mainstream, typically in crime-ridden inner-city neighborhoods that provided little cause for optimism. Wilson identified in this underclass a 'culture of poverty' characterized by low labor-market attachment, low educational attainment, high rates of teenage pregnancy and single parenthood, and high involvement in illegal activities.

This linkage of inner-city culture and other neighborhood-level characteristics to social breakdown sparked enormous research and funder interest. A voluminous multidisciplinary literature developed around hypotheses drawn from Wilson's cultural observations about urban poverty. Cultural explanations resonated so strongly with the growing neoliberal consensus in government circles that, during the 1980s and early 1990s, there was much emphasis on addressing the human capital deficits of poor urban communities. Self-help type programs such as job skills and job search training, drug treatment, leadership development and family self-sufficiency became dominant themes in the community revitalization agenda. Underclass research in its own way helped to re-legitimize reductionist interpretations of inner city disadvantage.

New localism

For contemporary community revitalization practice, recent ideological trends have translated into yet another round of neighborhood-focused activity that attaches low priority to fundamental problems of structural inequity. From a historical standpoint, Alice O'Connor notes that the American social policy tradition has been dominated by recurring, often contradictory, ideological themes ill-suited to the task of community revitalization.[10] She suggests that poverty reformers – driven by localism, philanthropic priorities, political expediency and other motives – have been wedded to the same basic set of localized experiments for the past 40 years. This, she observes, stands in sharp contrast to the early postwar period of federal government leadership in creating employment, providing middle-class housing and erecting a social safety net.

Social science has contributed to this bias toward inadequate local and individual solutions. A recent literature review by Michael Teitz and Karen Chapple (1998: 38) identified six major hypotheses about inner-city poverty in recent decades, only one of which squarely emphasizes non-local causes. Briefly, the reviewers listed inadequate human capital, racial and gender discrimination in employment, spatial mismatch between workers and jobs, inadequate social capital, low levels of minority entrepreneurship and access to capital, and the unanticipated consequences of public policy.

Since the brief interruption of the War on Poverty, there has a been a return to the non-governmental anti-poverty tradition. Interest in the social and human capital, personal mobility, local entrepreneurship and other reductionist diagnoses has led to a new consensus perspective that might be called 'new localism'. New localism basically holds that distressed communities need to develop indigenous resources, as well as initiate the kinds of collaborative relationships with outside institutions that could bring external resources into the inner city. Essentially, it leaves prevailing economic and political paradigms unchallenged and approaches urban poverty as, first and foremost, a local- and individual-level problem. 'People', 'places' and local systems are priority points for intervention by civic actors who recognize local assets and opportunities for synergistic benefits through program coordination, potential public–private partnerships, and 'leveraging' external resources. Local sustainability and individual economic self-sufficiency (and not structural change) are the new localism's primary goals.

New localism has proven useful in some respects. For instance, community builders today are much more interested in recognizing and enhancing local assets and agency. They are keenly aware that sustainable change can come only when local stakeholders are deeply invested in the revitalization process, and develop the capacity to engage the wider society's operating systems more effectively.

But in overemphasizing the catalytic roles of neighborhood, family and individuals in the revitalization process, this renewed interest in nongovernmental solutions has pushed the obligations of the larger society toward poor communities too far into the background. The danger of new localism is its implicit assumption that communities that have been systematically exploited and neglected for generations, and that have been isolated from lucrative job markets, public transportation networks and adequate educational and service systems, can nevertheless begin to revive themselves, essentially by their own efforts. Structural and institutional barriers that continue to block racial minority advancement can be overcome or made irrelevant, it is assumed, by denser collaborative networks – within neighborhoods and across institutional, functional and jurisdictional boundaries.

The challenge for new localism is, first, recognition that racialized values embedded in overarching social, political, economic and psychological structures play a critical role in limiting key collaborations and in sustaining the patterns of urban poverty we see. For instance, minority isolation in inner cities prevents formation of important 'weak ties' to white opportunity networks (see Granovetter 1973).

Furthermore, since new localism implicitly derives from a partial theory of urban poverty (that is, one that does not give sufficient weight to historical and other contexts), it needs to be aware that prescriptions may be only partial. It needs to be skeptical of local remedies that do not outline how poor individuals and communities can themselves become agents for reforming societal norms and institutions, or that do not simultaneously leverage other resources to promote systemic and structural change.

When these limitations are taken into account it becomes apparent that those who most influence the community revitalization field have made some shortsighted strategic choices in tackling inner-city poverty. The following 1995 statement by a group of leaders in this arena provides a glimpse of this:

> While most of its advocates recognize a continuing need for considerable outside assistance (public and private), *community building's central theme is to obliterate feelings of dependency and to replace them with attitudes of self-reliance, self-confidence, and responsibility* (emphasis added). It gives high priority to establishing and reinforcing sound values. And these are not ideas being imposed from the outside – they are what the leaders of distressed neighborhoods across the nation themselves are saying they want to see accomplished.[11]

This view of a race-neutral, benign, public policy environment is powerful, seductive and dangerous. It encourages us to cast our eyes downward when looking for the sources of the enduring racial group disparities that lie at the heart of urban poverty. In this way community characteristics, neighborhood effects and individual behavior come into sharpest focus, and state, federal and societal roles remain blurred. The broader society is relieved of accountability while an unfair burden is imposed on the relatively powerless. Worse still, it frustrates efforts to promote a comprehensive understanding of the meaning, manifestations and consequences of racism for those communities.

Future directions in comprehensive community building practice

The community revitalization enterprise is at a peculiar juncture in its history. It is interested in tackling urban distress from a 'comprehensive' perspective, but at the same time, reluctant or unable to integrate race meaningfully into the analytical or prescriptive aspects of the comprehensive agenda. The choice facing the field is continuation of what amounts to palliative work for the people and the places victimized by structural racism, or alternatively, expansion of its mission to include race-conscious goals on multiple levels.

All the evidence suggests that continuing to do business as usual may be irrational – even immoral. A 'comprehensiveness' that treats race as just another exogenous factor, thereby disregarding its foundational significance to the social distribution of opportunity and power in the US, flies in the face of all that is obvious about urban disadvantage. Moreover, there is a wealth of latent resources available to community builders for addressing issues of racial inequality. More than most civic actors outside formal politics, this field has great potential to act as a catalyst for progressive change. To make this possible, community building's practitioners, funders and researchers first need to be as interested in reshaping the broader civic context for public policy, as they are in refining localism.

One compelling reason why community building should take up a challenge that some see as better suited to the political sphere, is that impetus for racially progressive change must come from civil society.[12] History advises that we need not wait for transforming presidential and legislative leadership, or for the spontaneous emergence of a kinder, gentler version of the economic marketplace. Political and business elites have little incentive to initiate the reallocation of power, resources and privilege.

Neither can we afford to wait for the activation of that moral sense of which Gunnar Myrdal was so confident. Slavery's long tenure in a society founded on the rights to 'life, liberty and the pursuit of happiness' testifies to the inadequacies of moral consciousness alone when vested interests are at stake. To destroy that 'peculiar institution', elements within civil society had to mobilize on the basis of an alternative moral vision – civil rights – and actively pressure conservative interests. The black church provided critical leadership that eventually brought the civil rights paradigm shift. Regrettably, since the waning of civil rights activism, few of civil society's other anchoring institutions have made this sort of leadership a priority.

However, as community builders attempt to play a more leading role in this civic dimension, they must be mindful of the complexities and deep stratifications of American civil society.[13] Indeed, race-based privilege in civil society complicates prospects for the kinds of grassroots, cross-racial coalition building that many see as the civic antidote to structural forces (for instance, see Wilson 1999).

Nevertheless, informed by an appropriate understanding of the prospects and constraints within civil society, the community building field could be a highly effective leader of a renewed effort to extend democracy. Along with the reasons already offered, it enjoys significant comparative advantages over other would-be change agents in the civic sphere.

- CCIs, community development corporations, and a range of other non-profit advocacy and service organizations are firmly grounded in poor communities.
- Many community building organizations already play an intermediary role that links their clients to strategic institutions inside and outside the civic realm – that is, they possess invaluable 'bridging' social capital, as they are usually embedded in rich resource networks in which they are respected.
- Community building organizations are among the few civic institutions that interact with and gain the trust of immigrants coming to the inner city today.

What is to be done? First, community building could assume an intellectual leadership role in integrating race and structure in ways that deepen the popular understanding of urban poverty. We can begin by sketching out a research agenda for proceeding in that direction.

Three areas of work seem to be called for. Influential voices in the field could:

- redefine comprehensiveness and community building from a structural racism perspective for funders, practitioners and other stakeholders;
- encourage research into how structural racism manifests itself at each level (individual, civic, and institutional) in the domains of greatest significance to distressed communities;
- encourage practitioners and funders to integrate a structural racism consciousness (as opposed to race-neutral, liberal assumptions) into the 'theories of change' they use to plan and evaluate community building initiatives.

Redefining comprehensiveness from a structural racism perspective

A genuinely comprehensive framework would recognize the existence of cognitive, cultural and other intangible mediating structures between the state and its social groups and individuals. It would explicitly challenge myths about concentrated black and brown poverty, e.g. that its incidence depends entirely upon the interplay of individual attributes and 'natural' market forces. To be a legitimate strategy for change, notions of comprehensiveness must recognize all the barriers to equality associated with race – particularly how 'whiteness' as social resource and 'nonwhiteness' as social liability, limit opportunity and empowerment.

To counteract the racial inequity so deeply ingrained in American life, community revitalization must deploy an alternative paradigm that is cognizant of the significance of white privilege at every level. It must develop and promote a perspective that is also cognizant of the historical, institutional and psychological dimensions to race in American life. It must draw as much attention to the systemic sources of poverty – institutional and ideological – as it does to people and place.

Such a structural vision would provide community building a much-needed balance to the increasingly popular communitarian diagnosis of what ails American society. Influential scholars have rightly drawn dire conclusions from the declining political participation and increasing atomization in American political and social life. They have inspired an intellectual movement that promotes construction or reconstruction of the cooperative ties that bind communities together (see Glendon 1991; Etzioni 1993; Fukuyama 1995). This thinking has resonated with community builders, and there has been a rich recent history of local mobilizing in this spirit.

But as political scientist Mark Warren (1998b: 3) points out, the 'weakness of communitarianism infects the contemporary world of community building' because it lacks 'an adequate strategy for developing political power'. Echoing arguments offered earlier, Warren notes that:

> for communities historically excluded from power, and suffering from social and economic inequality as well, the health of their communities cannot be reclaimed solely by mobilizing their own internal, communal resources. They have to exert political power to demand a greater share, if not a restructuring, of societal resources. (p. 3)

It should be stressed that a structural analysis does not imply that community-level cooperation and social capital are irrelevant or detrimental to building community. Rather, the question it poses is: cooperation and networks of trust in pursuit of *what* visions of community change? It suggests that an exclusive focus on functional cooperation[14] is a serious self-limitation, given the heavy challenge posed by racial inequity.

Functional cooperation is one logical implication of the communitarian outlook. But its tendency to discourage issue definitions that highlight power asymmetries associated with race and class makes functionalism an inadequate tool. It appears strategically wise to identify interests that transcend race and to seek cooperation, first, around 'safe' issues, but there is no historical evidence that sufficient goodwill is generated by this approach to facilitate the empowerment of disadvantaged groups.

To end structural racism, it seems that cooperation should also seek more immediate social policy goals. Communitarian sensibilities could be blended with realistic appraisals of where the color line exists in facets of our society that heavily determine individual life chances. Warren has noted that in the American Southwest, reformers affiliated with the church-based Industrial Areas Foundation (IAF) mobilize communities around social justice issues and encourage them to utilize their social capital as a lever in the policy process. The IAF model has its limitations with respect to issue-definition and replicability (see Warren 1998a; 1998b), and does not really interrogate race forthrightly, but it does provide a glimpse of what might be possible if reformers were to expand their visions of community change.

Not only is it important to challenge non-racial conceptions of comprehensiveness, we need to be skeptical of change models that underemphasize the significance of politics and power. The simple reality is that sustained inner city viability and racial equity require institutional changes that can neither come quickly, nor be secured by community rebuilders alone. 'Power' coalitions need to be forged across unions, academic institutions, white and black churches, philanthropic organizations, trade and professional associations, political parties, progressive media and other civic institutions, to articulate and legitimize new social values. The call here is for leadership by the community revitalization field in constructing and socializing an ideological framework for such social change networks. And to reiterate the central argument, this ideological roadmap must be designed with the pervasive significance of race in America in mind. We already have solid scholarship interrogating the race-public policy connection (for example, see Shulman 1990; Bobo and Smith 1994; Oliver and Shapiro 1995). This linkage is also highlighted, albeit to a lesser extent, in the growing 'Smart Growth', urban sprawl and metropolitan sustainability literatures (e.g. Orfield 1997; Ross and Leigh 1998). The challenge is to translate these insights into strategies for policy and programmatic action.

Another point that bears clarification is that attitudes and ideas relating to race – the public 'common sense' – form an important and inseparable part of the institutional decision context. Comprehensiveness must also come to mean an interest in reshaping broad public perceptions of nonwhite poverty, and not just local and individual self-images. Since the psychological attributes of black and brown poverty extend to the macro-structural level, we should not confine our attention to local 'feelings of efficacy', 'self-esteem', and other individual-level indicators of the community well-being. The comprehensive approach should be redefined to seek changes in the civic institutions and other influences that maintain a permissive psychological environment for concentrated poverty beyond the local level.

Broadening the community rebuilding mission is important, but so is identifying the right audiences for the new message, and tailoring the communication for greatest effectiveness. Community builders need to reach a wider public and also to promote linkages across institutional and academic disciplinary boundaries. A broader array of civic organizations, social science researchers, professional organizations, labor unions, environmental groups and suburban allies across metropolitan regions, need to be pulled into the structural racism debate. For this to be feasible, the message must not just be redefined, but 'packaged' in ways that make it readily comprehensible.

Structural racism research in critical community building domains

One urgent task suggested by this new paradigm falls to social science. Critical domains of community building activity – employment, education, services, participation, neighborhood safety, youth development, etc. – need to be dissected in ways that uncover where the structural effects of race present the greatest barriers. To be useful, this investigation must take place at various functional levels of those domains – for example, the individual, community and institutional, making the task even larger and more complex.

High inner-city unemployment, for example, is a typical community revitalization concern that might be re-examined from a racial equity vantage point. Hypothetically, a structural approach might bring racial labor force stratification more into focus than more localized issues, such as job availability and individual work readiness. Racial labor force stratification might be understood as the disproportionate confinement of Americans of color to the lowest echelons of the labor force, where low incomes, little job security and meager employee benefits make them most vulnerable to cyclical fluctuations in the economy.

Arguably, the main issue this employment perspective raises is whether current workforce development strategies to boost inner city employment hold any real promise for solving this root problem of racial labor force stratification.[15] It challenges us to focus more on the values supporting our labor market (i.e the prevailing consensus relating to full employment, controlling inflation, the living wage, free trade and other production-related issues).

It might be worthwhile, for instance, for community builders to explore the institutional norms associated with the tenuous underclass–labor force connection, even as they pursue workforce development strategies. For example, collective bargaining, a labor market tool of great potential significance for today's growing 'workfare' army, has been severely weakened by federal and state institutional treatments of labor unions. Granted, the union movement has had a mixed history regarding minority inclusion (see Kelley 1998), and was already on the decline in the 1970s. Nevertheless, executive and legislative assaults at all levels during the 1980s contributed greatly to the anti-labor climate clearly evident today.

Recognition of employment issues like these bring the institutional and civic levels more into the picture and significantly expand the range of appropriate medium- and long-term employment outcomes for community practitioners. Policy-level reform appears as a higher priority. Also, it may seem appropriate to challenge the normalcy of the racial unemployment gap on an industry-by-industry basis. Strategically, public education and institutionally focused employment advocacy campaigns might receive more emphasis, and as a consequence, grassroots organizing and lobbying might receive greater tactical emphasis.

Finally, researchers in community building could advance theory-based program planning and evaluation techniques currently being explored in some CCIs (see Fulbright-Anderson, Kubish and Connell 1998) by incorporating the structural racism analysis. Again, this work might be elaborated at various functional levels and community building domains. The theory-building should be grounded in historical, regional and other contextual information. Conceivably, it might aim to create comprehensive racial equity templates for the key problem areas addressed by CCIs.

More specifically, the theoretical work could recommend sets of race-conscious outcomes that reformers might use as benchmarks in a given area of intervention. Practitioners desperately need these kinds of 'precision tools' as they address issues of race and equity in their community programs.

Notes

1. 'Urban' or 'community revitalization' is the generic term used throughout for the broad range of efforts aimed at halting the decline of inner-city neighborhoods. However important distinctions are made between similar terms used to describe these activities. For example, 'community building' aims more at fostering indigenous capacities for initiating and sustaining local improvements. References to 'the community revitalization field' or 'arena' here mean the constellation of practitioners, philanthropies, community-based service organizations, community development corporations, not-for-profit intermediaries and urban poverty researchers engaged in this work.
2. Race is understood as the social hierarchy of privilege in American society that is associated with ethnic and phenotypic characteristics. 'Whiteness' and 'blackness' constitute the top and bottom of this social scale, and Americans are assigned to various levels by enduring cultural norms and stereotypes.
3. Excellent recent sources of racial disparity information are the publications of the Clinton Administration's 'Commission on Race' (e.g. see Council of Economic Advisers 1998).
4. Zimmerman (1999) contends that empowerment theory has always included multiple levels of analysis, although, in the 1980s, its individual-level aspects received more research attention than its organizational and community dimensions (e.g. see Chavis and Wandersman 1990; Riger 1993; Israel et al. 1994).
5. Opinions vary, but over 50 initiatives may currently be called CCIs. Among the largest and best known are:

   Baltimore's Sandtown-Winchester program supported by the City of Baltimore and the Enterprise Foundation.

   The recently ended Atlanta Project initiated by former President Jimmy Carter to assist 20 neighborhoods address poverty.

   The Ford Foundation's Neighborhood and Family Initiative to improve neighborhoods in Detroit, Hartford, Memphis, and Milwaukee through interventions involving whole families.

   The Comprehensive Community Revitalization Program, funded initially by the Surdna Foundation to revitalize communities in the South Bronx area of New York City.

   The Rebuilding Communities Initiative (Annie E. Casey Foundation) in five cities: Boston, Philadelphia, Denver, Detroit, Washington, DC.

6. For a discussion of various conceptions of social capital see Warren, Thompson and Saegert (1999).
7. See sidebar on Power and Race in CCIs by Rebecca Stone, in Collaborating for Change by Winton Pitcoff (1997), in *Shelterforce* No. 97 (Jan./Feb. 1998): 15.
8. The 'color line' is W.E.B DuBois' still-powerful metaphor for the barriers constituted by race in America (and abroad). See O'Connor (1998) and Lopez and Stack (1998) for explanations of how social policy continually readjusts the color line to maintain white privilege.
9. See Steinberg (1995).

10. See Alice O' Connor, 'Swimming against the Tide: A Brief History of Federal Policy in Poor Communities', in (eds.), Ron Ferguson and Bill Dickens (Brookings Institution forthcoming).
11. In mid-1995, the Annie E. Casey Foundation, the Rockefeller Foundation, and the US Department of Housing and Urban Development jointly funded a project to broaden understanding of community building and its implications. The work of the project – implemented by the Development Training Institute (DTI) and the Urban Institute – centered around six seminars which examined the historic movements out of which today's community building practice is evolving. Seminar participants included community building practitioners, interested researchers, foundation representatives, and federal and local officials. See report at http://www.ncbn.org/directry/dirlay.htm.
12. 'Civil society' is a sphere of social interaction between the economy and the state, composed above all of the intimate sphere (especially the family), the sphere of associations (especially voluntary associations), social movements, and forms of public communication' (Cohen and Arato 1995: ix). It is the realm in which social values and beliefs are debated and legitimized, social hierarchies are enforced (by 'public opinion'), and racialized social policies are mediated and accommodated. For these reasons, many of those concerned about race, or the health of American democracy in general, call for renewed attention to the condition and potential of the civic sphere.
13. According to Dawson (1998), African Americans, women, social progressives and other marginal groups historically were denied access to the mainstream of political, economic and cultural discourse wherein society systematically allocated 'favorable outcomes to privileged groups' (p. 6). However, while many of these groups often were able to carve out alternative discursive spaces ('subaltern counterpublics') blacks were excluded from these also. Consequently, blacks developed their *own* civic sphere in response to the structural forces that enforced segregation, and out of a perceived need to develop black autonomy 'as an institutional principle and an ideological orientation' (ibid.).
14. This term here describes the widely recommended strategy of building social capital incrementally through collaboration on projects that promise universal benefits, or around carefully selected, uncontroversial issues. Functionalism's basic premise is that habits of cooperation developed through collaborations that accomplish tangible, mutually beneficial, outcomes or that focus on issues that lie 'outside politics', can eventually carry over to the resolution of more contentious problems.
15. Political scientist Jane Junn (1998) raises similar questions in relation to education. Is more access to education necessarily better for disadvantaged minorities given that system's tendency to reproduce racial hierarchies through its measurements of intellect, talent and merit?

References

Allen, R.L., Dawson, M.C. and Brown, R. (1989) A Schema-Based Approach to Modeling an African-American Belief System, *American Political Science Review* 83: 2 (June), 421–41

Annie E. Casey Foundation (1998) *The Eye of the Storm: Ten Years on the Front Lines of New Futures.* An interview with Otis Johnson and Don Crary, by Joan Walsh

Bobo, L.D. (1998) Mapping Racial Attitudes at the Century's End: Has the Color Line Vanished or Merely Reconfigured? Paper prepared for the Aspen Roundtable Project on Race and Community Revitalization

Bobo, L.D. and Smith, R.A. (1994) From Jim Crow Racism to Laissez-Faire Racism: An Essay on the Transformation of Racial Attitudes in America, in Wendy Katkin and Andrea Tyree (eds.), *Beyond Pluralism: Essays on the Conceptions of Groups and Identities in America,* (Eranston: University of Illinois Press)

Bobo, L.J., Kluegel and R.A. Smith (1997) Laissez-faire Racism: The Crystallzation of a Kinder, Gentler, Antiblack ideology, in S. Tuch and J. Martin (eds), *Racial Attitudes in the 1990s: Continuty and Change* (Westport, CT: Praeger)

Chapin Hall Center for Children (1996) *Core Issues in Comprehensive Community-Building Initiatives,* ed. Rebecca Stone (Chicago: University of Chicago Press)

Chaskin, R. and Brown, P. (1996) Theories of Neighborhood Change, in R. Stone (ed.), *Core Issues in Comprehensive Community – Building Initiatives* (Chicago: The Chapin Hall Center for Children)

Chavis and Wandersman (1990) Sense of Community in the Urban Environment: A Catalyst for Participation and Community Development, *American Journal of Community Psychology* 18, 159–62

Cohen, Jean and Andrew Arato (1995) *Civil Society nd Political Theory* (Cambridge, Mass: MIT Press)

Coulton, C. (1998) 'Comprehensive Approaches to Distressed Neighborhoods in the United States: Restoring Communities Within the Context of the Metropolis'. Paper prepared for Partnerships, Participation, Investment and Innovation – Meeting the Challenge of Distressed Urban Areas. OECD and the European Foundation for the Improvement of Living and Working Conditions. Dublin, June.

Council of Economic Advisers (1998) *Changing America: Indicators of Social and Economic Well-Being by Race and Hispanic Origin* (Washington, DC: US Government Printing Office)

Dawson, M.C. (1998) An Alternative Perspective on the Theoretical and Empirical Study of Race and Community. Paper prepared for the Aspen Roundtable Project on Race and Community Revitalization

DelliCarpini, M.X. (1998) Race and Community Revitalization: Communications Theory and Practice. Paper prepared for the Aspen Roundtable Project on Race and Community Revitalization

Dominelli, L. (1992) An Uncaring Profession? An Examination of Racism in Social Work, in P. Braham, A. Rattansi and R. Skellington (eds.), *Racism and Antiracism: Inequalities, Opportunities and Policies* (London: Sage Publications)

Etzioni, A. (1993) *The Spirit of Community: The Reinvention of American Society* (New York: Touchstone)

Fukuyama, F. (1995) *Trust: The Social Virtues and the Creation of Prosperity* (New York: Free Press)

Fulbright-Anderson, K., A. Kubisch and Connell, J. (eds) (1998) *New Approaches to Evaluating Community Initiatives* (Washington, DC: Aspen (Institute)

Glendon, M.A. (1991) *Rights Talk: The Impoverishment of Political Discourse* (New York: Free Press)

Granovetter, M. (1973) The Strength of Weak Ties, *American Journal of Sociology* 78, (May), 1360–80

Halpern, R. (1995) *Rebuilding the Inner City: A History of Neighborhood Initiatives to Address Poverty in the United States* (New York: Columbia University Press)

Israel, B.A., Checkoway, B., Schulz, A. and Zimmerman, M. (1994) Health Education and Community Empowerment: Conceptualizing and Measuring Perceptions of Individual, Organizational, and Community Control, *Health Education Quarterly.* 21: 2 (Summer), 149–170

Junn, J. (1998) Education, Race and Community Building. Paper prepared for the Aspen Roundtable Project on Race and Community Revitalization

Katz, M. (1989) *The Undeserving Poor* (New York: Pantheon)

Katznelson, I. (1981) *City Trenches: Urban Politics and the Patterning of Class in the United States* (New York: Pantheon)

Kelley, R. (1998) Building Bridges: The Challenge of Organized Labor in Communities of Color. Paper prepared for the Aspen Roundtable Project on Race and Community Revitalization

Kubisch, A.C., Brown, P., Chaskin, R., Hirota, J., Joseph, M., Richman, H. and Roberts, L.M. (1997) *Voices from the Field: Learning from the Early Work of Comprehensive Community Initiatives* (Washington, DC: The Aspen Institute)

Lopez, M.L. and Stack, C.B. (1998) Social And Cultural Theories of Poverty: Community Practices and Social Change. Paper prepared for the Aspen Roundtable Project on Race and Community Revitalization.

Naples, N.A. (1998) From Maximum Feasible Participation to Disenfranchisement, *Social Justice* (Spring)

O'Connor, A. (1996) Federal Policy in Poor Communities: A Brief History. Paper prepared for the NCDPAN Fall 1996 Conference, November

O'Connor, A. (1998) 'Historical Perspectives on Race and Community Revitalization'. Paper prepared for the Aspen Roundtable Project on Race and Community Revitalization

O'Connor, A. (1999) Swimming against the Tide: A Brief History of Federal Policy in Poor Communities, in R. Ferguson and W. Dickens (eds), *Urban Problems and Community Development* (Washington, DC: The Brookings Institution)

Oliver, M. and Shapiro, T. (1995) *Black wealth/White wealth: A New Perspective on Racial Equality* (New York: Routledge)

Orfield, M. (1997) *Metropolitics: A Regional Agenda for Community and Stability* (Washington, DC: Brookings Institution Press)

Patterson, O. (1991) *Freedom, Volume I: Freedom in the Making of Western Culture* (New York: HarperCollins)

Pincus, F.L. (1996) Discrimination Comes in Many Forms: Individual, Institutional, and Structural, *The American Behavioral Scientist* (Nov./Dec)

Putnam, R. (1995) 'Bowling Alone: America's Declining Social Capital'. *Journal of Democracy* 6: 1 (January): 65–78

Riger, S. (1993) What's Wrong with Empowerment, *American Journal of Community Psychology* 21: 3

Ross, C.L. and Leigh, N.G. (1998) Planning, Urban Revitalization and the Inner-City: An Exploration of Structural Racism. Paper prepared for the Aspen Roundtable Project on Race and Community Revitalization

Shulman, S. (1990) The Causes of Black Poverty: Evidence and Interpretation, *Journal of Economic Issues* XXIV: 4 (December)

Steinberg, S. (1995) *Turning Back: The Retreat From Racial Justice in American Thought and Policy* (Boston: Beacon Press)

Stone, R. (1996) *Core Issues in Comprehensive Community-Building Initiatives* (Chicago: University of Chicago, Chapin Hall Center for Children)

Teitz, M.B. and Chapple, K. (1998) The Causes of Inner-City Poverty: Eight Hypotheses in Search of Reality, *Citiscape: A Journal of Policy Development and Research* 3: 3

Thomas, June Manning (1997) Model Cities Revisited: Issues of Race and Empowerment, in J. Manning Thomas and M. Ritzdorf (eds.), *Urban Planning and the African American Community: In the Shadows* (Thousand Oaks, CA: Sage)

Warren, M.R. (1998a) The Contributions of Faith-Based Community Organizing. Paper prepared for the Aspen Roundtable Project on Race and Community Revitalization

Warren, M.R. (1998b) 'Community Building and Political Power: A Community Organizing Approach to Democratic Renewal', *American Behavioral Scientist* 42: 1, 78–92

Warren, M.R., Thompson, J.P. and Saegert, S. (1999) Social Capital and Poor Communities: A Framework for Analysis. Paper presented at the conference on Social Capital and Poor Communities: Building and Using Social Assets to Combat Poverty. City University of New York

Wilson, William Julius (1987) *The Truly Disadvantaged: The Inner City, the Underclass, and Public Policy* (Chicago: University of Chicago Press)

Wilson, William Julius (1996) *When Work Disappears: The World of the New Urban Poor* (New York: Vintage)

Wilson, William Julius (1999) The *Bridge over the Racial Divide* (University of California Press)

Zimmerman, M.A. (1999) Empowerment Theory: Implications for Research and Practice Paper presented at the Flemish Institute for Health Promotion. Brussels, 22 March

4

Housing as an Anchor for Community Building: Community Development Corporations in the United States

Mercer L. Sullivan

The community development movement in the United States, though it has deep historical roots, began its modern phase during the urban unrest of the late 1960s. By the end of the century, it has matured into an enduring and growing sector of the American housing market that provides both affordable housing and related services to individuals and families with low and moderate incomes. Though unresolved issues of institutional identity remain and meeting the substantial needs of those it seeks to serve has proved extremely difficult, community development has emerged as a distinctive field of social activity situated within a specific historical, political and cultural context.

This chapter describes the characteristics of the community development movement within its national context, focusing on its emblematic organizational form, the community development corporation (CDC). The CDC has proved an adaptable, versatile mechanism through which low-income areas have been successfully revitalized. Two characteristics in particular have proven responsive to a fast-changing economic and policy environment. First, in large measure CDCs are locally controlled and to varying degrees local residents and their organizations participate in decision-making. Second, they have become adept in leveraging capital which in an era of low public funding has often meant that they are the only institution with the capacity to build or renew low-income housing.

CDCs learned to develop effective capacity in providing low-cost housing in poor urban neighborhoods. Increasingly, however, on the back of their prominent role as developers of housing they have expanded their community building activities. This 'more than housing' approach contains important lessons for urban revitalization. Because CDCs serve not just poor people but poor people with high levels of prior disadvantage such as homelessness increasingly the impact of the work of specific CDCs in highly disadvantaged areas is attracting national and international attention. It is this expanded role and the impact that CDCs are having in terms of community building that is the focus of the chapter. It looks at the work of the some of the most well-known CDCs and draws on important recent evaluation of their work and then discusses some of the major issues for the future of these organizations.

History of community development corporations

One early observer of the CDC movement traced its underlying ideas back to the utopian communities of the nineteenth century, which combined ethics of self-sufficiency and communal solidarity along with various religious and political ideologies (Berndt 1977). The modern community development movement, however, has its roots in efforts by private foundations and the federal government to address the deterioration of poor urban neighborhoods that became evident as early as the 1950s and later of intense national concern at the time of the urban riots of the mid-1960s. From the beginning of this modern phase, the combination of extra-local support and grassroots organizing at the neighborhood level has characterized the growth and evolution of CDCs. The earliest experiments were supported by the Ford Foundation's Gray Areas program, so named in reference to the deteriorating slums that at first seemed invisible to the rest of a country enjoying the rapid economic expansion following the Second World War (Marris and Rein 1967).

Many observers date the take-off point of the modern community development movement to Robert F. Kennedy's walk through Brooklyn's Bedford-Stuyvesant neighborhood in 1965 (O'Connor 1995; Halpern 1996). Community leaders accompanying him responded to his questions about what to do by asking him to get things built in their decaying neighborhood. This answer has resonated throughout the subsequent expansion of community development in the United States both because of the evident physical deterioration of the ghettos and the fact that building things, doing something, is a characteristically pragmatic American response to social problems. Kennedy subsequently co-sponsored

Federal legislation that created the Special Impact Program (SIP) within the then recently established Office of Economic Opportunity. The SIP was aimed specifically at neighborhoods with low-income minority residents giving CDCs tax exempt status and required the participation and control of their programs by local residents. Thus from the outset there was the intention of legislators that CDCs would adopt residents' priorities.

CDCs represented a sharp shift in the direction of federally supported social experimentation, away from support for efforts called community action programs. For a brief period in the early and mid-1960s, the federal government had provided direct support to community groups engaging in political action, often directed against local government. This produced considerable resentment amongst local political leaders and in the wake of the ensuing politically disastrous results, the notion of funding local development rather than local agitation held special appeal for federal planners (Moynihan 1969; O'Connor 1995; Halpern 1996).

In the next few years, SIP funded about 40 organizations across the country which became the prototypes for what are now known as CDCs. Originally CDCs drew on a variety of development strategies that included developing local businesses, investment in local infrastructure or supplying technical assistance to local enterprises. The creation of this new type of organization, directed toward a broader goal of improving the economic well-being and quality of life of residents of lower-income areas, was an important turning point in the anti-poverty efforts of that era, often referred to collectively as the War on Poverty. Most prior efforts had tried to accomplish goals such as the improvement of education, housing and social services through the delivery vehicles of large government bureaucracies. The CDC movement, in contrast, attempted to attain similar goals through the creation and support of locally based non-governmental organizations, enticing private industry to provide information and resources through low-cost loans, grants or tax abatements.

CDCs became a focus of contention at local level as local activists viewed them as instruments through which to expand political influence. They viewed CDCs as the first step toward reviving depressed local economies and that local minority economic control could alter the structures that produced poverty in the inner cities. It aspired to combine a politically progressive institution, firmly under local control, with an economically dynamic, market focus. This duality at the heart of the CDC concept has been both the source of its adaptability and of limitations which critics have not hesitated to point out. Although the stimulus provided by the federal government and large private foundations, especially the Ford Foundation, was undoubtedly crucial to the emergence of the movement, the movement also drew on other, more radical sources with deeper roots than the community action experiments. These included the community organizing movement pioneered by Saul Alinsky (see chapter 5), a veteran of earlier labor movement organizing, and various isolated black separatist attempts to establish economically self-sufficient institutions and communities (Alinsky 1972; O'Connor 1995).

As historian Alice O'Connor notes, the sudden influx of capital from government and foundations to the locally controlled CDCs 'de-radicalized' these traditions. This de-radicalization was not immediate, however, nor, according to some, has it ever been completed. To the present day, the record of demonstrations and blockades during the formation of some of the older and more established CDCs remains an important founding story that validates the organizations' legitimacy as representatives of their communities. The stories of yet other CDCs show how success has flowed from the shift from confrontational to cooperative tactics.

The activism of the federal government as reflected in the War on Poverty in the United States is now long past, supplanted, according to critics, by the War on the Poor (Gans 1995; Katz 1989). Yet the community development movement remains and has grown progressively larger, accelerating during the past two decades. The number of CDCs grew rapidly in the 1970s as low-income neighborhoods organized themselves around the production of low-cost housing which attracted the greatest level of financial and political support from the federal government. This support base for CDCs has changed a great deal since the early days when the federal government provided generous core support for the early SIP-funded prototype organizations with their broad range of social objectives. Job creation in particular was a prized goal in the early days, and remains an important goal today, but bringing jobs into poor neighborhoods simply proved too daunting a task to fuel the growth of the movement. The historical outflow of jobs from central cities to the suburbs was too powerful a trend.

When the SIP was wound up in the early 1970s CDCs were compelled to find activities that would attract new sources of funding. The majority consolidated themselves by developing housing with support from the federal government under section 8. Section 8, so named from its origin in the 1937 Housing Act, from 1974 onwards provided project-based development money for the construction and rehabilitation of low-cost housing, along with, crucially, a commitment to long-term rent subsidies for tenants. Section 8 subsidy required that no more than 30 percent of a family's income should be spent on rent. Since the gap between this and rents set at the market rate could be quite large, this program provided generous support. CDCs capitalized on the changing nature of federal subsidies for low-income housing. By dedicating themselves to building and managing low-income housing, they were able to generate real profits that could then be invested in further development or in other community activities.

Although this structure of funding was phased out during the Reagan era in the 1980s, CDCs had established themselves firmly as major housing providers particularly in the older cities of the northeast and midwest. A national survey in 1991 reported the existence of between 1,500 and 2,000 CDCs that had participated in the development of over 125,000 units of affordable housing (NCCED 1991). A follow-up only four years later reported cumulative housing production of 400,000 units (NCCED 1995). The size, productivity, capitalization and structure of these organizations varied tremendously, from fledgling efforts that have not yet closed a development deal to established CDCs that have produced hundreds of units and manage millions of dollars in assets. Today they produce some 23,000 units a year or about 13 per cent of all federally subsidized housing, although many are small, producing between 4 and 10 units.

In recent years, the funding base for community development has become much broader and the development process has become more complicated. The federal government still provides a great deal of this funding, but it does so through structures that provide tax incentives for private investment. Philanthropic foundations have also expanded their financial support through a series of complex financial mechanisms that leverage private funds. While the resulting capitalization has underwritten a rapid expansion of development activity, the complexity of the financial structures has led to a number of problems that are widely discussed within the movement (Dreier 1999; Weir 1999). The sheer complexity of development makes it difficult and expensive, while the resulting financial support structures can be quite fragile, imperiling the long-term viability of the projects. Some critics also complain that, in order to provide public monies to support development for disadvantaged communities, it is necessary to provide lucrative opportunities for already wealthy investors. Others counter that this is the only practical strategy in a corporatist state.

A crucial aspect of the emergence and growth of CDCs has been the creation of national, non-governmental organizations that coordinate, aid and support the efforts for local CDCs. Referred to as national intermediaries, these organizations have been especially instrumental in connecting national fund-raising efforts to the local level. These intermediaries function as a kind of community development clearing bank. The creation of LISC in particular in 1980 proved a catalyst for CDC funding in an era of severe cutback in federal spending on housing (LISC 1997; Gittell and Vidal 1998). The two largest intermediaries, the Local Initiative Support Corporation (LISC) and the Enterprise Foundation, work with prospective funders to facilitate the flow of resources. They themselves receive funding from a range of institutions such as foundations, banks, corporations and in turn provide grants, loans and other credit to CDCs as well as carry out feasibility studies. The effect is to diminish the risk for funders of investing in any one project.

Structure and activities of CDCs

In the 1990s a number CDCs, using their track record in local housing management and roots in local communities, began to provide services that focused on people, not property. This turn to a 'more than housing' strategy arose broadly from the realization that the strength of a neighborhood's social fabric was as important as the quality of its housing. Indeed without that fabric the housing development, now matter how new, soon fell into a familiar pattern of decay (Sullivan 1993). In this CDCs were responding to the same growing awareness that social problems in poor urban neighborhoods were interlinked as the new range of comprehensive community intiatives (see chapter 1).

The involvement of CDCs in non-housing activities such as social service delivery and broad-based advocacy varies considerably. In neighborhoods with relatively well-funded services, for example, CDCs are less inclined to expend energy duplicating those efforts. Conversely, some CDCs in service-poor neighborhoods have become major service providers. Similarly, CDCs in neighborhoods with active advocacy organizations may avoid the exposure and risk of confrontational advocacy by leaving such activities to the specialized advocacy groups. At the local level, then, a particular CDC may be the major community organization and take on a wide range of functions directly, or it may coexist with other organizations whose functions it complements.

None of these characteristics absolutely differentiates CDCs from other community building organizations. There is wide variation in the extent to which CDC activities overlap with those of other types of organizations and in the ongoing working relationships between CDCs and other organizations. Comprehensive community initiatives for children and families, or CCIs, for example, have come into being in the 1990s primarily under the sponsorship of private foundations, including many of the same ones that historically and to the present have supported CDCs. (See chapter 1 in this volume.) CCIs share a community focus and involve a network of neighborhood organizations. While CCIs typically include aspects of physical development in their mission statements, they are more focused on the delivery of social services than CDCs (Connell et al. 1995b).

The period of narrowing focus on housing development, as noted above, had produced strains and controversy within the movement. In order to pursue the development opportunities that were becoming increasingly available, CDCs had to develop technical expertise in the financial, political, architectural and management aspects of housing development. Many came to feel that this increasing emphasis on technical expertise was diverting CDCs from two central aspects of their original vision: comprehensive approaches to neighborhood needs and broad-based neighborhood participation in CDC activities. These concerns have come to the fore over the course of the 1990s and led to a number of efforts to redress the situation, in the form of renewed emphasis among CDCs on programs to involve neighborhood residents directly, whether through organizing, education and job training, or social services. These efforts are generally referred to in the aggregate as community building initiatives. The two principal changes in the community development movement over the last decade have been the accelerated growth of the movement and the renewed emphasis on community building.

In order to take a closer look at what community development means in practice, it is useful to examine some of the activities undertaken by prominent CDCs. For that purpose, I draw on the findings of a large study of CDCs undertaken in the 1990s, the Social Impacts of Community Development Corporations Study, which the author of this chapter directed at the New School for Social Research (Briggs, Mueller and Sullivan 1997; Sullivan 1993; Sullivan 1998). This study was designed to answer the difficult question of whether CDCs actually changed the lives of the people they served, and, if so, how. Because our interest was in the best practices in the field, our selection strategy was intentionally skewed toward established CDCs with proven track records. We also explicitly sought out CDCs that were known for engaging in activities beyond housing development, a reflection of the intense interest in community building that was emerging (Sullivan 1993).

We looked initially at 12 well-established CDCs which varied along a number of dimensions. Their annual budgets varied from $500,000 to more than $70 million, although the low end of that spectrum is deflated because some organizations contract out property management and other operations. In terms of housing production, the CDCs had developed between 300 and 2,700 units. Their defined service areas ranged from about 0.25 square miles to 4 square miles in size. The levels of family poverty in these areas ranged from around fifteen to over 50 per cent. Their governing boards all included local residents but varied in the extent to which they also included non-residents such as planning experts, clergy and members with connections to powerful interests such as private foundations, corporations and political interests.

A second phase of research followed in the mid-1990s and focused in depth on the work of three long-established CDCs: 1) Urban Edge Housing Corporation in Boston which manages 475 rented housing units in a low-income neighborhood populated primarily by African American and Latino residents; 2) Whittier Alliance in Minneapolis which is based in a mixed neighborhood with both a large white population in modest owner-occupied dwellings and a growing minority population living in rented units which the Alliance was converting into larger family apartments suitable for low income families; 3) New Community Corporation in Newark, New Jersey, which served an extremely poor, predominantly African American neighborhood with 3,300 housing units concentrated in a small area of several blocks.

We were particularly interested in what we considered to be the most exciting elements of the CDCs' activity, namely their moving beyond housing development into areas that strengthened the social fabric of low-income neighborhoods. The results were fascinating and diverse, requiring new perspectives to assess this activity. We finally concluded that these efforts could be grouped into three broad categories: property management, social services and community organizing and advocacy.

Property management

Most CDC housing was developed on a rental basis, although some programs for moderate-income ownership were in progress. We quickly discovered that the manner in which properties are managed once they were built is a crucial stage in CDCs, efforts to transform their neighborhoods. One aspect of this has to do with the long-term viability of the properties as decent and affordable housing. The two terms, 'decent' and 'affordable', are crucial. If properties are to remain decent, residents must not abuse them, managers must be competent, and there must be a sufficient income stream from rental payments and subsidies. If properties are to remain affordable, the rental portion of this stream must remain below a certain level. The struggle to balance all these considerations, we found, was often intense.

Another crucial aspect of property management is that it is the direct point of contact between the CDC and residents of the CDC's housing. The residents may or may not participate in other aspects of the CDC's activities, depending on what those activities are and the lifestyles, attitudes and other commitments of the residents. Rents must be paid each month, however, and property managers get called when toilets clog or basements flood, as well as when neighbors quarrel or apartments get broken into or raided by the police. Property managers in non-profit, community-oriented housing developments can also serve as points of reference to job training and education programs and community organizing efforts, even though such referrals are rarely part of their explicit job descriptions.

The property management role in CDC housing thus includes the roles of mediator, an agent of social control and social worker. We found a great deal of recognition of the multifunctional nature of this role, along with considerable variation in the extent and effectiveness with which this multifaceted role was accepted and enacted.

Not all CDCs managed their own housing units directly after the development phase. Some retained ownership interests but then hired outside firms to manage the property, including both non-profit and for-profit firms. In some cities with significant CDC activity, there were citywide, nonprofit organizations that specialized in providing this kind of management and training and technical assistance. Whether CDCs manage their properties directly or indirectly, finding, training and retaining capable property managers is a difficult and necessary part of maintaining viable housing. Some groups have struggled with this issue. In some groups, we found high rates of tenant turnover, and in others, crisis-provoked shifts from in-house to external management or between different external management companies.

We found in almost all our case studies a history of struggling over what to do when a poor family is unable to pay the rent. This becomes an agonizing issue for CDCs attempting to maintain both decent, affordable housing and a commitment to social goals. Almost without exception, CDCs report learning the hard way to resist the temptation to simply ignore delinquent payments, along with stories from those that collapsed precisely because they did ignore the matter of rent arrears. CDCs and their property managers may bend over backwards to find solutions. Indeed, they may find ways to raise income subsidies or other kinds of help that allow the residents to remain, but the policy of insisting on regular payment of rent appears to be one that all successful groups eventually adopt.

One CDC director described three stages in his organization's development: first, wide-eyed optimism: 'Good housing makes good people'; then cynical landlords: 'Follow the rules or get out'; and finally realistic compassion: 'Work with people'.

While one challenge of CDC property management derives from internal difficulties such as retaining committed and competent managers, another serious challenge derives from the perilous nature of maintaining an adequate stream of financial support for the properties. Despite the great success of CDCs in increasing housing production in the past years, analysts continue to point to a high degree of fragility in the financial health of the resulting developments (Vidal 1997).

Social services

Though most CDCs define their missions in terms of housing development rather than services, there is a range of positions on service provision. Some groups are actively involved in providing social services while others overtly reject the notion they should provide social services. Such groups maintain that their mission is self-help. Others are not very involved in services, not because they reject the notion but because their efforts are consumed with development and property management.

Among the CDCs we studied that provided some social services, the extent and range of their involvement varied enormously. Some of the smaller CDCs operated one or two youth programs, serving at most a few dozen people, while two of the larger groups operated extensive social services programs attracting millions of dollars in funding, usually from municipal agencies for which they operated as local contractors. CDCs also varied in the manner in which they linked their social service departments to their other activities. Some, generally the smaller programs, provided services directly and exclusively to residents of their own housing. The larger social service operations delivered services to a broad cross-section of residents of their local neighborhoods, most of whom were not residents of CDC housing.

The types of social services delivered in these settings included social work and counseling, employment and training, day care, youth recreational programs, services for senior citizens, health services and services for special populations such as the formerly homeless or battered women. Among these, services for youth were not prominent and were noted by some as a conspicuous lack and need. More recently there has been considerable new activity in job placement and employment training. Although CDCs have not been able to generate the kind of local business development that would reverse the flow of jobs out of central cities or poor urban neighborhoods the importance of job finding and job creation as the core of any anti-poverty strategy has never disappeared from view. In recent years, efforts have been redirected from direct job creation to training people for jobs outside their neighborhoods.

One issue is what, if any, added benefit comes to the area when CDCs deliver social services. In some neighborhoods, as mentioned, CDCs have picked up this function simply because they were the only organizations in the area capable of doing so. In other cases, relatively few in number but quite intriguing, CDCs have been able to demonstrate direct synergies in linking social services directly to housing. In one example, tutoring programs for children also served to help parents get to know one another and assume collective responsibility for monitoring children. In another, resident organizers were used to recruit participants in job training programs, and in another, day care homes programs, in which CDCs trained people to provided licensed child care in centers also developed by the CDC. The recent emergence of a new kind of program, Comprehensive Community Initiatives for Children and Families, probably reflects a feeling among activists and funders that CDCs are not always the best type of organization for improving neighborhood-level integration of social service delivery (see chapter 1).

Organizing and advocacy

The recent trend in community development has been away from the kind of confrontational community organizing originally advocated by the followers of Saul Alinksy and briefly catapulted to the level of Federal policy during the tumultuous days of the community action programs of the early 1960s. Even the Industrial Areas Foundation, the bearer of the Alinsky legacy, engages in non-confrontational, CDC-style housing development activities in its Nehemiah homes projects in Brooklyn and elsewhere. CDCs are constrained by both practical and legal considerations from engaging in the kinds of overtly political and confrontational community organizing that are still available to other kinds of groups. They have to respond to the legal proscriptions against using funds granted for other purposes for direct political activity. The major private foundations, great benefactors of the CDC movement, faced losing their tax-exempt status during the 1960s over these kinds of issues and are particularly wary of granting funds that could be seen to be used for such purposes. The recent attention paid to the conduct of foundations from a conservative, Republican-controlled Congress has only heightened this sensitivity. In addition, to the extent that CDCs are successful, they develop working partnerships with banks, city agencies and other powerful interests that it is not in their interest to jeopardize through alliances with combative, argumentative local political organizing.

While this situation has generated accusations from among some critics on the left that CDCs have sold out and been co-opted by the establishment, it is also true that organizing and advocacy, in less confrontational forms, remain vital aspects of the mission of many CDCs. LISC's demonstration project has explicitly adopted 'consensus organizing' as it seeks to promote and strengthen the work of CDCs in low-income urban areas. Consensus organizing places greater weight on what Gittell and Vidal call 'bonding' – trust and cooperation within the neighborhood – and 'bridging' – working relationships between poor neighborhoods and external sources power, resources and influence (Gittell and Vidal 1998: 53). This emphasis on two kinds of organizing undertaken simultaneously distinguishes the approach from that of the more combative, broad-based organizing, say of the Industrial Areas Foundation (see chapter 5).

Some kinds of advocacy, then, are not confrontational, legally prohibited or threatening to ongoing partnerships with powerful interests. Possibilities for this kind of advocacy arise when CDCs demonstrate their efficacy by accomplishing various projects and when they project an image of local support. Under these conditions, city officials and others can come to see CDCs as valuable partners. The extent to which CDCs actually achieve this presence appears to vary between cities and administrations. We found various examples of organizing at the local level. These included both organizing directed toward residents of the CDCs own housing and organizing of the broader community. The emphasis on local organizing varied among the CDCs in the sample, from low to high priority. Some CDCs had full-time staff positions for organizers while others merely organized occasional meetings. Among those CDCs engaging in resident organizing, the stated objectives included getting control of their buildings; promoting ownership, leadership and self-governance; assisting and monitoring property management; maintaining connections with buildings under outside property management; crime prevention; beautifying buildings and grounds; and providing recreation and social events. For those engaged in organizing the broader community, objectives included building coalitions with other local organizations, neighborhood crime prevention and neighborhood social events. Yet even confrontational advocacy is not entirely out of picture. There are instances when both confrontational and non-confrontational tactics are employed by the same people, appearing in different capacities. CDC staff reported taking part in demonstrations and protests as individuals or as members of separate advocacy groups, but not as representatives of the CDCs for which they worked.

Neighborhood safety

The efforts of CDCs in Boston, Newark and Minneapolis had a substantial impact on neighborhood safety. That each had engaged in specific activities which aimed to responded to concerns about rising crime and residents' fear of crime paid some dividends when looking at the level of victimization, residents' perception of safety and the fear of crime and perceptions of physical and social disorder.

Comparing the impact on residents' perception of crime and on rates of actual victimization reveals a number of important effects. First, residents held a lower fear of crime compared with residents in non-CDC housing in the cities and had the feeling that something was being done to make the area safer. Residents were also significantly more likely to feel safer than in their previous housing. But in general these effects were established indirectly through the dedicated, at times risky, work of small groups of committed residents and not through mass meetings or mass involvement in 'community policing' initiatives. Property and management issues, not community safety, continued to dominate most of the large gatherings within the area. However, the mere occasion of public meetings, street gatherings or cook-outs from time to time, together with the wide range of CDC activities, did seem to impact on residents' feeling of safety. Knowing more neighbors even casually makes people feel safer in the neighborhood. In the area covered by Urban Edge housing, the Jamaica Plain/Roxbury area of Boston, an astounding 40 percent of the residents knew ten or more people well enough to speak to occasionally (Briggs et al. 1997: 167).

Community safety seemed to respond to a number of mechanisms for change. As housing managers and housing developers and, increasingly, social service providers CDCs have substantially more capacity to affect residents' feelings of safety than for example, neighborhood watch schemes. They were able to work with police, organize residents around other issues that connect with community safety, displace criminal activity through further property development and provide services designed to curtail crime. It is likely that the effects of all these activities were greater on safety and perceptions of safety than conducting meetings or other anti-crime activity during periods of crisis or heightened concern (Sullivan 1998). In only one of the three CDC areas, however, Urban Edge in Boston, did the level of victimization significantly decline and this is attributable to a number of activities such as instituting youth programs, redesigning residential buildings and public space.

The evaluation seemed to suggest that the ways community groups may improve levels of safety are different from those put forward in the 'broken windows' theory (Wilson and Kelling 1982). The latter argues that criminal activity is attracted to spaces where there is a perceived lack of public order – of which unrepaired broken windows are the first sign. Even low levels of criminal activity scares away law-abiding citizens and this only leads to increased disorder. The theory emphasizes responding swiftly to repair the visible signs of damage, neglect and vandalism which will in turn have a positive effect on the preservation of public space and the interactions that take place there.

The data on the CDCs' impact, however, suggested rather that the reduction in the levels of crime and in the fear that residents felt had more to do with the work of committed individuals and influencing the institutional practices of housing managers and police. Such individuals, the 'saints' (Keyes 1992) of the neighborhood, often undertook risky but effective work in identifying dangerous apartments, buildings and situations and to facilitate evictions and police raids (Briggs et al. 1997: 11–12; 166–7).

Repairing the social fabric

At least two of the CDCs studied in depth provided evidence that they can 'build community' within realistic limits. Their activities were most able to affect casual ties and acquaintances, not close ties or personal friendships. A condition of leasing from Whittier Alliance CDC required participation in residents' associations and there was a significantly higher number of acquaintances within buildings than in the other comparative areas. Urban Edge's organizing efforts apparently increased the size of acquaintance networks at neighborhood level. Three-quarters or more of all residents thought it was likely that a neighbor would 'do something' to help in a variety of threatening situations such as breaking into a building, a significant finding that contradicts general fears that urban neighbors have no interest in repulsing threats.

On the broader matter of 'empowerment' there were few observed differences in residents' activism whether attending a neighborhood meeting, signing a petition, calling the media or the police. Majorities of New Community and Urban Edge agreed with the statement: 'I have no influence over what this neighborhood is like' – an indicator that they held little confidence in their individual power. Conversely, each of the CDCs were acknowledged as effectively representing resident interests whether with city government or through brokering area interests.

Current issues in community development

The present state of community development in the United States is one of rapid growth and a renewal of commitment to people as well as housing structures. The growth, however, is accompanied by concern about the financial viability of the resulting developments. At the same time the current emphasis on community-building involves a good deal of searching to define just what this means in an era of increasing mobility and decreasing dependence on the local neighborhood as a source of personal or familial identity. Community development is vibrant, active and continually in search of its own identity, while at the same time facing important issues for the future.

Community development versus dispersion

The most important of these is whether place-based investments have the undesirable side effect of anchoring the poor and thereby reinforcing class and especially racial segregation. African Americans are more residentially segregated than any other cultural group in the United States, and this segregation has been shown to interact with economic disadvantage to calamitous effect (Massey and Denton 1993). Ending this intractable problem of residential segregation by race is the goal of fair housing activists who share a great deal of their political orientation with community development activists. Yet the agreement on ends – economic equality – coexists with their disagreement on means – development or dispersion. Research on the Gautraux experiment in Chicago has also shown that children of former inner-city residents who receive housing subsidies in middle-class suburbs do better in school and on other measures than their matched peers remaining in the inner-city neighborhoods (Rosenbaum et al. 1991). Advocates of community development usually counter that by saying that, rather than wait for someone to solve the intractable problems of discrimination in the private housing sector, they intend to keep trying to improve life in low income urban areas.

The limits and obstructive complexity of the development process

Although the recent history of community development makes a persuasive argument that this approach can produce significant amounts of decent, affordable housing, that level of production still falls far short of the need. The development process as presently constituted is undoubtedly quite expensive as a result of the variety of funding sources, the length of time and number of parties required to produce a deal, and the high burden of subsequent reporting requirements. Even allowing full credit for what has been or is being accomplished, it is doubtful whether this approach alone is sufficient to solve the problems (Dreier 1999; Weir 1999).

Critics on the left describe the function of CDCs simply as agents for 'directed capitalism' trying to repair the failure of the market to provide jobs and services in the inner cities. This has, according to Marquez (1993), proved a false promise in part because of the low level of funding from the federal government which never rose above $75 million in a year and partly because they never attained the level of political support needed to give them independence of action. As a consequence, these critics argue, CDCs have been forced to accommodate themselves to the free market, relying themselves on profit-maximization to survive, rather than restructure it and appearing to be community oriented while their funding is controlled by forces outside the community (Stoecker 1997). This description has generated its own debate. Others cite precisely these mediating activities as sources of strength. Because they are both a landlord with links to outside capital *and* an organization for the expression of local needs they have developed a proven community building capacity (Bratt 1997).

Defining and defending the community participation element

The sense in which community organizations represent their communities and the extent to which this representation makes a difference in the effectiveness of the activities undertaken remain insufficiently understood. Although all CDCs include some community members on their management boards, the extent to which community and CDC housing residents define the direction and agendas of their organizations varies a great deal. Further, communities are by no means united in their vision of what a local organization should be doing. During our investigation, for example, one of strongest CDCs fell apart in a brief period after a take over of the board by a group of homeowning community residents who then formally disavowed everything the organization had stood for up to that point (Briggs, Mueller and Sullivan 1997).

There is then a legitimate question over how much and in what sense a CDC represents its local area. There is the further question about whether the element of participation itself makes any difference in outcomes such as the production and maintance of decent and affordable housing, the effectiveness of social services, and the like (Weiss 1995). While the concept of local democracy has undoubted appeal, especially in the current US environment of disillusionment with mainstream electoral politics, the meaning and significance of this concept in action remain in need of further study and understanding.

Evaluating community interventions

Although rigorous standards for scientific evaluation of various kinds of social program have been established over the past few decades, the methods used for evaluating interventions serving individuals are not readily applicable to evaluating interventions designed to change communities (see chapter 6). The Social Impacts study is the most extensive effort to evaluate CDCs to date. Using a combination of ethnographic case studies and a quasi-experimental survey of residents of CDCs and residents of matched comparison areas, we assessed change along a number of dimensions, including residential satisfaction, feelings of safety and community engagement. While our findings were almost all in favor of the CDCs, we did not find that any individual CDC accomplished everything it had set out to achieve. Rather, the CDCs that focused on particular objectives produced results in those areas. Thus, while we found positive effects, we did not necessarily find comprehensive ones (Briggs, Mueller and Sullivan 1997; Sullivan 1998). There were other limits. One key consideration is that our design did not allow us to ask whether any of these things might have been accomplished as well or better through other means than community development. The problems of evaluating community initiatives have been addressed in depths by a group of researchers convened by the Aspen Institute (Connell et al. 1995a). As the trend toward community interventions encompasses a range of efforts in addition to community development, further work on evaluation strategies is clearly needed.

Conclusion

The experience of the community development movement in the United States to date is one of impressive achievements along with a number of uncertain implications both for its own future and for other countries. The nature of the effort can be understood only with respect to the historical, political and economic circumstances under which the movement emerged and evolved. The transferability of the US experience to other places will inevitably depend on the particular relationships among the state, the private sector, and the non-governmental organizational sector in those places. If there is one key lesson of the US experience, it is probably that locally based entrepreneurship on behalf of social causes can work and can evolve into a significant institutional sector, even in the context of a corporatist state.

References

Alinsky, S. (1972) *Rules for Radicals* (New York: Vintage Press)
Berndt, H.E. (1977) *New Rulers of the Ghetto: The Community Development Corporation and Urban Poverty* (Westport, CT: Greenwood Publishing)
Bratt, R. (1997) CDCs: Contributions Outweigh Contradictions, a Reply to Randy Stoecker, *Journal of Urban Affairs* 19: 1, 23–8
Briggs, de Souza, X., Mueller, E.J. and Sullivan, M.L. (1997) *From Neighborhood to Community: Evidence on the Social Effects of Community Development Corporations.* (New York: Community Development Research Center, New School for Social Research)
Connell, J.P., Kubisch, A.C., Schorr, L.B. and Weiss, C.B. (eds.) (1995a) *New Approaches to Evaluating Community Initiatives* (Washington, DC: The Aspen Institute)
Connell, J.P., Kubisch, A.C., Schorr, L.B. and Weiss, C.H. (1995b) *New Approaches to Evaluating Community Initiatives: Concepts, Methods, and Contexts* (Washington, DC: The Aspen Institute)
Dreier, P. (1999) Comment, in R.F. Ferguson and W.T. Dickens (eds.), *Urban Problems and Community Development* (Washington, DC: The Brookings Institution Press), pp. 178–86
Gans, H.J. (1995) *The War against the Poor: The Underclass and Antipoverty Policy* (New York: Basic Books)
Gittell, R. and Vidal, A. (1998) *Community Organizing. Building Social Capital as a Development Strategy* (Thousand Oaks: Sage Publications)
Halpern, R. (1996) Neighborhood-Based Strategies to Address Poverty-Related Social Problems: An Historical Perspective, in Alfred J. Kahn and Sheila B. Kamerman (eds.), *Children and Their Families in Big Cities: Strategies for Social Reform* (Cross-National Studies Research Program, Columbia School of Social Work)
Katz, M.B. (1989) *The Undeserving Poor: From the War on Poverty to the War on Welfare* (New York: Pantheon)
Keyes L. (1992) *Strategies and Saints: Fighting Drugs in Subsidized Housing* (Washington, DC: Urban Institute Press)
LISC (1997) *1996 Annual Report* (New York: Author)
Marquez, B. (1993) The Industrial Areas Foundation and the Mexican-American Community in Texas, *Contributions in Political Science* 33: 3, 127–46
Marris, P. and Rein, M. (1967) *Dilemmas of Social Reform: Poverty and Community Action in the United States* (New York: Atherton Press)
Massey, D.M. and Denton, N.A. (1993) *American Apartheid: Segregation and the Making of the Underclass* (Cambridge, Mass: Harvard University Press)
Moynihan, D.P. (1969) *Maximum Feasible Misunderstanding: Community Action in the War on Poverty* (New York: The Free Press)

NCCED (1991) *Changing the Odds: The Achievements of Community-Based Development Organizations* (Washington, DC: National Congress for Community Economic Development)

NCCED (1995) *Tying it All Together: The Comprehensive Achievements of Community-Based Development Organizations* (Washington, DC: National Congress of Community-Based Development Organizations)

O'Connor, Alice (1995) Evaluating Comprehensive Community Initiatives: A View from History, in J.P. Connell, A.C. Kubisch, L.B. Schor and C.H. Weiss (eds.), *New Approaches to Evaluating Community Initiatives: Concepts, Methods, and Contexts* (Washington, DC: The Aspen Institute)

Rosenbaum, J.E., Popkin, S.J., Kaufman, J.E. and Rusin, J. (1991) Social Integration of Low-Income African-American Adults in Middle-Class White Suburbs, *Social Problems* 38, 448–61

Stoecker, R. (1997) The CDC Model of Urban Redevelopment: A Critique and an Alternative, *Journal of Urban Affairs*

Sullivan, M.L. (1993) *More than Housing: How Community Development Corporations Go about Changing Lives and Neighborhoods* (New York: Community Development Research Center, New School for Social Research)

Sullivan, Mercer L. (1998) Evaluating the Effects of Community Development Corporations on Conditions and Perceptions of Safety, *Security Journal* 11, 51–60

Vidal, A. (1997) Can Community Development Re-Invent Itself? The Challenges of Strengthening Neighborhoods in the 21st Century, *Journal of the American Planning Association* 63, 429–38

Weir, M. (1999) Power, Money, and Politics in Community Development, in R.F. Ferguson and W.T. Dickens (eds.), *Urban Problems and Community Development* (Washington, DC: The Brookings Institution Press)

Weiss, C.H. (1995) Nothing as Practical as Good Theory: Exploring Theory-Based Evaluation for Comprehensive Community Initiatives for Children and Families, in J.P. Connell, A.C. Kubisch, L.B. Schorr and C.H. Weiss (eds.), *New Approaches to Evaluating Community Initiatives: Concepts, Methods, and Contexts* (Washington, DC: The Aspen Institute)

Wilson, J.Q. and Kelling, G. (1982) Broken Windows, *The Atlantic Monthly*, February, 35–50

5

Evaluating Complex Comprehensive Community Initiatives: Theory, Measurement and Analysis

Anne C. Kubisch, James P. Connell and Karen Fulbright-Anderson

As described in this volume by Kubisch and Stone, comprehensive community initiatives (CCIs) are a new and promising approach to the revitalization of distressed inner-city neighborhoods in the United States. These initiatives are made of multiple programs, such as housing, economic development, human services, recreation, culture and education, that simultaneously target individual, family, neighborhood and institutional change. They are based on the premise that combining the various interventions will stimulate greater and faster improvements in the life circumstances of residents of chronically poor urban neighborhoods than might otherwise occur.

CCIs, however, are more than simply a collection of traditional programs. They are also designed to address the political, social and economic isolation that seems to plague the inner city. As a result, CCIs have explicit goals of individual and community empowerment; they attempt to re-weave the social fabric of the neighborhood; and they forge alliances between the neighborhood and outside political and economic resources. They operate according to principles of mutual respect, social justice and racial equity. The relationships that are forged, the capacity that is developed in individuals and institutions, and the 'sense of community' that is created are all highly valued in a CCI.

Why is good evaluation of CCIs so important?

For political, practical and policy reasons, CCIs bear an enormous responsibility to ensure that as much as possible is learned from their collective experience.

Politically, CCIs are public efforts intended to be democratic in process while, at the same time, committed to producing results. As such, they benefit from the support of a wide range of constituents, all of whom need to be kept informed of progress and outcomes. Foundations and other funders, for example, look for evidence that their investments are 'paying off', quite often within the time frame of their funding cycles. Neighborhood residents and 'influentials' outside the community are equally important audiences for information about the CCIs. They too need evidence that their investments – whether in time, energy, or social or political capital – are having an effect. Other partners in the public, nonprofit and corporate sectors also need to be kept informed of progress.

The practical need for good evaluation is to guide implementation. Any good program or agency manager wants formative feedback to inform planning, management and administration, and mid-course correction. In CCIs, this need is intensified by the defining mandate to create new and different ways of doing business at the neighborhood level. No blueprint or program design shows how this should happen: structures and activities must be tailored to individual neighborhood circumstances. Thus, contemporaneous learning from each CCI's unique, progressive experimentation is necessary to guide practitioners' decisions and actions, to help ensure that CCIs have the best chance of success.

The policy demand for good evaluation stems from what Alice O'Connor (1995) calls the need for 'social learning' over the longer run. CCIs are essentially laboratories for applying the best lessons from previous inner-city revitalization efforts. They offer opportunities for practitioners and researchers to test their knowledge and experience and to examine some of the most fundamental and cutting-edge questions in the antipoverty field today – questions concerning the configuration of model programs, for example, or the role that 'social capital' and 'neighborhood capacity' play in promoting healthy communities. This information, ultimately, cycles back to inform and shape both policy and research agendas.

The challenge of evaluating CCIs

Broad interest in the principles underlying CCIs means that CCI evaluations are being asked to serve multiple purposes for a host of audiences. Fortunately, many CCI funders have recognized the value of investing in learning as much as possible from the current cohort of interventions, and a number of evaluations are underway. At the same time, the defining characteristics of CCIs that energize stakeholders and observers are also the ones that challenge our ability to evaluate and learn from these initiatives. In their introduction to the first Aspen Roundtable volume on evaluation, Kubisch and colleagues (1995) describe the CCI features that challenge traditional evaluation approaches:

- *Horizontal complexity.* They work across multiple sectors (social, economic, physical, political and others) simultaneously and aim for synergy among them.
- *Vertical complexity.* They aim for change at the individual, family, community, organizational and systems levels.
- *Community building.* They aim for strengthened community capacity, enhanced social capital, an empowered neighborhood and similar outcomes.
- *Contextual issues.* They aim to incorporate external political, economic and other conditions into their framework, even though they may have little power to affect them.
- *Community responsiveness and flexibility over time.* They are designed to be community-specific and to evolve in response to the dynamics of the neighborhood and the lessons being learned by the initiative.
- *Community saturation.* They aim to reach all members of a community, and therefore individual residents cannot be randomly assigned to treatment and control groups for the purposes of assessing the CCI's impact; finding equivalent comparison communities is also not feasible. (The lack of suitable comparison groups in CCI evaluations is discussed at greater length in Hollister and Hill 1995.)

These conditions have meant that, throughout the evaluation enterprise, CCI evaluators have been confronted with challenges for which traditional evaluation tools have seemed inadequate. These challenges can be summarized in the following three questions.

1. Given the breadth, complexity and evolving nature of CCIs, what can be done to clarify the short, interim and long-term outcomes of an initiative, as well as the projected pathways for achieving them, in a way that guides initiative evaluation?
2. Given the value that CCIs place on community building, on the process of change and on community-level change, what are compelling indicators of *all* CCI outcomes – early, interim and long-term – and how should they be measured?

3. Given the community-specific and community-wide goals of CCIs, how should data be collected and analyzed to ensure that the causal links between initiative activities and outcomes – and the role of contextual variables in those links – are as fully understood as possible?

The remainder of this chapter attempts to answer these three questions. In the interest of full disclosure, we warn here that our discussion of these issues is cast in a particular light. We attempt to answer these questions by referring and responding to the *multiple* purposes of evaluation. That is, while we fully respect the need for evaluation to provide evidence about whether outcomes are achieved or not, we believe evaluations can and should be designed to provide other information, about how, why and under what circumstances an initiative is working. We also believe that an evaluation can be designed in a way that empowers participants and furthers the community building agenda of many of the current generation of community change initiatives.

What can be done to clarify the outcomes sought by a complex initiative – as well as the pathways for reaching those outcomes – in a way that guides evaluation?

In her 1995 paper, 'Nothing as Practical as Good Theory: Exploring Theory-Based Evaluation for Comprehensive Community Initiatives', Carol Weiss hypothesized that a key reason that CCIs and other complex programs are so difficult to evaluate is that the 'theories of change' that underlie the structures, strategies and goals of CCIs are poorly articulated. This is, perhaps, not surprising given that CCIs are meant to be 'co-constructed' by multiple stakeholders: as funders and communities enter into agreements to work together toward neighborhood transformation, they deliberately leave many aspects of the initiative open so that a collaborative process of planning and implementation can unfold. But Weiss has challenged CCI designers to be specific about theories of change guiding CCIs and suggests that doing so would improve their overall evaluation plans while also providing guidelines for data collection and analysis.

The 1998 volume on evaluation published by the Aspen Institute, *New Approaches to Evaluating Community Initiatives, Volume 2: Theory, Measurement and Analysis*, expands upon and develops the notion of a theory of change as a launch point for evaluation. In the volume, Connell and Kubisch define a theory of change approach to CCI evaluation as 'a systematic and cumulative study of the links between activities, outcomes, and contexts of the initiative'. They go on to describe the steps in a theory of change approach. These include: 1) working with all key stakeholders to articulate the initiative's theory of change; 2) unpacking that theory into a set of ultimate and interim outcomes and activities hypothesized to achieve them; 3) clarifying how external or contextual factors will affect both activities and outcomes; 4) identifying and measuring indicators of activities being implemented and their intended outcomes; 5) analyzing the resulting data with respect to the initiative's theory of change. The authors point out that these steps resemble the steps any good evaluator would take in designing the evaluation strategy for a complex program, but the theory of change approach is distinguished by several key attributes.

- It delineates the *pathway* of the initiative by emphasizing the activity–outcome sequences along the way to the longer-term outcomes.
- It aims to identify the *assumptions or theory underlying* the activity–outcome sequences; thus, it integrates a theory of change in outcomes (what will occur) with a theory of change-making (how the changes in outcomes will occur).
- A theory of change considers *how much* change is expected to occur, the *timing and sequencing* of change, and the *interactions* among various types and levels of change.
- A theory of change examines expectations for *outcomes in light of available and potential resources* (financial, institutional, technical, political).
- A theory of change process is participatory throughout. It encourages *multiple stakeholders* to co-construct the theory by drawing upon multiple sources of information, including program experience, scientifically generated knowledge, and community residents' insights.
- A theory of change approach can *span the design, implementation and evaluation* of the initiative. It requires specifying, evaluating and then revisiting the pathways of change – that is, the relationship between activities and outcomes – at multiple levels throughout the course of the initiative. Thus, a theory of change can *evolve* as the initiative incorporates lessons learned over time.

Practitioners who have begun to apply this approach are beginning to report that defining an initiative's theory of change is no easy task. In general, they find that stakeholders in an initiative can more easily describe what they are doing than where they are going. Philliber (1998) describes how 'some agencies or programs are almost defined by their processes or strategies', and warns that 'process' can become confused with outcomes and can even begin to substitute for them.

At the same time, in CCIs the 'process' *is* important. This means their evaluations attend not only to *what* activities are carried out in order produce desired outcomes but also *how* they are carried out – emphasizing principles and seeking evidence of empowerment, capacity building and social capital formation while carrying out more programmatic activities. Milligan et al. (1998) describe trying to walk the fine line between being concerned about process and letting it substitute for outcomes by adding rigor to the process dimensions of the initiative: 'We have tried to describe processes in terms of observable outcomes that can serve as signs that the processes have been accomplished well.' Asking about CCI activities and presenting activities through the lens of the outcomes they produce, including resident empowerment and social capital formation, is one of the fundamental building blocks of a CCI theory of change evaluation.

Even when CCIs succeed in articulating the component parts of their theories of change, they tend to be clearest about either the very long-term goals of the initiative or the most immediate outcomes associated with activities underway. The lack of a specified continuum of steps over the mid-course of an initiative – for example, between forming a representative community collaborative to govern the initiative in the first year of the CCI and reducing poverty in year 10 – is a problem that looms large in many evaluators' experiences. There appears to be no simple solution to this 'Grand Canyon' problem (Philliber 1998), in part because of the inherent tension between the need for a clearly articulated theory up front and the need for flexibility to modify the theory over time based on early results and lessons. Nonetheless, there seems to be consensus that CCIs benefit from support and structure to ensure that theory articulation is taken as far as possible; that stakeholders are provided with a framework for planning their initiative that demands clarity about linkages and alignments between activities and early, interim, and long term outcomes (Connell and Klem, 2000).

In complex initiatives, evaluators often find that the multiple stakeholders can, and often do, hold different theories about how goals of the initiative are likely to be achieved. These differences may have political or ideological sources, or they may reflect genuine differences about how to bring about community-level change. For example, people might differ in their views of how to reduce crime in their neighborhood – one might take a defensible space approach, another a youth development approach, and another a law enforcement approach – each legitimate and based on knowledge gained from research or experience. Evaluators of complex initiatives are often in the position of needing to reconcile differences among the various theories.

How do we identify compelling indicators of CCI progress and outcomes, and how do we measure them?

Evaluating CCIs invariably implies heavy measurement because the initiatives work across so many sectors and at so many levels, attending both to how activities are implemented and their outcomes. First, as Gambone (1998) notes, even the most basic tasks of measuring change in a CCI can be daunting. Simply assembling the array of potential measures for the long-term outcomes can be overwhelming. No catalogue or data base combines various sources of information on the full range of social, economic, physical and political outcomes sought by community change initiatives.

In the United States, the census is probably the most important source of detailed small area data but it is only conducted every ten years. Administrative data can be a cost-effective source of information for calculating baseline and ongoing measures for many long-term CCI outcomes. In the United States, the possibilities are particularly rich in the areas of housing, health, employment, economic activity, safety, education and transportation. Although sources such as these present opportunities for evaluators, Coulton and Hollister (1998) identify several areas in which they may be problematic, including their definition of neighborhood or community, their accuracy, confidentiality restrictions, and data extraction and management issues.

Whether they are drawn from administrative, census or survey sources, most 'published' measures assess individual outcomes, which represent only one level on which CCIs operate. Although some desired community outcomes can be measured by aggregating individual-level information (such as the percentage of residents above the poverty line), other types (such as the quantity and quality of supportive relationships for youth) are more difficult to derive since they do not conform to traditional psychometric criteria for reliability and validity. In any case, the individual-level measures that are available have rarely been tested with the demographic groups that are typically the focus of CCIs: African Americans, Latinos, Asians and various immigrant populations.

Because tracking change over both the short and long term is critical to evaluating CCIs, measures that are truly sensitive and accurate reflections of progress are critical. In some instances, this requires measurement activities that are amenable to repetition, such as monitoring the number of new or rehabilitated houses, conducting windshield surveys of neighborhood conditions, counting the number of neighborhood youths participating in after-school programs, or tracking resident participation in planning and decision-making (Milligan et al. 1998). But measures of progress identified during one phase of the initiative may need to be refined or new ones added over the course of an evaluation. For example, a useful measure of participation during the early stages of an initiative, such as the number of people attending collaborative governance meetings, may need to change as it becomes clear that who participates and the nature of their participation are more important over the longer term.

Moreover, the timing of measurement is critical. Fixed interval measurement is unlikely to capture the sequence and timing of changes crucial to a CCI's the theory of change. If the key linkages in the theory are to be tested and the integrity of the overall evaluation design maintained, there appear to be few shortcuts around deliberate and *timely* measurement of CCI activities and their intended outcomes. Milligan and colleagues (1998) allude to methods that might be used to vary the intensity of measurement according to the particular aspect of the theory under study: stronger activity–outcome sequences might be easier to monitor or need less sensitive measures than weaker sequences. At this point, there is little experience upon which to base those decisions.

One critical challenge is setting threshold levels of change for desired early, interim and long-term outcomes. In CCIs and other initiatives that emphasize empowerment and community building, a collaborative process may be the best way to establish thresholds of change for planning and management as well as for evaluation purposes. In this case, an important role for the evaluator might be to help ensure that the projected magnitudes of change are reasonable and meaningful. Some evaluators (Hebert and Anderson 1998) warn that stakeholders might be 'tempted to define the evaluation framework to ensure that the initiative will not be seen as "failing"'. They might set performance goals low or describe them in terms of inputs, activities, and outputs rather than outcomes.

Finally, measurement strategies must attend to contextual factors that will affect the CCI's pathway of change. Gambone (1998) makes this challenge concrete by identifying the particular elements of 'context' that should be included in the measurement strategy: the historical trajectory of a community and the conditions at the time a CCI gets underway; surrounding social, political, economic and other dynamics;

and discrete, powerful events that can affect the progress and outcomes of a CCI.

How can a CCI evaluation be designed to ensure that the causal linkages between activities, processes and outcomes are as fully understood and explicated as possible?

Analysis challenges are likely to plague evaluators of comprehensive community initiatives for the foreseeable future. These challenges fall into two main categories: if individual and neighborhood circumstances in a CCI neighborhood improve, evaluators will need to make the case that the initiative itself has been the cause of the changes; if no change occurs or circumstances worsen, evaluators will need to help disentangle the contributions of flawed theory, flawed implementation and unmeasured contextual influences.

As to the first challenge, the method preferred by evaluators for establishing causal linkages – experimental design – is simply not feasible in the context of complex community-wide initiatives and cannot be counted upon as the primary approach to assessing a CCI's impacts. (See Hollister and Hill 1995.) As a result, evaluators approach the CCI enterprise knowing that experimental methods will have a limited role to play. At the same time, they are acutely aware of their responsibility to build strong cases for making judgments about the value of initiatives or their component parts. Granger (1998) suggests that the nature of social science knowledge about community change requires that evaluators adopt a 'modest standard about causal inferences'. He acknowledges that, although it may be possible to say that certain outcomes are the result of a CCI, it is unrealistic to believe that we can determine the precise effects of the CCI and which aspects of the intervention caused them. Instead, he suggests that CCI evaluations must produce 'credible and generalizable results'.

One emerging view is that a strong theory will be an important building block in making the case for attributing outcomes to activities that form part of the CCI (Connell and Kubisch 1998; Granger 1998). Based on their first phase of work evaluating national Empowerment Zones/ Enterprise Communities, Hebert and Anderson (1998) suggest: 'The theory of change cannot provide statistically generated confidence levels, but it can provide compelling, detailed descriptions of the unfolding of the interventions and an argument regarding the apparently logical connections between theories, activities, and outcomes.' They admit that such descriptive arguments may not be convincing to researchers 'who see experimental or quasi-experimental methods as the only reliable approaches to impact analysis', but believe they will be 'welcomed by staff of community organizations and other practitioners'. Results of these evaluations will be credible to policy-makers and other researchers who hold more pluralistic views of what constitutes compelling evidence of causal effects.

The second major analysis challenge is how to track unfolding events closely enough to make distinctions regarding the failure (or success) of implementation, the failure (or success) of theory and the influence of external events. Reminiscent of a distinction made by Weiss (1997) between implementation failure and program or theory failure, Milligan and colleagues (1998) write that 'compelling evidence must distinguish between strategies that were incompletely implemented and strategies that were done according to the standards but did not produce the desired changes'. They add to this distinction the importance of context; that is, identifying whether a correctly implemented strategy based on sound theory did not work because of an external force or circumstance.

To respond to these challenges, Connell and Kubisch (1998) recommend that equal attention be paid, early on in an evaluation, to assessing whether and how well CCI activities are implemented and whether their intended early outcomes occur. By doing so, failures of implementation and failure of theory can be more easily disentangled in time to make adjustments to both if necessary. Disentangling the role of contextual factors in undermining predicted CCI effects demands that planners and evaluators try to anticipate and measure as best they can these conditions events. This challenge is not unique in any way to CCI evaluation, however.

For these reasons, good analysis of the effects of a CCI will likely make the use of multiple methods a necessity, not an option. Because the field of complex community initiatives is simultaneously building and testing change models as initiatives unfold, using multiple methods is an important way to seek convergence of results. Granger (1998) suggests that a strong CCI theory should be reinforced by creatively integrating methods, such as blending quasi-experimental designs or explicating and testing for patterns.

A note on the evolving role of the evaluator

The recent experience of evaluators of CCIs and other complex community initiatives has shown that the role of the evaluator is evolving in this context. Traditionally, the prescribed role of the evaluator was that of outside and 'unbiased' observer. In many CCIs, evaluators are engaged quite early in the process, generally because theory development, initiative planning and evaluation design overlap. In these cases, evaluators work with other constituents as collaborators, and the evaluator's skills of inquiry are used to help specify and even accelerate the theory articulation and initiative planning process.

Brown (1998) notes that 'once the line between evaluation and technical assistance is crossed', however, an evaluator can face a 'range of dilemmas associated with the new role for which there are few models or agreed-upon standards'. Evaluators may be asked to bring to bear their knowledge base in a way that strengthens the plausibility of the theory of change or affects the stakeholders' choice of outcomes or strategies. Or, they might be drawn into the theory articulation process to bring a neutral, more scientific view and 'provide focus and momentum when local political differences [seem] to overwhelm the conversation' (Brown 1998). These differences may occur among local stakeholders or between stakeholders, funders and/or technical assistance providers. There are critics, however, who question whether this is an appropriate role for evaluators and ask whether strategic planners or technical assistance providers are better placed to carry out this function (Connell 1997; Rossi 1999).

Current CCI evaluators warn (Brown 1998; Hebert and Anderson 1998) that the evaluator should be wary of engaging to the point where the evaluation framework and its hypotheses belong as much to the evaluator as to the site. The negative consequences of this situation are both immediate, in that local stakeholders may not feel ownership of the theory, and long-term, in that the evaluators themselves may have trouble being objective about their findings. As Brown (1995) stated, this high degree of involvement in the initiative does not 'release the evaluator from the right or obligation both to maintain high standards of scientific inquiry and to make judgments and recommendations as warranted'.

Thus, this generation of complex community initiatives presents the field of evaluation with new challenges regarding purpose, methodology and roles. At the same time, it opens up new opportunities for a collaborative process that is consistent with the community building principles that are so central to the work of CCIs.

Conclusion: the contribution of a 'Theory of Change Approach' to the field of evaluation

How do we define a CCI's theory of change? How should we measure the change? How can we be sure that the CCI caused the change? What is the role of the evaluator in this new approach? This chapter describes the progress that has been made in the field as a whole on each of those questions over the last five years. Greater advances have been made in some areas than in others, and in some cases the progress has been more conceptual than applied. Nonetheless, innovations in evaluation design, data collection and analysis offer new ways of thinking, new insights and new information, which together can help CCI stakeholders approach the evaluation enterprise with greater confidence that the result will meet their various needs.

How well does the progress that has been made – especially in defining a theory of change approach to evaluation – respond to the three purposes of CCI evaluation described at the beginning of this chapter?

On the political issue of keeping all stakeholders involved, informed and invested, the newer approaches appear to have been quite successful. Participants from residents to corporate partners find that their perspectives are valued and infused through all aspects of the process and their sense of ownership expanded. Momentum generated at the outset of an intervention has a vehicle for sustaining itself, while interim information about what is working can reinforce the commitment of funders, residents and other partners. The theory of change approach to evaluation has even served to convert some of the most skeptical participants in the evaluation process, especially residents who feel they have been 'burned' by evaluations of previous community revitalization efforts.

As regards formative feedback, the theory of change approach offers a way to combine 'process' and 'outcomes', both conceptually and in practice. Activities and their qualities are tracked, but always with a view of the outcomes they are intended to produce. The CCI manager can learn about effective components as they are happening and, if a strategy is not producing the anticipated pathway of change, correct the course or attempt alternative action.

In terms of the social learning function of CCI evaluation, the theory of change approach examines how and why change occurs, thus providing much richer information than evaluations that focus exclusively on whether or not the presence of the intervention results in change over the long term. By linking activities to the outcomes they produce throughout the initiative, knowledge is generated that can guide future adaptations of the initiative in different settings, including understanding the contextual conditions that favor an initiative's taking hold and being sustained. The failure to confirm hypotheses with this approach will also highlight topics for additional research and practical experimentation.

Gambone (1998) describes how a theory a change produces a different type of knowledge and how that knowledge advances the field:

> The progress of 'normal science' is rooted in the principle that knowledge development occurs *only* when high-quality, reliable measurement strategies are combined with well-specified theories so that hypotheses can be tested. As the resulting information is used to confirm or discard hypotheses, new 'knowledge' is gained, and disciplines make progress in their ability to explain and predict phenomena. Constructing research designs that yield valid and reliable information, therefore, is more than a matter of methodological mechanics. From this perspective, data collected without a theory has the status of 'information' and is limited to describing phenomena, while data collection guided by theory produces what can be called 'knowledge'.

As Connell and Kubisch (1998) have stated, 'the major strength of the theory of change approach is its inherent common sense'. Any good evaluation should begin with clear information about the outcomes sought by the initiative under study and how it intends to pursue them. From that perspective, 'theory of change' is an elegant term that describes the starting point of any responsible evaluation, and one that some evaluators have been using – through methods such as results mapping, theory of action or logic models – for years. A distinguishing feature of the theory of change approach is its guiding philosophy of collective responsibility among all CCI participants for developing and implementing the theory of change and then using the theory to bring rigor to the work of the CCI. This mirrors the 'community building' philosophy that guides CCIs in all dimensions of their work. The harmony between the philosophy of the initiative and the philosophy of the evaluation may be the most enduring feature of the theory of change approach.

References

Brown, P. (1995) The Role of the Evaluator in Comprehensive Community Initiatives, in J. Connell, A. Kubisch, L. Schorr and C. Weiss (eds.), *New Approaches to Evaluating Initiatives: Methods and Contents* (Washington, DC: The Aspen Institute)

Brown, P. (1998) 'Shaping the Evaluator's Role in a Theory of Change Evaluation' in Karen Fulbright-Anderson et al. (eds.), *New Approaches to Evaluating Community Initiative Vol. II: Theory, Measurement, and Analysis* (Washington, DC: The Aspen Institute)

Chapin Hall Center for Children (1997) *The Partnership for Neighborhood Initiatives: Report of the Chapin Hall Center for Children at the University of Chicago* (Chicago: Chapin Hall Center for Children)

Chaskin, R. (1992) *The Ford Foundation's Neighborhood and Family Initiative: Toward a Model of Comprehensive Neighborhood-Based Development* (Chicago: Chapin Hall Center for Children)

Chaskin, R., Chipenda Dansokho, S. and Joseph, M. (1997) *The Ford Foundation's Neighborhood and Family Initiative: The Challenge of Sustainability* (Chicago: Chapin Hall Center for Children)

Chaskin, R. and Joseph, M. (1995) *The Neighborhood and Family Initiative: Moving toward Implementation* (Chicago: Chapin Hall Center for Children)

Chen, Huey-tsyh (1990) *Theory Driven Evaluations* (Thousand Oaks, CA: Sage Publications)

Connell, J.P. (1997) Render unto Evaluators . . . : Some Cautions from Early Experience with a Theory of Change Approach. Paper presented at the Annie E. Casey Foundation Evaluation Conference, Baltimore.

Connell, J.P. and Klem, A. (1996) Using a Theory of Change Approach to Evaluate Investments in Public Education. Paper presented at a meeting convened by Independent Sector, Washington, DC.

Connell, J.P. and Klem, A. (2000) You *Can* Get There from Here: Using a Theory of Change Approach to Plan Urban Education Reform, *Journal for Psychological Consultation*, 11, 1, 93–120.

Connell, J.P. and Kubisch, A.C. (1998) Applying a Theory of Change Approach to the Evaluation of Comprehensive Community Initiatives: Progress, Prospects, and Problems, in Karen Fulbright-Anderson et al. (eds.), *New Approaches to Evaluating Community Initiatives Vol. II: Theory, Measurement, and Analysis* (Washington, DC: The Aspen Institute)

Coulton, C. and Hollister, R. (1998) Measuring Comprehensive Community Initiative Outcomes Using Data Available for Small Areas, K. Fulbright-Anderson et al. (eds.), In *New Approaches to Evaluating Community Initiatives Vol. II: Theory, Measurement, and Analysis* (Washington. DC: The Aspen Institute)

Ferguson, R. and Dickens, W.T. (eds.) (1999) *Urban Problems and Community Development* (Washington, DC: Brookings Institution)

Fulbright-Anderson., Kubisch, A.C. and Connell, J.P. (eds.) (1998) *New Approaches to Evaluating Community Initiatives Vol. II: Theory, Measurement, and Analysis* (Washington, DC: Aspen Institute)

Gambone, M.A. (1998) Challenges of Measurement in Community Change Initiatives, in K. Fulbright-Anderson et al. (eds.), *New Approaches to Evaluating Community Initiatives Vol. II: Theory, Measurement, and Analysis* (Washington, DC: The Aspen Institute)

Granger, R.C. (1998) Establishing Causality in Evaluations of Comprehensive Community Initiatives, in K. Fulbright-Anderson et al. (eds.), *New Approaches to Evaluating Community Initiatives Vol. II: Theory, Measurement, and Analysis* (Washington, DC: The Aspen Institute)

Hebert, S. and Anderson, A. (1998) Applying the Theory of Change Approach to Two National, Multisite Comprehensive Community Initiatives, in K. Fulbright-Anderson et al. (eds.), *New Approaches to Evaluating Community Initiatives Vol. II: Theory, Measurement, and Analysis* (Washington, DC: The Aspen Institute)

Halpern, R. (1994) *Rebuilding the Inner City: A History of Neighborhood Initiatives to Address Poverty in the United States* (New York: Columbia University Press)

Hirota, J.M., Brown, P. and Butler, B. (1998) *Neighborhood Strategies Project: Report on Initial Implementation, July 1996–March 1998* (Chicago: Chapin Hall Center for Children)

Hollister, R.G. and Hill, J. (1995) Problems in the Evaluation of Community-Wide Initiatives, in J. Connell et al. (eds.), *New Approaches to Evaluating Community Initiatives: Concepts, Methods, and Contexts* (Washington, DC: Aspen Institute)

Jackson, M.-R. and Marris, P. (1996) *Collaborative Comprehensive Community Initiatives: Overview of an Emerging Community Improvement Orientation* (Washington, DC: Urban Institute)

Kingsley, T.G., McNeely, J. and Gibson, J.O. (1997) *Community Building: Coming of Age* (Washington, DC: Urban Institute)

Kubisch, A.C., Brown, P., Chaskin, R., Hirota, J., Mark Joseph, M., Richman, H. and Roberts, M. (1997) *Voices from the Field: Learning from Comprehensive Community Initiatives* (New York: Roundtable on Comprehensive Community Initiatives for Children and Families, The Aspen Institute)

Kubisch, A.C., Weiss, C.H., Schorr, L.B. and Connell, J.P. (1995) in J. Connell et al. (eds.), *New Approaches to Evaluating Community Initiatives: Concepts, Methods, and Contexts* (Washington, DC: Aspen Institute)

Leiterman, M. and Stillman, J. (1993) *Building Community* (New York: Local Initiatives Support Corporation)

Milligan, S., Coulton, C., York, P. and Register, R. (1998) Implementing a Theory of Change Evaluation in the Cleveland Community-Building Initiative: A Case Study', in K. Fulbright-Anderson et al. (eds.), *New Approaches to Evaluating Community Initiatives Vol. II: Theory, Measurement, and Analysis* (Washington, DC: The Aspen Institute)

Nathan, R.P. (1997) *Empowerment Zone Initiative: Building a Community Plan for Strategic Change: Findings from the First Round of Assessment* (Albany: Nelson A. Rockefeller Institute of Government, State University of New York)

O'Connor, A. (1995) Evaluating Comprehensive Community Initiatives: A View from History, in J. Connell et al. (eds.), *New Approaches to Evaluating Community Initiatives: Concepts, Methods, and Contexts* (Washington, DC: Aspen Institute)

O'Connor, A. (1999) Swimming against the Tide: A Brief History of Federal Policy in Poor Communities, in *Urban Problems and Community Development* (Washington, DC: Brookings Institution)

OMG, Inc. (1998) *Final Assessment Report: Comprehensive Community Revitalization Program in the South Bronx* (New York: Comprehensive Community Revitalization Program)

OMG, Inc. (1995) *Final Assessment Report: The Planning Phase of the Rebuilding Communities Initiative* (Baltimore: Annie E. Casey Foundation)

Philliber, S. (1998) The Virtue of Specificity in Theory of Change Evaluation, in K. Fulbright-Anderson et al. (eds.), *New Approaches to Evaluating Community Initiatives Vol. II: Theory, Measurement, and Analysis* (Washington, DC: The Aspen Institute)

Pitcoff, W. (1998) Redefining Community Development, Part II: Collaborating for Change, *Shelterforce* 20: 1, 2–17

Pitcoff, W. (1997) Redefining Community Development, *Shelterforce* 19: 6, 2–14

Rossi, P.H. (1999) Evaluating Community Development Programs: Problems and Prospects, in R.F. Ferguson and W.T. Dickens (eds.), *Urban Problems and Community Development* (Washington, DC: The Brookings Institution)

Schorr, L. (1997) *Common Purpose* (New York: Doubleday)

Stillman, J., Butler, B., Brown, P. and Henderson, L.J. (1996) *Sandtown-Winchester Community Building in Partnership: 1990–1994: Interim Evaluation Report* (New York: Conservation Company)

Stone, R. (1996) *Core Issues in Comprehensive Community-Building Initiatives* (Chicago: Chapin Hall Center for Children)

Sviridoff, M. and Ryan, W. (1996) *Investing in Community: Lessons and Implications of the Comprehensive Community Revitalization Program* (New York: Comprehensive Community Revitalization Program)

Walsh, J. (1996) *Stories of Renewal: Community Building and the Future of Urban America* (New York: Rockefeller Foundation)

Weiss, C.H. (1997) How Can Theory-Based Evaluation Make Greater Headway?, *Evaluation Review* 21: 4

Weiss, C.H. (1995) Nothing as Practical as Good Theory: Exploring Theory-based Evaluation for Comprehensive Community Initiatives for Children and Families, in James Connell et al. (eds.), *New Approaches to Evaluating Community Initiatives: Concepts, Methods, and Contexts* (Washington, DC: Aspen Institute)

Wright, D.J. (1998) Comprehensive Strategies for Community Renewal, *Rockefeller Institute Bulletin*, pp. 48–66

6

'Power before Program': Broad Base Organizing and the Industrial Areas Foundation

Frank C. Pierson

Five thousand leaders from broad-based community organizations gathered in San Antonio, Texas, on 7 November 1999 to celebrate 25 years of Industrial Areas Foundation (IAF) organizing in the southwest United States. They came by bus, plane and automobile from 27 cities and rural areas. They were united in one purpose: to build a base of power to represent the interests of their families and communities. The gathering of 5,000 leaders in turn had been built on thousands of house meetings, research actions, assemblies and direct actions conducted by Southwest IAF organizations. Some of the organizations, like Citizens Organizing for Public Service (COPS) in San Antonio, were decades old. Others like West Texas Organizing Strategy and Yuma County Interfaith Sponsoring Committee, only a year or two. All had a history of connecting community institutions like churches, synagogues, mosques, and schools together to organize for power. Each had built local leadership teams, raised budgets from membership dues to hire at least one professional organizer and established a track record of accomplishment.

The leaders of Southwest IAF, representing over 1,000 churches, synagogues, labor unions, schools and nonprofit organizations, had a great deal to celebrate. Over a period of 25 years their network had grown from a single organizing drive in San Antonio to 27 broad-based organizations. Successful organizing drives had brought together communities as diverse as Dallas, Texas; the rural Rio Grande Valley of south Texas; Houston, Texas; Tucson, Arizona; Los Angeles, California; Omaha, Nebraska; and New Orleans, Louisiana. Together with the IAF organizations in places like Chicago, Illinois, New York City, Baltimore, Maryland, Albuquerque, New Mexico, and Boston, Massachusetts the IAF had become by far the largest and most powerful community-based organizing network in the United States. On 7 November, Southwest IAF leaders celebrated their growing capacity to raise money, to train and hire an expanding cadre of professional organizers, and to impact major issues affecting families. They celebrated their diversity – African-American, Native American, Anglo, Latino – one of the few large-scale embodiments of cross-racial organizing in the United States.

The event marked a clear passage beyond community and civic organizing to what the modern generation of IAF organizations call 'broad-based'. The IAF had left behind many of the small-scale community efforts, including those first pioneered by Saul Alinsky in the 1930s and had developed the power to take up the major issues impacting families, especially poor and working families across metropolitan regions and state. A number of victories were achieved as a result. These included job training programs for thousands of living wage jobs, a statewide alliance for school reform in Texas and an investment of several hundred million dollars in water and sewerage in South Texas *colonias*. Other successes were the setting up of living wage campaigns in five cities across the southwest involving work place organizations, faith communities, and low income neighborhoods and a sharp expansion of after school programs for children and youth in cities and towns throughout the region.

Finally the 25th celebration established the political will to move forward with an ambitious Human Development Agenda that Southwest IAF seeks to establish throughout the region which will be the most comprehensive campaign yet undertaken. In order to strengthen the Development agenda 500 leaders gathered some weeks before the celebration to study a series of papers on the economy and the family. An important paper on democracy by Amartya Sen, whose recent work (1999) helped stimulate the idea of a human development agenda in the first place, was at the centre of deliberations. The ensuing discussion provided a framework for developing the central themes for the 25th celebration. Thus did the IAF become a political force to be reckoned with throughout the southwest.

This chapter thus has two important aims. First, it explains the light which broad-based organizing throws on our understanding of two key elements in the regeneration process – citizen engagement and the exercise of political power. To do this it examines the activities of the Industrial Areas Foundation among Anglo, Hispanic and African-American communities in the southwest United States.

Second, the chapter reflects on the role of social services in regeneration and anti-poverty strategies and on the tension between broad-based organizing and the social service ethos embodied first in the settlement house traditions and subsequently in the 'professionalization of compassion' of social service bureaucracies.

The objective here is to rework the relationship between the two: minimally to diminish the behaviors of public bureaucracies which are destructive of citizen engagement, maximally to achieve a constructive engagement between broad-based organizing concepts and a new ethos for social service delivery.

Organizing universals

The scale and energy of the IAF network was only achieved by paying patient attention over many years to a number of organizing 'universals':

- organize for power before initiating program;
- relentlessly teach skills of public engagement such as individual meetings and house meetings;
- build networks of dues paying institutions where families congregate such as churches, synagogues, schools and unions;
- build relationships with an emphasis on story not task or issue;
- maintain a bias for action;
- and the iron rule of the IAF: 'Never ever do for people what they can do for themselves. Never.'

IAF organizations are, perhaps, best conceived as institutions through which citizen leaders learn and practice the craft of successful engagement in public life. The large numbers of leaders which IAF organizations bring together reflect not a pattern of ongoing mobilizations but a deep commitment to face-to-face relationship building. Relationships in turn become the foundation for the development and exercise of public, political skills of debate, discussion, argument and compromise. These are the skills that build the capacity of IAF leaders and organizers to cross lines of difference like race and class.

At the heart of the IAF practice of relationship building is the willingness to probe and share the stories of families and communities often disregarded, overlooked or actively dismissed by power elites. In fact, each of the leaders present at the celebration had been 'discovered' through relational meetings in which an exchange of stories occurred. Most had a story of powerlessness, anger or humiliation at the hands of powerful institutions whether corporate, political or bureaucratic. Their stories run the gamut from humiliation as a child in school for speaking with an accent, to brutal dismissal from a job as corporations become lean and mean, to explicit discrimination by race.

The scale and breadth of the Southwest IAF organizations' work contrasts sharply with government-backed neighborhood revitalization initiatives. Indeed, one aspect of its organizational accomplishment is the fact that they are now able to tackle major economic and political issues precisely because of their independence from government funding. In this respect 'neighborhood revitalization' efforts in the US and the UK have a lot to learn from the IAF theory and experience. Indeed, as this chapter will make explicitly clear, neighborhood revitalization efforts not founded on organizing universals are often counter-productive and even demoralizing to participants.

The current emphasis on 'local participation' in neighborhood regeneration policy in the UK and the US has focused attention on both the mechanisms for this to happen and the ability of communities to engage in a process dominated by political elites, private–public corporatism and professional services. The IAF critique of these efforts bluntly suggests that power inequalities guarantee that revitalisation efforts, dependent as they are on outside money and talent, constrained as they are with respect to the exercise of power, will consistently fail.

Civic organizations and neighborhood revitalization efforts are caught in a power vice. On the one hand, because their autonomy is limited they can impact only on small local issues with relative autonomy and, on the other, they are political captives of their funders, including government, on major issues affecting their families. The challenges facing local organizations, such as reaching financial independence, developing strong alliances for power, developing a confident leadership and acquiring some measure of political power cannot be addressed by government supported revitalization efforts. IAF experience suggests that 'neighborhood revitalization' merely confirms the power of major players over the neighborhood and the disinterest of such efforts in the core issues at the center of real community building.

The introduction of service-led renewal strategies such as some comprehensive community initiatives in the US and the range of 'joined-up' initiatives in the UK only further muddies the waters. Invariably these efforts are controlled by strong vested interests, whether political, economic or professional and bureaucratic in motivation. The tension between social service professionals and local community institutions is one form in which the conflict over the degree of political power held locally is fought out. Indeed, the ongoing legacy of distrust and conflict, dating back to the late nineteenth century between a service agency culture that professionalizes compassion and local forces that would wish to exert control over service programs indicates that this is one of the prime arenas of struggle.

Broad-based organizing and the Industrial Areas Foundation

Saul Alinksy founded the IAF in the late 1940s as a training institute for community organizers. It became a priority for Alinsky as he struggled to develop a cadre of professionals capable of organizing communities because he understood that the organizing work was directly limited by the available pool of talented organizers. The curriculum for Alinsky's IAF emerged from his experience building an 'organization of organizations' in the neighborhoods around the stockyards, slaughterhouses and packing houses of Chicago, Illinois in the 1930s. In this pioneering effort the Back-of-the-Yards Neighborhood Council, Alinksy emphasized the central importance of local institutional relationships (churches, unions) and the development of a collective leadership which could tie those institutions together into a political force to address issues identified by themselves. In the process Alinsky learned how to mobilize around specific neighborhood grievances, drawing on local discontent, using unconventional even confrontational tactics, and above all the necessity of building networks with institutions rooted in the neighborhood (Alinksy 1972).

Alinsky was a democratic pluralist and did not seek to overthrow capitalism but gain recognition and power for families and communities overlooked, or actively undercut, by political and economic elites. Though sometimes saddled with the charge of being 'left-wing' Alinsky's ideological pragmatism allowed the IAF to raise both substantial funds and support from mainstream, even socially conservative institutions such as the Catholic Church. This has been a continuing feature of IAF strategy, a fact that left-wing critics of the IAF have routinely held against it (Marquez 1998).

Another important aspect of the Alinsky legacy derives from early struggles in urban neighborhoods with deep religious and ethnic divisions. In his first organizing effort, in the 1930s the Back of the Yards Neighborhood Council (BYNC), Alinsky's success in developing relationships of power across the dividing lines of ethnic communities was distinctive. Horwitt (1989), in his biography of Alinksy, notes that until then, labor organizing in the stockyards had consistently failed. This was in part 'because the meat-packers were able to drive a wedge between the organizers and the community by playing on ethnic rivalries and

on the hostility of the Catholic churches to labor radicals and commun-
ists'. Alinsky skilfully drew on the support of both the Catholic parishes
and packinghouse workers that had historically been antagonistic.
The Southwest IAF has deepened this dimension of the Alinsky legacy.
While respecting the diversity of its constituents: Latino, African-American,
Anglo with significant participation by Asians and Native Americans,
like Alinsky, it refuses to organize around race and ethnicity. Ernesto
Cortes, Jr., Southwest Supervisor of IAF organizations, describes race based
organizing as '. . . a trap. That strategy cannot produce enough power
to address the major issues impacting working families of all races'
(personal communication). Communities Organized for Public Service
(COPS), the first IAF organization in Texas, was put together by Cortes
in primarily the Catholic, Hispanic section of San Antonio. Later, a sister
organization, Metro Alliance, was established to extend the base of
IAF power to African-American and Anglo parts of San Antonio. Having
learned from this experience, modern generation IAF organizations organized since COPS/METRO ethnically reflect the communities in which
they are located. None is organized around race. The ability of IAF to cross
the racial divide in part is a function of the base of the organization in
churches, synagogues and schools. All of these institutions are called by
their founding documents to build relationships across lines of race.
   The contemporary IAF now combines some of the approach that
Alinksy developed with newer strategies of the last 25 years. It uses the
term 'broad-based organizing' to describe this newer approach, going
beyond the connotation of community organizing which was concerned
with local issues in a relatively small area. It explicitly aims to overcome
the fragmentation which prevents effective expression of community
power through action campaigns initiated and sustained by 'organizations of organizations' in which as wide a possible representation is
achieved – civic organizations, churches, labor unions, schools, nonprofit
agencies and ethnically based mutual aid societies. The intent of these
broad-based organizations is both to build powerful regional institutions
capable of acting on major issues confronting communities and to teach
the public skills necessary to promote and sustain such action.

Political power

IAF understanding of political power assumes that self-interest rather
than altruism shapes human behavior. But this view of 'self-interest' is
based on physical and psychological needs for human growth – literally,
what people need to develop a healthy sense of self. For their own

integrity they need some visibility, or power, in political arrangements (Rogers 1990). The role of broad-based organizing is precisely to nurture the development of a collective leadership's understanding of what those interests are, to teach how they can be effectively articulated, and to enter into negotiations with major centers of political and economic power to effectively realize them.

The main aim of broad-based organizing is to rebuild the democratic life of urban and rural communities through the development and exercise of political and economic power. The IAF seeks to develop the political capacity and political skills of congregation and neighborhood leaders to reach beyond their neighborhoods in order to have an impact on powerful political and economic institutions. The approach suggests that the revitalization of urban neighborhoods cannot occur only in the realm of civil society (as moralists and communitarians have argued) but also requires a local political capability that will have an effect on political and economic institutions. The IAF understands that politics is a realm of conflict and power – an inescapable realm for communities and families that are historically excluded from political power and have experienced the effects of long term social and economic inequality. Equally, the IAF understands that political parties for the most part have lost their connection with community-based institutions and that politics is a vastly wider, more compelling field than the popular understanding of party politics assumes. The IAF is non-partisan in relation to political parties but partisan with respect to public agendas for family and community betterment.

One of the major influences on senior levels of IAF thinking is Bernard Crick's *In Defense of Politics* (1963). Crick laid out the importance of political activity to rounded social development both for individual citizens and local community. Politics is a complex activity Crick wrote. 'It is not simply the grasping for an ideal, for then the ideals of others may be threatened; but it is not pure self-interest either, simply because the more realistically one construes self-interest the more one is involved in relationships with others. . . . The more one is involved in relationships with others, the more conflicts of interest, or of character and circumstance, will arise. These conflicts, when personal, create the activity we call "ethics" . . . ; and such conflicts, when public, create political activity . . .' Politics while the expression of conflicting interests also depends on a settled order and conciliation of those interests.

Ernesto Cortes who, with Ed Chambers, is generally considered the architect of the modern IAF, draws on Crick's themes. He describes the kind of politics broad-based organizations practice:

True politics is not about polls, focus groups and television ads. It is about engaging in public discourse and initiating collective action guided by that discourse. In politics it is not enough to be right or to have a coherent position; one also must be reasonable, willing to make concessions, exercise judgement, and find terms that others can accept as well. So politics is about relationships that enable people to disagree, argue, interrupt, confront, and negotiate, and, through this process of conversation and debate, to forge a consensus or compromise that makes it possible for them to act. (Cortes 1993: 1)

The concept of relational power resides at the heart of IAF political thinking. Drawing on Bernard Loomer's (1976) reflections on two kinds of power IAF teaches a distinction between relational and unilateral power. The former involves acting and being acted upon, give and take, confrontation and compromise. The later is top-down, hierarchical, one-way, often unaccountable. While unilateral power has its place in modern political and social institutions it must be kept in its place. The very word power, derived from the Latin root *posse* – to be able – is defined as 'the ability or capacity to act'. This definition leads to specific and precise conclusions about who does and does not have a seat at the table where decisions are made, and who is and who is not engaged in public conversation about matters of central importance to communities. The IAF understanding of power in turn is grounded in its perspective on the human person. Learning to exercise relational power is central to the development of the whole person. In this sense learning to engage in public life is a vital ingredient in full human development.

The IAF believes that significant power is unattainable unless power itself is carefully studied. Part of what distinguishes a power organization from activism on issues is the careful study of the diverse interests that make up a given power structure. At the beginning of an organizing drive and periodically thereafter leaders in broad-based organizations perform a power analysis to situate themselves and others accurately inside of an existing power grid. This analysis in turn promotes the ability to understand others interests, negotiate around those interests, confront and compromise.

Relational organizing

In building the broad-based organization the IAF employs what it calls relational organizing, defined by Mark Warren as 'the deliberate building of relationships for the purpose of finding common ground for political action' (Warren 1998: 78). Through this patient and long-term work the organizers and leaders promote discussions that may lead to identification of additional leadership talent and a deep understanding of issues as they impact individual families. Meetings are small and informal, often no more than between two individuals in a person's home and are the principal work of organizing. The intention is to generate on-going conversation that explores family stories and values, sustains participation and uncovers issues of concern to local residents. This contrasts with an activist approach that moves directly to mobilize as many residents as possible around a potentially explosive issue.

IAF organizers work through local institutions such as congregations, schools, unions, nonprofits and adult learning centers. The invitation of a pastor, principal or governing board is a prerequisite for an exploration of an organizational relationship. IAF organizations build on the social capital within religious institutions, churches, schools, unions, synagogues, mosques, as a foundation for initiating strategies which positively impact the public, political life of communities. By enhancing the trust in relationships and in the moral frameworks already present in religious and educational organizers strengthen the capacity of community institutions and networks to help shape responses to pressures on families and, where appropriate, challenges these toward constructive, non-partisan political engagement (Wood 1997).

The first step taken by community leaders toward a relationship with IAF is to build a sponsoring network of institutions to raise money to hire a full-time organizer (or a team in larger metro areas) and pay for an IAF training contract. A sponsoring committee is established whose primary purpose is to raise funds, hire the lead organizer and initiate relationships with a broad spectrum of community institutions. This is done primarily through relational meetings, house meetings and training for leaders in the fundamentals of broad-based organizing. As the organizing drive progresses, assemblies occur: first, to establish a dues base of institutions committed to work for justice across lines of race and class; second, to initiate research into an action agenda based on issues growing out of the thousands of grass-roots conversations.

As issues of concern and urgency emerge it is common for the broad-based organisation to investigate them much more fully. This happens through grass-roots consultation, research meetings with city staff, business leaders, government bureaucrats, academic experts and consultants and the organisation's own research efforts (Wood 1997). The focus then is to locate where the authority lies to implement a solution to the problem – these may be corporate officials, city administrators, elected council members or members of the state legislature. The signature event – always well rehearsed and worked toward over a period of time – is the 'accountability session' where the targeted decision-maker is asked before a public audience to endorse the suggested solution and to commit to working with the organisation to achieve it (Wood 1997).

IAF carefully distinguishes between levels of leaders for purposes of selectively identifying and developing leadership talent. But individual capacity is not the only criterion; so also is the social networks and strength of connections that potential leaders have. For IAF, *primary leaders* are individuals with a large following who have broad vision and a willingness to work hard on themselves to develop leadership skills. *Secondary leaders* have an institutional base of support and an appetite for power but are less inclined to invest long term in their own development. *Tertiary leaders* are issue-specific and task-oriented. All levels of leaders are required for a broad-based organization to become powerful. Leadership training includes learning how to understand power, distinguishing between different kinds of power, learning how to conduct relational meetings, learning and practicing the craft of negotiation, and developing confidence in a public self. Training sessions and seminars with outside experts as well as consistent mentoring help fuse these skills into a coherent whole.

Rather than be limited to a single issue, as so many community organizations are, IAF organizations are multi-issue. They aim to build their political capacity over time to address a broad range of issues: job training, wages and benefits, school reform, community safety, public health, housing, community infrastructure. The Southwest IAF now conducts its relational organizing in the context of metropolitan-wide organizations networked together at the state and regional level with ongoing connections to public officials, business leaders, denominational executives, bishops, union presidents and policy experts at the state and national level. 'Its local affiliates can now address quite large-scale issues of workforce development, community wage scales and public school reform' (Warren 1998: 87).

Thus over six decades of organizing the IAF has undergone a series of transformations that have led to its present wide level of engagement.

First, the organizations themselves are larger, often metropolitan in scope. The most recent organization in the midwest – United Power in Chicago – now has an institutional membership of several hundred churches, synagogues, mosques, unions and nonprofit [voluntary] organizations. United Power, like Dallas Area Interfaith (DAI), Pima County Interfaith (Arizona) and other contemporary IAF organizations, include member institutions that cut across lines of race and class in metropolitan regions. DAI, for example, in a city known for deep racial divisions, comprises in equal parts Hispanic, Anglo and African-American members.

Second, the IAF has begun to link broad-based organizations through statewide networks. Efforts to build power on a statewide basis were pioneered by the IAF in Texas, which began its work in one city, San Antonio, with one organizer, Ernesto Cortes, in 1974. Texas IAF now organizes in all major cities and many rural areas. Since passing a state equalization formula for investment in poor schools Texas IAF has been a force in school reform statewide (IAF 1990). The Texas Alliance Schools network now comprises over 125 public schools committed to parent engagement and school improvement while the Texas state legislature has committed tens of millions of dollars to individual schools in the Alliance network. William Greider (1993) observes that

> the IAF network is a strange new force in their [state politicians] midst, potentially capable of disrupting their own power relationships because it includes so many real people. Something is being built in Texas politics that does not respond to the usual alignments of money and influence . . . when IAF speaks to power they listen respectfully. After all, those are live voters going to all those IAF meetings.

Third, the issues addressed by IAF organizations are significantly greater in complexity and duration than those tackled by early generation IAF organizations. School reform, infrastructure construction in poor neighborhoods, housing, local and regional economic development, job training, community living wage standards, health care delivery and welfare reform are all issues regularly taken on by southwest IAF organizations. IAF has the staying power and depth to engage successfully in public deliberations of high impact in these and other issue areas of its choosing.

Fourth, the contemporary IAF regularly draws on the work of intellectuals and theoreticians capable of challenging leaders, organizers and members from diverse, independent perspectives. These seminars are central to the development of a collective of professional organizers. The Southwest IAF, under the direction of Ernesto Cortes and Associate Director Sr. Christine Stephens holds regular seminars with leading economists, philosophers, educationists, theologians and historians whose work probes the history, values and strategies of civic engagement and the exercise of political power. Nationally recognized scholars like economists Frank Levy, Richard Murnane and James Tobin, political theorists Charles Lindblom and Michael Sandel, and historian Alan Brinkley have made the journey from their academic redoubts to the southwest to engage organizers and leaders in two and three day seminars in their thinking. In conjunction with rigorous intellectual development, the IAF encourages independent evaluation and critique of its programmatic initiatives. Professor Paul Osterman, at Massachusetts Institute of Technology, for example, has conducted a study of the job training initiative QUEST, which evaluated all aspects of the programme (Osterman and Lautsch 1996).

William Greider (1993) in *Who Will Tell The People? The Betrayal of American Democracy*, describes broad-based organizations as one of American democracy's best hopes:

> The quality that makes the IAF organizations so distinctive is their relentless attention to the conditions that ordinary people describe in their own lives. Their authority is derived from personal experience, not from the policy experts of formal politics. Most other varieties of citizen politics start at the other end of the landscape – attaching to the transient storms of 'public opinion' or 'policy debate' that play out abstractly on the grand stage of high-level politics. IAF gives up short-term celebrity on 'hot issues' in order to develop the long-term power of a collective action that is real.

Conflict with service-dominated community initiatives

Because of its understanding of how power functions IAF organizations have been skeptical of service-led neighborhood initiatives. In fact, tension between IAF organizers and public bureaucracies and nonprofit social service providers is long-standing and deeply rooted. Indeed community organizing as developed by Alinksy in the 1930s originated in part as a reaction to the persistent thread of institutional humiliation of individuals and families running through decades of social service practice – both professional and voluntary – in the United States. An examination of these historical tensions and the mutual hostility between organizers and service providers, which have only intensified in the past decade, offers important insights into the markedly different understanding of politics and its role in community development. In turn, these insights may help in re-establishing theoretical basis for compassionate services which encourage rather than undercut citizen engagement in public life.

From the first, organizers faced the hostility of the social work establishment. Horwitt (1992) notes that Alinsky's BYNC had two natural enemies in Chicago: the professional social work establishment and the Kelly Nash democratic party machine. Horwitt writes:

the social workers felt threatened and offended by 'the minimizing of the part that can be played by professional people' in solving problems in lower-class industrial communities. This misleadingly restrained criticism – misleading because it masked the depth of antagonism felt by many in the Chicago social-work establishment – appeared in a confidential report filed by the executive committee of the division on education and recreation of the council of social agencies of Chicago. (1992: 135)

The root of the conflict stemmed in part from the different understanding of human development and an altogether different political culture from that of the work of the settlement, Hull House, the social service arm of the University of Chicago. While the BYNC was learning to acknowledge ethnic differences and developing a new appreciation of the possibilities of communal action and local accountability for that action (1992: 83) the settlement house could accomplish little in the world of the immigrants. 'Standing on the outside, they tried to break down walls and heal the socially ill, but they never reached the heart of the neighborhood enclaves. For this reason, they could not help those people to build a democratic, stable society' (Slayton 1986).

The issue of local control versus professional control became the crux of hostility. The emergence of a leadership among the ethnic communities 'contradicted one of the basic assumptions behind the settlement idea, namely, the leading role of the American middle class "better element" in the reorganization of the slums and the reunification of the segmented American society' (Lissak 1989). 'In accordance with this perception of the primary role of American-born workers, foreign leaders were never invited to represent their groups on the Hull House board of trustees or given any role in the policy making and direction of Hull House.' The key to the policy of 'control through alliance' therefore lay in securing the cooperation of the enlightened members of the immigrant colonies. This included transferring the control of immigrant adjustment to American Society from the immigrant lower-middle class leaders and their allies and immigrant welfare and ethnic institutions, to American governmental and upper middle class.

This early history of antagonism helps clarify the fact that far from simply omitting the skills of active citizenship and public engagement the professional social workers of the settlement house were actively threatened by any institution capable of teaching such skills. In this sense social service professionals viewed organizers' attempting to build institutions through which public skills were learned as 'natural enemies'.

Slayton notes that university of Chicago social workers were informed by a set of assumptions dependent on their mostly upper middle class and mostly Protestant roots. Social class along with religious practices and beliefs separated the 'helpers' from their clients. Indeed, the Protestant outsiders viewed part of their mission to be diminishing their clients' family stories, undermining their beliefs and severing their institutional relationships. In contrast, BYNC's leaders and organizers considered these family stories, beliefs and institutional relationships a positive asset to be protected and fostered.

The dominant institutions, including media and business, then shaping American understanding of what was good for the residents of urban slums clearly sided with the social work profession and its battery of experts. Settlement houses of elite, Protestant origin served clients in immigrant, mostly Catholic communities all over the urban United States to the applause of local and national media. Secure in the political quiescence of modern social work, business money and organizational backing flowed. Powerful mainline Protestant denominations set up 'missions' to cleanse and convert at least to Americanism urban Catholics. This major fault line still persists and organizers have to deal with it.

This early history is important because it graphically highlights the phenomenon of 'institutional humiliation'. Avishai Margarlit, in *The Decent Society* (1996), makes the important distinction between a society which treats individuals in a civil manner and institutions within such a society which humiliate. At its core, he argues, humiliation is a consequence of institutional failure to grasp the central importance of politics. It is not necessary, he asserts, for individuals operating inside a humiliating institution to intend such humiliation. In fact, motives such as pity and altruism may lead to humiliation in a manner that is quite unintended. That is, humiliating behavior can be perpetrated by individuals with the most noble intentions. Indeed, the central paradox Margalit would have us confront is the likelihood that pity and altruism by virtue of their fundamental lack of reciprocity consistently lead to humiliating acts. He asserts, 'There can be no humiliation without humans to bring it about, but there can be humiliation without humiliators, in the sense that the people causing the humiliation did not intend to do so' (1996: 10).

In the democratic tradition, the term commonly used since the establishment of Athenian democracy for a non-humiliating relationship with public life is 'citizen'. Margalit observes that Aristotle thought humanity's defining trait is as a political animal. The more we strip away a person's political characteristics the more animal he or she becomes. They are rejected from the human commonwealth. Taking away a person's political features means, in Aristotle's view, 'preventing them from being a citizen – that is, an active participant in the life of the polis'.

With Margalit's framework, it is possible to grasp how well-intended, even noble, individuals operating inside the institutions of professional social service may still function in a humiliating manner. Outside professionals who established helping outposts are motivated by the best of intentions: pity and altruism. Neverthless they frequently engaged in humiliating behavior by denying local residents opportunities for political engagement, including self-governance, and by rejecting the very institutions around which their family life was built.

One of the limits which neighborhood service providers have accepted in return for funding is the de-politicization of local citizens who are thereby reduced to clienthood. The unwritten contract that defines this bargain is that providers agree to disengage in anything recognizable as political activity – such as the registration of new voters. In return, these providers gain meager resources with which to help the deserving poor and minorities. In Tucson, Arizona, a major social service leader described in detail the financial consequences to his organization if he registered his clients to vote. Acknowledging that legal restraints in this domain no longer applied, he stated, 'none of my board will let any politics happen, even the simplest acts in a democratic society such as registering to vote, as long as they're footing the bill' (personal communication to the author).

The Tucson example is consistent with what Janet Poppendieck considers a nationwide pattern. In *Sweet Charity* she develops what she calls the Wenceslas syndrome to describe the substitution of charitable activity for public engagement and public policy. 'The Wenceslas syndrome is not just something that happens to individuals and groups that become deeply involved in charitable activity; it is a collective process that affects our entire society as charity replaces entitlements and charitable endeavor replaces politics' (Poppendieck 1998: 19). An example of this dynamic is the fact that business now views food banks as important marketing devices.

Regrounding service relationships: the IAF experience

Over a 60-year period of building citizens' organizations, the IAF have learned a great deal about how to build democratic institutions and to develop services under democratic control. The experience of the IAF in Texas and Arizona with job training is especially useful. Communities Organized for Public Service and a sister IAF organization in San Antonio, the Metro Alliance, initiated Project Quest in response to plant closures by Levi Strauss which left thousands of families in COPS/Metro member institutions unemployed. It is important to note that the patient groundwork of many previous years now came into play: gathering in hundreds of house meetings, organized through relationships established over a period of 15 years, listening to thousands of families. On this basis COPS/Metro began to research alternative strategies to address employment and wage issues.

Their first discovery was that existing job training did not work. Public money was spent on training that was not appropriate for finding decent paying work in the area. The battle was waged on two fronts: with existing training service providers who were threatened by 'broad-based upstarts' and with an existing political leadership tied to prevailing job training services through patronage and other political deals. The political struggle was intense as COPS/Metro ran one public action after another over a year-long period to convince city officials to fund the new and highly creative strategy. Finally, in the face of massive numbers, highly competent research and a range of new allies including employers, the city of San Antonio, and subsequently the state of Texas, agreed to fund Project Quest. From this experience three aspects of the service/politics interface are important to note.

- The emphasis placed on community ownership of services sharply distinguishes broad-based organizing from professional social service delivery. Broad-based organizations attempt to turn upside down the unequal power relationships which typically undergird service delivery in poor and working-class communities by linking together those institutions most responsible for shaping the habits and practices of community life.
- Exploration of family stories between equals is a better starting point for any relationship, including service relationships, than bureaucratic needs assessments and 'intakes' which are fundamentally unequal and humiliating in nature.
- For service delivery to promote active citizenship a continuous focus on leadership development and teaching the skills of public engagement is a requirement. Service delivery, even programmatic initiatives of IAF organizations, slip into client/provider relationships when habits and practices associated with the identification and training of leaders

are pushed aside in favour of tasks connected to particular programs. In San Antonio, the fact that a large cadre of local leaders developed the skills and capacities to represent their own and their neighbors interests in public forums distinguished Project Quest from conventional social service appeals by paid staff backed by the pleadings of an occasional 'client'

From the experience of the layoffs there was a shift in understanding self-interest. Families discovered their own struggle was connected to others. They discovered that as their private distress became public it was connected to economic pressures also experienced by others. They also discovered, unexpectedly, that their interests coincided in important ways with employers who were seeking highly trained workers in the San Antonio area. They further discovered that social service agencies, far from being benevolent providers, operated within their own set of highly specific interests which were tuned to their own institutional survival.

Perhaps the core insight of IAF experience relevant to creating citizen control over services is the vital role of struggle. Where struggle – or victory – occurs, a deeper understanding of power, self-interest and solidarity is likely to emerge. What people don't fight for they don't own and what they don't own they don't fight for. The experience of struggle is repeated over and over in IAF history; and it is the thread connecting past and present strategies. From the beginning in the back-of-the-yards neighborhood campaign in Chicago in the 1930s the sense of struggle was there – between workers and meat-packing companies between local immigrant organizations and social work professionals, and between residents and city machine politics. The nature of 'struggle' may have changed but its educative and energizing role have not.

Service agencies typically have no comparable proving ground, either in terms of what 'clients' will fight for or what agency and bureaucratic leaders value. At issue here is the sharp difference in organizational culture: one puts tension at the center of organizational life and uses it creatively while the other considers tension as a kind of enemy and understands conflict to be unhealthy and dangerous to service interests.

Rethinking service delivery

Programmatic ventures into service, even those embedded in their communities, are not without internal dangers to broad-based organizations. Two in particular have emerged with respect to Project Quest and other major service intitiatives by the modern IAF. First, service delivery strategies tend to individualize organizational thinking and narrow the breadth of vision of the broad-based organization. In the case of Quest for example, attending to the development of 1,000 individuals' training may lessen the willingness of COPS/Metro to explore the larger economic forces which produce layoffs and low-wage work in the first place. The danger is that a strategy for dealing with these will wither, leaving those without access to Project Quest without remedy. Second, service delivery strategies compete for the time and energy of leaders and organizers with a high degree of tasks to be performed.

The dangers to broad-based organizations notwithstanding, three areas appear especially fruitful for exploration if services under political/citizen control are to be developed. Each has implications for service agencies who are trying to re-examine their own relationship to clients as well as for broad-based organizations.

1. *Mission.* IAF experience suggests that it is possible to introduce the teaching of skills to clients appropriate to active engagement in public life by applying the principles of relational organizing to strengthening the power/control/engagement of clients/citizens. Pima County Interfaith Council in Tucson, Arizona holds training workshops aimed at helping individuals understand the specific economic pressures on their families. The workshops also examine the role of politics in creating opportunities embodied in Jobpath, a local job training service modeled on Quest, and challenges participants to give something back to their community, for example by giving time to a volunteer youth program once their training is complete and employment obtained.

2. *Active citizenship.* Service organizations have a shared interest with broad-based organizations in leveraging funders, public and private, to place active citizenship skills at the center of contractual relationships with service providers. Such skills include the relational work of identifying resources, connecting people, coaching/mentoring, training, agitating, follow up; the conceptual work of inquiry, policy development, initiation, argument, confrontation, compromise. Currently any leveraging works in the opposite direction; funders consistently discourage teaching and learning skills associated with a reinvigorated public life.

3. *New institutions.* New institutions, such as associations for self-improvement, offer promise for linking individual service recipients. Both COPS/Metro and PCIC are experimenting with such associations in their job training initiatives.

Only in such arduous patient long-term work will organizations amass the power and leverage necessary to produce structuralist change from the ground up.

References

Alinsky, S. (1972) *Rules for Radicals A Pragmatic Primer for Realistic Radicals* (New York: Vintage)
Arizona Daily Star (1997) 1 March
Cortes, E. (1993) Reweaving the Social Fabric, in H. Cisneros (ed.), *Interwoven Destinies Cities and the Nation* (New York: W.W. Norton)
Cortes, E. (1999) personal interview
Crick, B. (1963) *In Defense of Politics* (London: Pelican)
Greider, W. (1993) *Who Will Tell the People? The Betrayal of American Democracy* (New York: Touchstone, Simon and Schuster)
Horwitt, S.D. (1989) *Let Them Call Me Rebel* (New York: Knopf)
Horwitt, S.D., (1992) *Let Them Call Me Rebel: Saul Alinsky, His Life and Legacy* (New York: Random House)
Lissak, R.S. (1989) *Pluralism and Progressives: Hull House and the New Immigrants, 1890–1919* (Chicago and London: University of Chicago Press)
Loomer, B. (1976) Two Kinds of Power, *Criterion* (Winter); 11–29
Margalit, A. (1996) *The Decent Society* (Cambridge, Mass. and London: Harvard University Press)
Marquez, B. (1993) The Industrial Areas Foundation and the Mexican-American Community in Texas, *Contributions in Political Science* 33: 3, 127–46
McKnight, J. (1991) Services are Bad for People: You're either a Citizen or Client, *Organizing* (Spring/Summer)
Osterman, P. and Lautsch, B. (1996) *Project QUEST: A Report to the Ford Foundation* (New York: Project QUEST)
Poppendieck, J. (1998) *Sweet Charity?* (New York: Viking Press)
Rogers, M.B. (1990) *Cold Anger: A Story of Faith and Power Politics* (Denton, Texas: University of North Texas Press)
Sen, A. (1999) *Development as Freedom* (New York: Knopf)
Slayton, R. (1986) *Back of the Yards: The Making of a Local Democracy* (Chicago and London: University of Chicago Press)
Texas Industrial Areas Foundation (1990) A Vision for Texas Schools
Warren, M. (1998) Community Building and Power: A Community Organizing Approach to Democratic Renewal, *American Behavioral Scientist* 42: 1, 78–92
Wood, R. (1997) Social Capital and Political Culture: God Meets Politics in the Inner City, *American Behavioral Scientist* 42: 1, 595–605.

7
Community Participation in Strategic Partnerships in the United Kingdom

Sarah Pearson and Gary Craig

In the late 1990s partnership appears to be the organizational strategy strongly espoused by government for UK regeneration and anti-poverty policy. An emphasis on joint working between organizations is, of course, not new; the UK has a 30-year history of initiatives that have aimed to combat poverty at the local level (Alcock et al. 1998, esp. Ch. 2), and throughout this period, greater or lesser policy emphasis has been placed on fostering relationships between and amongst central government, local government, private enterprise, public bodies, voluntary organizations, quasi-public agencies and local communities. Some of these relationships have merited the description of partnership whereas others have not, but there has nevertheless been an identifiable strand of joint working running through urban and anti-poverty policy throughout this period.

This chapter considers community involvement in recent central and local government partnerships in the UK in relation both to the appropriateness of partnerships as a mechanism for fostering community participation, and to the ability of communities to respond to such initiatives.

The policy context in central and local government

Skelcher et al. (1996) have identified three phases of partnership in urban regeneration, each associated with changing emphases in policy. They characterize the 1970s as the 'single agency period' where the key role in developing and implementing the urban policy agenda was taken by local authorities. They identify the late 1970s and 1980s as a period when bilateral public–private partnerships dominated a policy agenda concerned mainly with physical regeneration, and call the 1990s a period when multilateral partnerships of public, private, voluntary and community sectors have contributed to a widening of the urban regeneration agenda to incorporate both economic and social foci.

This broadening approach to regeneration, which includes support for local partnership activity, community development, and social as well as economic regeneration, reflects a changing policy approach that has focused attention on issues of social exclusion and social integration rather than on physical and economic development. The problem of social exclusion has been the subject of considerable academic deliberation in both the UK and in the wider European policy arena from which the debate largely originated (for further reading see Room 1995; Oppenheim 1998) and as a term social exclusion has been taken to mean many things, from a euphemism for poverty to a conceptualization of disadvantage as a denial of citizenship rights. The notion of social exclusion that now dominates the UK policy agenda falls between these two poles. It acknowledges the multi-dimensional nature of disadvantage and the processes through which difficulties such as low income, unemployment, poor skills, bad health, crime and family breakdown are compounded so that individuals and families experience marginalization and detachment from mainstream society. Yet it is also, to some extent, a limited definition, with a strong emphasis on issues linked to welfare dependency and on spatial concentrations of exclusion, such as the so-called 'sink estates' or poor neighborhoods (SEU 1998).

Nevertheless, the importance of combating social exclusion has been recognized at central government level. The New Labour government, elected in 1997, created the Social Exclusion Unit, formed in the Cabinet Office in 1997 to coordinate activity around a number of specific issues, and social exclusion is now expected to inform policy planning and implementation across all government areas, including regeneration.

For local government, the focus on social exclusion has meant a renewed emphasis on ensuring that regeneration activity achieves maximum benefits for poor communities and focuses on the social and community contexts of development work. This, in turn, has highlighted the importance of linkages between regeneration and anti-poverty work. Local authorities that have undertaken anti-poverty work have sought to combat social exclusion through ensuring improved and subsidized access to local services, support for community economic and social development, the provision of welfare rights and debt advice services, and support for job creation and training. In developing strategies to combat social exclusion, regeneration partnerships, then, will need to recognize the important connections between urban policy and anti-poverty work. These links are already apparent in policy. In 1998, the government announced that the Single Regeneration Budget would be 'refocused' to target 80 per cent of spending to the 50 most deprived areas. The SRB is supplemented by the 'New Deal for Communities' (NDC), a policy response to the Social Exclusion Unit's report 'Bringing Britain Together; A Strategy for Neighbourhood Renewal' (SEU 1998), which will provide an extra £800 million to be spent on projects targeted to the most deprived estates between 1999 and 2002. Seventeen target areas, designated as 'Pathfinders', have been able to bid for funds to target money on their most deprived neighborhoods, to create employment opportunities, improve health, tackle crime and raise educational achieve-ment. Together, the revised SRB and the NDC developments are being hailed by the government as a 'New Deal for Regeneration'.

Within this most recent policy context, attention has also shifted toward the greater involvement of local communities (through their representative organizations), not merely as recipients of central or local government action, but also as key partners in the development of stra-tegic responses to poverty and exclusion. In recent years, a large body of academic and policy literature has highlighted the need to involve local people in sustainable regeneration initiatives (Fordham 1995; Taylor 1995; Thake 1995; Hastings 1996; Alcock et al. 1998). Some of these research findings have begun to filter through to policy guidance. Bidding Guid-ance to Round 4 of the Single Regeneration Budget Challenge Fund (a competitive bidding process for the allocation of central government regeneration funds), for instance, advises that bids should 'secure the real involvement of communities, including ethnic minority communities, both in the preparation and implementation of bids' (DoE 1997: 2). A community-based approach to regeneration is also a fundamental tenet of the NDC.

In other policy areas too, greater importance is being placed on joint working with local people. For local government this has been high-lighted in the Best Value initiatives (the duty of 'best value' requires that authorities commission local services according to quality, value for money and local need; see DETR 1998a) and in the recent government White Paper on developing local democracy (DETR 1998b). The implicit policy target, in theory at least, is for local communities not only to maintain a role in project implementation, but now also to influence policy development and direction. In short, the processes of government should aim to be 'inclusive' and not to reproduce and reinforce social exclusion. In urban policy, one mechanism through which this is to be achieved is the participation of local people in strategic regeneration and anti-poverty partnerships.

Community involvement in strategic partnership has the potential to promote forms of empowerment that differ greatly from the rather limited interpretation that has dominated community involvement in consultation exercises and project implementation to date (Taylor 1995). Indeed, Taylor observes that it could result in a realignment of power distribution within partnerships:

> In theory it provides the community with the right to a seat at the table on an equal basis with other partners, which in turn requires other partners to negotiate rather than pulling rank, to develop alliances and coalitions, to mediate consensus building and compromise. (ibid.: 61)

Central and local government approaches to community participation

An analysis of power relations is crucial to a delineation of the role of partnerships in urban policy. In the 1980s and early 1990s, Conservative governments sought to rectify the problems of urban decay through fostering physical renewal and the creation of economic opportunity. The dominant paradigm throughout this period was that private sector-led economic regeneration would be the motor to create competitive conditions within inner cities and facilitate the operation of markets. The key to urban regeneration was seen to be in fostering private enterprise, supported by public funds. The effect of this approach, underpinned by financial incentives and an attack on the roles and functions of local government (Stewart and Stoker 1995), was to ensure that partnerships in urban regeneration were generally dominated by private sector partners and by central government policy (Hastings 1996; Lawless 1996). The creation of local partnerships was considered as neither necessary nor desirable.

This approach was also apparent in the creation of a number of prominent 'single-purpose' agencies (dominated by private sector involvement), such as Urban Development Corporations (UDCs) and Training and Enterprise Councils (TECs), whose agendas were, in many ways, precisely to circumvent the compromises which partnerships, joint ventures and consensus building inevitably require (Stewart 1994). Within this political context, many potential partners found themselves at the margins of regeneration work, and this was particularly true for those at whom much regeneration work was targeted; people living in deprived communities. Some have gone so far as to describe themselves, in the words of a review of black community involvement in the Single Regeneration Budget, as 'Invisible Partners' (Crook 1995). This marginalization has been reflected, in Crook's view, throughout the process of regeneration, from initial planning and identification of needs and programme bidding, through to the allocation and control of resources and service delivery.

The failure of urban policy to engage local communities in this period contributed to a parallel development in the local government policy response to poverty, the growth of local authority anti-poverty strategies. The emphasis on private enterprise in the 1980s and early 1990s was in direct contrast to the more 'welfarist' approach to urban policy that had been evident in the 1960s and 1970s through the Urban Programme and Community Development Projects (Deakin and Edwards 1993), when areas of 'social need' where mainstream welfare provision was inadequate to meet the needs of people living in acute poverty were targeted for special help (see Alcock 1993). This approach had come under criticism, particularly from those working in the CDPs, who pointed out that without additional policy solutions to unemployment and poverty, the targeting of supplementary welfare provision to communities that were experiencing severe economic and structural decline was a largely fruitless exercise (CDP 1997).

Many local authorities had experienced direct involvement in locally-based anti-poverty initiatives through the Community Development Projects and Urban Programme in the 1960s and 1970s, and in some authorities these initiatives were absorbed into mainstream service delivery programmes when central government funding for projects ended. In the 1980s and early 1990s, many more local authorities, marginalized in urban policy dominated by the private sector, and faced with evidence of increasing social polarization and worsening levels of poverty amongst local communities, expanded service commitments to poor local citizens and began to coordinate them into strategic programmes to combat local poverty (Alcock et al. 1995). Anti-poverty strategies and initiatives are now a significant feature of the local government landscape; 161 local authorities responding to a survey of local authorities in England and Wales conducted in 1997, indicated that they were active in anti-poverty work. Forty-seven per cent of these operated a corporate anti-poverty strategy (Pearson et al. 1997). These authorities have recognized that, working alone, their abilities to combat poverty are limited, and therefore partnership, with other organizations and with local people, has become an important element of local authority anti-poverty strategy.

As discussed above, since the late 1990s, the policy environment is changing again and these hitherto dissonant approaches to combating poverty and promoting economic development are coming together under a new focus on social exclusion. The recent developments discussed above, toward addressing the needs of the most deprived communities through urban policy and for representatives of those communities to participate in strategic partnerships – including the new local strategic partnerships for policy development – means that it is now essential to assess what benefits the experiences of partnerships in anti-poverty work have offered these communities.

Local authority anti-poverty strategies and community partnerships

As noted above, in 1997, 180 local authorities out of a total of 412 authorities in England and Wales responded to a survey on anti-poverty work in local government administered through the Anti-Poverty Unit at the Local Government Management Board. This survey was part of a research project concerned with developing tools for the evaluation of anti-poverty work (Pearson et al. 1997). Of these authorities 161 indicated either that they were active in anti-poverty working or had formally adopted an anti-poverty strategy. More than 90 per cent also indicated that partnership working was an important element of this work.

The survey asked local authorities to indicate which of a range of organizations they engaged with in partnership working on anti-poverty issues. Local voluntary and community organizations were the most popular choice of partner, followed in order by health authorities, other local authorities, national voluntary organizations, police and (in a minority of cases), the Benefits Agency, central government departments and the local offices of government departments.

Local authorities were also asked to differentiate between the involvement with these partners in arrangements concerning either the delivery and implementation of specific anti-poverty initiatives ('specific' partnerships) and arrangements concerned with strategic development and service planning ('generic' partnerships). Local voluntary and community organizations were again the most popular choice of partner in specific partnerships, with over 45 per cent of responding authorities indicating joint working arrangements of this nature. In relation to generic partnerships, however, the involvement of local and community organisations

Table 7.1 Generic and Specific Partnerships

Partner Agency	Specific	Generic	Both
Other Local Authorities	35	10	15
Central Government Departments	17	5	3
Health Authority	45	11	16
Benefits Agency	24	10	3
Police Authority	24	7	8
Local Employer	16	7	7
National Voluntary Organization	23	11	9
Local Voluntary or Community Organization	46	11	22
Local Office of Central Government Department	26	8	3

was less prevalent. Only 10 per cent of responding authorities indicated that they engaged in generic partnership arrangements with local voluntary and community sectors, making these organisations less frequently involved in generic partnerships than either health authorities or national voluntary organisations.

Table 7.1 indicates the percentage of responding local authorities working with different partner organisations in relation to generic and specific partnerships.

Clearly, then, whilst there has been substantial involvement of communities in relation to specific anti-poverty initiatives, this involvement has been more limited where strategic anti-poverty partnerships are concerned. There is also evidence to suggest that in urban policy, despite the increasingly strong steer from policy guidance, widespread involvement of communities in project implementation has not generally been matched by a strong community presence at the strategic level (Robson et al. 1994; Alcock et al. 1995; Mawson et al. 1995). This finding has been reflected in more recent policy developments, there being little evidence to demonstrate the involvement of local people in the planning processes of welfare-to-work schemes (Brown and Passmore 1998).

In a review of Local Partnerships for Social and Economic Regeneration across the EU, Geddes and Martin (1996: 31) have suggested that whilst partnership working has provided:

> better co-ordination and integration of the policies of the many local public and quasi-public agencies involved in local regeneration, it is less clear either that local partnerships have actively engaged local community partners, or that the economic benefits claimed to derive for local communities from partnership working have been significant.

They conclude that:

> while some commentators suggest that partnerships may be leading
> to a significant reshaping of the structure and processes of local eco-
> nomic governance, reflecting fundamental shifts in relations between
> market, state and civil society, in at least some contexts partnership
> is a far less grandiose product of a rather desperate search for rela-
> tively cheap means of managing the worst of our urban and rural
> problems. (ibid.: 33; see also Pike 1996)

Despite this evidence, there appear to be compelling reasons, not least
to make them more sensitive to local needs and conditions, and to
address one aspect of the 'democratic deficit', to advance community
participation in strategic programmes addressing local needs. If this is
to be achieved then, as Taylor (1995) points out, these 'new rules of
engagement' create the need to revisit some familiar questions about
community participation; questions about the relative power of various
partners; about procedures, structures and agendas for participation;
and about communication.

Issues in community participation in strategic partnerships

Defining the community

Regeneration programs generally target resources to spatially defined
areas. The choice of these areas has often been circumscribed by the
boundaries of external funding criteria; suitable targets for current regeneration programs need not only exhibit characteristics of widespread
deprivation but also demonstrate capacity to benefit from regeneration
resources. Local authorities and their partners have identified these areas
through a combination of local knowledge and the use of secondary
data analysis to measure, for example, unemployment levels and recipients of benefits. The use of data to measure levels of local deprivation
has also been a common element of local authority anti-poverty strategies. A large number of authorities have produced 'poverty profiles' or
social audits of local areas in order to identify, and subsequently target,
those experiencing the most severe economic and social disadvantage
(Alcock and Craig 1999).

For policy planners, the restriction of policy interventions within
clearly delineated geographical boundaries makes sense: for regeneration partnerships it is much easier to keep track of resources and prove
the 'success' of regeneration programs through analyses of numbers of

jobs, training places, etc. created within the targeted area. And it has been these qualities that have appealed to local authorities seeking to direct extra resources to poor communities through anti-poverty strategies. In the harsh climate of local government finance in the UK, in the 1980s in particular, the allocation of resources to areas which could be identified through statistical analyses as experiencing widespread and acute deprivation and where the impact of these resources could be more readily measured, has often been an attractive strategy to local councillors (Alcock et al. 1995). This has meant that some areas are the target of both regeneration programs and anti-poverty strategies (and frequently a host of other initiatives). In other cases, however, areas targeted through anti-poverty strategies have missed out on regeneration programs because very deprived areas have lacked the capacity to meet regeneration targets (Alcock et al. 1998).

The technical difficulties involved in defining the boundaries for the spatial targeting of resources have been well documented (see, for instance, Alcock and Craig 1999 for a discussion of local poverty profiles and the use of variables to map urban and rural poverty). A more germane debate concerns the merits of geographical targeting and the effects that this can have on those population groups, and spatial areas, that are the targets of policy. Most regeneration and anti-poverty practitioners are aware of the main drawback to geographical targeting, identified since the creation of Educational Priority Areas in the 1960s, of the so-called 'ecological fallacy', that not all people living in targeted areas are poor, nor do the majority of poor people live in areas of concentrated deprivation. This is an inevitable, and unavoidable, dilemma for those undertaking targeted work of this nature. Similarly, where social groups are targeted, there is a tendency for some groups, the unemployed, elderly, minority ethnic communities, etc., to feature frequently as the targets of anti-poverty and regeneration initiatives. Other groups vulnerable to poverty and with limited access to the labour market, for example people with mental ill-health or people with drug and alcohol addictions, are less often targeted for special attention. The danger is, therefore, that some groups receive widespread attention and that other groups are nobody's priority (Balloch and Jones 1990).

There are a number of other difficulties inherent in targeting spatial locations and social groups. These include:

- *Pathologization* – the identification of certain areas and certain groups as poor is often all too readily translated into blame for their poverty. This has been experienced in different ways by many groups such as lone parents, young people and members of minority ethnic groups or by those who through, for example, housing allocations policy, end up concentrated in particular areas.

- *Disincentives for local investment* – the paradox of targeting certain spatial locations for special treatment is that the public identification of these areas as disadvantaged, and therefore experiencing all the concomitant difficulties of low skill levels, high crime rates and poor environment, can act as a deterrent for private investment. Local authorities and regeneration partnerships can find themselves in a double bind, emphasizing local poverty and deprivation in order to attract central government and European regeneration funds on the one hand, and 'talking up' local areas and emphasising opportunity in order to attract investors on the other.
- *Resource distribution* - the selective allocation of resources to targeted areas and social groups raises questions about the legitimacy of an approach that includes only relatively small sections of the population. Political support for targeted initiatives can waver if other sections of the population feel that their needs are not also being met.

As mentioned earlier, the key benefit from targeting is the potential for the effective use of scarce resources. An issue for the involvement of local people in spatially targeted strategic anti-poverty programmes, however, is that the external drawing of boundaries bears no necessary relation to the real or experienced sense of community of those living in targeted areas. Real communities do not follow administrative boundaries and will change over time. People may also identify more readily with other spatial areas, or experience allegiances to social groups, which are stronger than geographical ties.

For many people living in deprived areas, the concept of identifying with anything that could be recognized as community in the traditional sense – individuals bound by kinship or geography with shared values, experience and expectations – may itself be alien. Duffy and Hutchinson (1997: 357) have argued that policy planners have failed adequately to consider the implications of a decline in the traditional concept of community. They point out that deprived communities that are targeted by regeneration policies and anti-poverty strategies are precisely those that 'demonstrate the least characteristics of community life in the classical or anticipated sense' and that urban policy which seeks to recreate these communities is inevitably bound to fail. This view has obvious implications for the Social Exclusion Unit's approach to deprived communities which, in moving toward a 'national strategy for neighbourhood renewal', not only adopts spatial targeting as an approach to policy delivery but also perpetuates the aim of rebuilding of cohesive local communities as a desirable policy goal (Kleinman 1998; Social Exclusion Unit 1998).

The difficulties involved in spatial targeting have led many local authorities with anti-poverty strategies to target social groups (rather than areas) vulnerable to poverty; and later rounds of the SRB Challenge Fund have enabled regeneration partnerships to include initiatives which take particular social groups, for instance young people or black and minority ethnic people, as their target populations. One of the advantages of targeting entire social groups is, of course, that the benefits of regeneration programs and anti-poverty strategies are more likely to reach a larger number of people in a particular local authority area. Amongst the disadvantages is the fact that resources are more thinly spread and their effects more difficult to measure.

Even where social groups are targeted, however, politicians and practitioners have faced difficult decisions over which groups to target. A wide range of social groups in the UK are generally recognized to be at greater risk of experiencing poverty: older people, young people, women, children, minority ethnic communities and people with disabilities are the groups that are most commonly identified in the research literature (e.g. Alcock 1993; Oppenheim and Harker 1996). These groups are frequently the target of local authority anti-poverty strategies and less frequently, though increasingly, the focus of regeneration initiatives. Such groups, however, rarely constitute a homogeneous community; black and minority ethnic 'communities', for instance, are often subdivided, sometimes reflecting faith or political divisions, sometimes national or cultural origins.

Other groups reflect parallel differences in experiences and expectations. In terms of social allegiances, people do not often recognize these broad social groupings – women, older people, people with disabilities – as representing a community to which they belong. More often, people identify with much smaller networks of people connected by common interest, for instance; employment (for those in work); gay, lesbian and bisexual groups; medical campaign and support groups linked to a particular illness or disability; and groups linked to schools or care providers. Issues such as these provide commonalities around which people mobilise into action. They are also a source of social connections. Perri 6 (1997) highlights the importance of these connections in overcoming, and preventing, social exclusion and Skelcher et al. (1996) argue that involvement in social networks is an important precursor to successful regeneration partnerships. These kinds of groupings are rarely, however, the targets of strategic anti-poverty and regeneration programs.

It would appear, therefore, that current strategic approaches to local poverty operate on an ill thought-out concept of community. In consequence, local people do not easily identify with the aims of these programs and may not readily get involved. This has been an issue for some local authority anti-poverty strategies where local people have not understood strategy aims and have been reluctant to participate in partnerships and consultation fora (Alcock et al. 1995). It may also be the case that people may be discouraged by the negative connotations associated with programs concerned with poverty and deprivation. There is, nevertheless, much scope here to revisit interpretations of community in policy development so that regeneration and anti-poverty programs can effectively target both geographically and to communities of interest.

Partnerships and representation

The failures of policy adequately to consider interpretations of community have been directly reflected in debates about the 'representativeness' of local people working within regeneration and anti-poverty partnerships. Representation on strategic partnerships tends often to comprise a similar range of key local players, although with some variation at the margins according to circumstances. In most localities, there are a number of organizations whose members, although ultimately only able to speak on behalf of their organisation, are also accepted as being able to stand as a proxy for sectoral opinion: Training and Enterprise Councils and Chambers of Commerce for the business sector; Councils for Voluntary Service and other voluntary sector umbrella organizations for the non-profit sector; and, in the public sector, local authorities, health authorities and education establishments. Various combinations of representatives from these organizations serve on almost all regeneration and anti-poverty partnerships, although it has generally been the case that those partners with a social agenda have been more commonly represented on anti-poverty partnerships.

In most communities (of whatever definition), however, there are typically no such representative structures in existence and strategic partnerships must set about building appropriate channels for facilitating the inclusion of local people. This requires time and resources, particularly when individuals and organizations are not readily equipped with the skills and resources for participation (see below). In areas where there is a complex mix of local communities it also requires negotiation between the demands of project and funding timetables and the desire to encompass as broad a range as possible of community voices. In some cases, the pursuit of 'representative' local people has resulted in complex structures for participation; sometimes with the consequence that, when there is only a limited number of spaces available at the board table, community representatives have become further and further removed from their constituencies (Duffy and Hutchinson 1997).

Ultimately, the pursuit of local people to represent unified local communities is fruitless. As Thake (1995) points out, participation in community regeneration is something of a 'minority sport'. Participation in strategic programs is even more exclusive, and representatives will probably be drawn from a very limited pool of people who may be untypical of the community sector (CDF 1996). It is important, therefore, that time and resources are invested more widely in developing good channels of communication between community 'representatives' and local people.

Participation and process

A number of commentators have argued that strict enforcement of representation is less important than a partnership's ability to reflect local priorities (McFarlane and Mabbott 1993; Taylor 1995) and it has generally been true that a very limited number of community representatives have been active in anti-poverty work. Indeed, it is almost a truism for many local authorities that a small number of familiar faces regularly turn up at public meetings. This raises crucial questions about the nature of participation in strategic partnerships and the expectations of other partners in relation to the roles and responsibilities of community representatives.

There is a large literature outlining the necessary processes to enable local people to participate successfully in local initiatives and service programs; much of this literature relates to local regeneration projects and tenant participation in housing management schemes (e.g. Wilcox 1994; Zipfel 1994; Stewart and Taylor 1995; Cole and Smith 1996; WECH 1998). A common theme is the need for a more equitable distribution of power in partnerships which appear dominated by 'top-down' working methods. Local people can feel excluded from the processes of partnership working when they sense they are ill-equipped to contribute or where partnerships function only as ratifying bodies, and important decisions are made through informal contact elsewhere. In partnerships with a strategic focus these issues can become magnified when local people are faced with negotiating the agendas and practices of not just one, but several, formal agencies. Participation in strategic partnerships is hard work for community representatives who need to keep up to speed with events in several different organizations. It is critical, therefore, that strategic partnerships keep open channels of communication which keep community representatives fully informed of all developments, not just those that take place at the board table.

The participation of community groups can also be constrained by external agendas which do not facilitate 'bottom-up' approaches to policy development. Local groups, often comprising unpaid volunteers, can hardly cope with being on the receiving end of an ever-changing panoply of interventions. If there is to be sustainable involvement of local people in the planning and development of these policies, then it is not only strategic partnerships, but also the policies which they are implementing, that need to recognise community priorities. The processes involved in submitting bids to the SRB Challenge Fund, for instance, have been criticized as being disempowering to local communities (Alcock et al. 1998). The short timescales available for consultation, coupled with the fact that programs are predefined by external criteria, have often meant that community groups have found it difficult to participate, and as a consequence have felt they have had little real influence on local development agendas. Anti-poverty strategies have been subject to the same criticisms where they have been developed internally in local authorities with little consultation and involvement from local communities.

The principles for effective partnerships involving residents in estate-based regeneration, cited by Taylor (1995), also seem appropriate for the involvement of communities in strategic partnerships with a wider focus. Effective strategic partnerships should:

- involve local people from the outset;
- have an agreed and negotiated agenda, with clear terms of reference;
- ensure that all partners are committed to community empowerment;
- develop appropriate structures and procedures for community participation, which are acceptable to all partners; and
- address issues of conflict and power.

Resources and organizational capacity

The counterbalance to the creation of appropriate structures for participation is that the communities themselves need to have the necessary resources and capacity to be able effectively to utilize these channels. Participation in strategic programs is a time- and resource-consuming business. Unlike other partners, local people often do not come to the board table readily equipped with skills for participation in meetings.

Skills such as negotiation, presentation and time management can, however, be learned with the appropriate support and access to training and much of the literature outlined above gives useful guidance on providing local people with opportunities to acquire these skills. What has also been crucial in disempowering many community representatives is that they have not approached the board table backed by the same levels of resources and organizational capacity as other, more powerful, partners. Senior figures in key formal or statutory organizations are able to bring significant institutional and personal 'clout' to strategic partnerships. This means that they are likely to be in positions to act on decisions made. These organizations may also have access to financial resources which can be assigned to projects, an important element of power within a policy climate which emphasizes the importance of additionality and leverage.

Community representatives are unlikely to be backed by the same level of personal and institutional resources. This can have two effects; first, community representatives may feel under pressure to legitimize their existence on strategic partnerships in a way that other 'partners' do not, and this exacerbates issues of unequal power; second, community groups may find it difficult to sustain meaningful involvement in partnerships. The point has already been made that community involvement in strategic partnerships will probably involve only a limited number of people. It is important that these people are not overwhelmed by the demands of participation, but that the community is resourced and empowered to develop the capacity to extend involvement and offer support to local representatives (Cole and Smith 1996). This is especially important in deprived communities, where organizational capacity is unlikely to be extensive but where local people are being asked to contribute to an increasing number of local, national, and even international programs and initiatives.

Centrally-driven regeneration programs such as the SRB, European initiatives such as URBAN, local authority anti-poverty strategies and partnership-based initiatives for the improvement in local governance and the delivery of services, for instance Best Value and Health Action Zones, all require substantial involvement of local communities for successful implementation. Communities are reaching saturation point in terms of their ability to respond to this succession of initiatives, and there is an urgent need for infrastructure support both to enable effective participation to develop, and to explore alternative methods for participation which place more manageable demands on local activists. It is probably appropriate that this support be independent of the local authority; in deprived communities the relationship between local government and its electorate is not always easy, and local authorities are often seen as part of the problem, not part of the solution (Alcock et al. 1995). Community development or capacity-building may result in local communities challenging decisions of the council, and whilst many local authorities have come a long way in developing 'community-friendly' approaches, there is still some way to go. Anti-poverty strategies have aimed to provide for more sensitive delivery of services in deprived communities but for many people with low incomes, contact with local government frequently has predominantly negative associations, linked to demands for rent or the interventions of social services.

In many strategic regeneration programs, the framework does exist for capacity building in communities to take place. However, the demands of pressured funding regimes and the working styles of partners, have made it difficult to effect. Capacity building in communities has also been a goal of anti-poverty strategies, but most anti-poverty strategies do not carry large budgets and the impact in terms of the development of community resources has therefore been limited. In order for communities to sustain involvement in strategic programs and partnerships, local authorities and their partners may need to make substantial investment in developing community capacity (Craig and Mayo 1995; Fordham 1995) before the parameters of strategic programs are set. Alternatively, communities will continue to have a limited influence on the regeneration of local areas and will struggle to develop their own organisations or engage with other partners.

Social and economic focus

It was suggested above that regeneration programs in the 1980s and early 1990s had an almost exclusively economic focus but that the gradually increasing involvement of local people in regeneration programs has gone some way toward broadening the regeneration agenda (Taylor 1995). Whilst communities do recognize the importance of job creation and physical redevelopment, there are also often other issues, for instance poor schools, lack of community facilities, fears about safety, poor transport networks, lack of access to childcare, high levels of ill-health coupled with poor health facilities, that are equally important to the sustainable regeneration of deprived areas. These issues have formed part of the focus of anti-poverty strategies which have addressed social needs in poor communities.

In many strategic regeneration programs, however, the priorities of regeneration are still inward investment and business development, and social issues often merit less attention (Alcock et al. 1998). Capacity building in these cases has often been about developing economic capacity and less about building up social capacity. In very deprived communities, however, the renewal of social capacity may be necessary before economic development can succeed. People whose relationship with the labor market is tenuous may need assistance to develop confidence and assertiveness skills before they are able to take up training and employment positions; others may be unable to benefit from increased employment opportunities if these are not matched by affordable (i.e. highly subsidized) and good quality local childcare facilities (Clarke et al. 1996).

Much more then needs to be done to develop the social agenda in regeneration and to enable local people to benefit from economic renewal. Local authority anti-poverty strategies have gone some way toward developing social capacity through the development of sensitive local services in deprived communities and through involving local people in the planning and development of service delivery. But they have too often operated in parallel to, and not in conjunction with, regeneration programmes (Alcock et al. 1998). If strategic partnerships are to offer an adequate reflection of the concerns of local communities, the agendas of anti-poverty strategies and urban policy need to come together and the range of strategic partners – and the support given them – needs to reflect this more holistic approach.

Black and minority ethnic communities

A final, critical point of discussion is in relation to the problems experienced by black and minority ethnic communities wishing to participate in strategic anti-poverty and regeneration programs. Such communities have a particular interest in regeneration and anti-poverty policies because black and minority ethnic groups live predominantly in the urban areas that constitute the major focus of such programs (Dorsett 1998). They are also more likely than other social groups to be living in deprived circumstances (Oppenheim and Harker 1996; Craig 1999).

There is some evidence that black and minority ethnic groups have been involved in regeneration initiatives, most notably in the inner London boroughs and other major urban conurbations. The concentration of black and minority ethnic communities in urban deprived areas has also meant that groups representing these communities are the subject of frequent consultation on regeneration and anti-poverty issues. As with local community members more generally, however, their involvement at strategic level has been limited and these groups have been largely excluded from access to policy development networks (Crook 1995). As a result, black and minority ethnic groups have felt that area-based regeneration frameworks have not often reflected their priorities (Skelcher et al. 1996). For these reasons, black and minority ethnic communities have also not featured largely in anti-poverty partnerships, although equalities issues should in principle be an important feature of an anti-poverty approach to local government work. This policy failure has been especially true of areas where there are not significant concentrations of black and minority ethnic groups, local authorities (and other policy-makers) often arguing that their sparsity requires no coherent policy response (Rai 1995; Craig et al. 1999).

The ability of strategic partnerships to meet the needs of possibly the most vulnerable minorities, refugee communities, may be even more circumscribed. There has been very little research which addresses the participation of refugee communities in strategic regeneration and anti-poverty programmes but the more generalized exclusion experienced by many of these communities suggests that their involvement will be limited.

In many cases, small-scale black and minority ethnic groups have even less capacity than other community groups for participation in strategic programmes. The concerns of these groups can be overlooked if 'universal' representative structures do not adequately reflect the needs of diverse communities. It is not appropriate for general voluntary and community sector representatives to be asked to represent black and minority ethnic group interests (Crook 1995; Craig et al. 1999), and where this practice occurs it may act to reinforce exclusion processes. It is important, therefore, that strategic partnerships recognize the needs of black and minority ethnic communities and that this is reflected in appropriate representation and resources to enable their participation.

Partnerships and power

Research examining partnership in a wide range of policy arenas suggests that the critical issue underpinning partnership between local and central government on the one hand and the voluntary and community sectors on the other, is that of resources and power (Alcock et al. 1999). Well-resourced organizations – in terms of human and financial resources – have expected poorly resourced community groups to engage with them on equal terms, often within compressed timetables, and in the context of complex and multi-faceted programmes. This engagement has, not surprisingly, appeared to many local groups to be tokenistic and oppressive. Effective partnership working – which takes the concerns and needs of local communities seriously rather than dragging them along in the slipstream of policy programs – requires enabling these communities to organize and respond as much on their terms and at a pace which is manageable, as at the speed determined by overarching political and policy imperatives. This, in turn, requires flexibility in budgeting and timetabling from government and its agents. Moving from the rhetoric of partnership to the reality of partnership requires government and those holding power to engage in a major shift not only in thinking but also in their practice.

References

Alcock, P. (1993) *Understanding Poverty* (London: Macmillan)

Alcock, P. and Craig, G. (1999) Mapping Local Poverty, in J. Bradshaw and Sainsbury, R. (ed.), *The Experience of Poverty* (Aldershot: Ashgate)

Alcock, P., Craig, G., Dalgleish, K. and Pearson, S. (1995) *Combating Local Poverty* (Luton: Local Government Management Board)

Alcock, P., Craig, G., Lawless, P., Pearson, S. and Robinson, D. (1998) *Inclusive Regeneration: Local Authorities Corporate Strategies for Tackling Disadvantage* (Sheffield Hallam University/University of Lincolnshire and Humberside/Department of Environment, Transport and the Regions, Sheffield/Hull)

Alcock, P., Craig, G. and Harvey, A. (1999) *Local Action on Poverty* (Basingstoke: Macmillan)

Association of Metropolitan Authorities Urban Policy Group (1996) *A New Deal for Regeneration* (London: AMA)

Balloch, S. and Jones, B. (1990) *Poverty and Anti-Poverty Strategy: The Local Government Response* (London: Association of Metropolitan Authorities)

Brown, T. and Passmore, J. (1998) *Housing and Anti-Poverty Strategies: A Good Practice Guide* (London: Chartered Institute of Surveyors/Joseph Rowntree Foundation)

Clarke, K., Craig, G. and Glendinning, C. (1996) *Small Change* (York: Joseph Rowntree Foundation/Family Policy Studies Centre)

Cole, I. and Smith, Y. (1996) *From Estate Action to Estate Agreement* (Bristol: Policy Press)

Combat Poverty Agency (1995) *Planning for Change: A Handbook on Strategic Planning for Local Development Partnerships* (Dublin: Combat Poverty Agency)

Community Development Foundation (1996) *Regeneration and the Community: Guidelines to the Community Involvement Aspect of the SRB Challenge Fund* (London: CDF)

Community Development Project (1977) *Gilding the Ghetto: The State and Poverty Experiments* (London: CDPIIU)

Craig, G. (1999) 'Race' Poverty and Social Security, in J. Ditch (ed.), *Poverty and Social Security* (London: Routledge)

Craig, G. and Mayo, M. (1995) *Community Empowerment* (London: Zed Books)

Craig, G., Taylor, M., Szanto, C. and Wilkinson, M. (1999) *Developing Local Compacts* (York: Joseph Rowntree Foundation)

Crook, J. (1995) *Invisible Partners: The Impact of SRB on Black Communities* (London: Black Training and Enterprise Group)

Deakin, N. and Edwards, J. (1993) *The Enterprise Culture and the Inner City* (London: Routledge)

Development Trusts Association (1997) *Here to Stay: A Public Policy Framework for Community-based Regeneration* (London: Development Trusts Association)

Department of the Environment (1997) *Partnership in Regeneration: the Challenge Fund, Round 4* (London: The Stationery Office)

Department of the Environment, Transport and the Regions (1998a) *Modernising Local Government: Improving Local Services through Best Value* (London: The Stationery Office)

Department of the Environment, Transport and the Regions (1998b) *Modern Local Government: In Touch with the People* (London: The Stationery Office)

Department of the Environment, Transport and the Regions (1997) *Building Partnerships for Prosperity: Sustainable Growth, Competitiveness and Employment in the English Regions*, Cm. 3814 (London: The Stationery Office)

Dorsett, R. (1998) *Ethnic Minorities in the Inner City* (Bristol: Policy Press)

European Commission (1995) *Community Involvement in Urban Regeneration: Added Value and Changing Values* (Brussels: EC)

Duffy, K. and Hutchinson, J. (1997) Urban Policy and the Turn to Community, *Town Planning Review* 68: 3, 347–62

Fordham, G. (1995) *Made to Last: Creating Sustainable Neighbourhood and Estate Regeneration* (York: Joseph Rowntree Foundation)

Geddes, M. and Martin, S. (1996) *Local Partnerships for Social and Economic Regeneration* (London: Local Government Management Board)

Hastings, A. (1996) Unravelling the Process of 'Partnership' in Urban Regeneration Policy, *Urban Studies* 33: 2, 253–68

Kleinman. M. (1998) *Include Me Out?*, CASE Paper No. 11 (London: Centre for Analysis of Social Exclusion, LSE)

Lawless, P. (1994) Partnership in Urban Regeneration in the UK: The Sheffield Central Area Study, *Urban Studies* 3.1: 8, 1303–24.

Lawless, P. (1996) The Inner Cities; Towards a New Agenda, *Town Planning Review* 67: 1, 21–43.

London Borough Grants Unit (1997) *Vision and Visibility: Regeneration and Ethnic Minority Communities in London* (London: London Borough Grants Unit)

Mawson, J. et al. (1995) *The Single Regeneration Budget: The Stocktake* (Birmingham: Centre for Urban and Regional Studies)

McFarlane, R. and Mabbott, J. (1993) *City Challenge: Involving Local Communities* (London: National Council for Voluntary Organisations)

Medas, M. (1994) *From City Challenge to The Single Regeneration Budget: A Black Perspective* (London: Sia)

NCVO (1993) *Community Involvement in City Challenge* (London: National Council for Voluntary Organisations)

Oppenheim, C. (ed.) (1998) *An Inclusive Society: Strategies for Tackling Poverty* (London: Institute of Public Policy Research)

Oppenheim, C. and Harker, L. (1996) *Poverty: The Facts* (second edition, London: Child Poverty Action Group)

Pearson, S., Kirkpatrick, A. and Barnes, C. (1997) *Local Poverty, Local Responses*, Discussion Paper No. 2 (Sheffield Hallam University/University of Lincolnshire and Humberside, Sheffield/Hull)

Perri 6 (1997) *Escaping Poverty: From Safety Nets to Networks of Opportunity* (London: Demos)

Pike, A. (1996) *In Partnership: Subject to Contract* (Swindon: Economic and Social Research Council)

Rai, D. (1995) *In the Margins*, Social Research Paper No. 2 (University of Lincolnshire and Humberside, Hull)

Robinson, F. (1997) *The City Challenge Experience: A Review of the Development and Implementation of Newcastle City Challenge* (Newcastle City Challenge West End Partnership Ltd, Newcastle)

Robson, B. et al. (1994) *Assessing the Impact of Urban Policy* (London: HMSO)

Room, G. (ed.) (1995) *Beyond the Threshold: The Management and Analysis of Social Exclusion* (Bristol: Policy Press)

Scottish Office (1996) *Partnership in the Regeneration of Urban Scotland, Central Research Unit* (Edinburgh: Scottish Office)

Skelcher, C., McCabe, A., Lowndes, V. and Nanton, P. (1996) *Community Networks in Urban Regeneration – 'It all depends who you know . . . !'* (Bristol: Policy Press)

Social Exclusion Unit (1998) *Bringing Britain Together: A National Strategy for Neighbourhood Renewal* (London: SEU)

Stewart, J. and Stoker, G. (1995) *Local Government in the 1990s* (London: Macmillan)

Stewart, M. (1994) Between Whitehall and Town Hall: The Realignment of Urban Regeneration Policy in England, *Policy and Politics* 22: 2, 133–45

Stewart, M. and Taylor, M. (1995) *Empowerment and Estate Regeneration* (Bristol: Policy Press)

Taylor, M. (1995) *Unleashing the Potential: Bringing Residents to the Centre of Regeneration* (York: Joseph Rowntree Foundation)

Thake, S. (1995) *Staying the Course: The Roles and Structures of Community Regeneration Organisations* (York: Joseph Rowntree Foundation)

Thake, S. and Staubach, R. (1993) *Investing in People: Rescuing Communities from the Margin* (York: Joseph Rowntree Foundation)

Walterton and Elgin Community Homes (1998) *Walterton and Elgin: From Campaign to Control* (London: Walterton and Elgin Community Homes (WECH))

Wilcox, D. (1994) *Guide to Effective Participation* (London: Partnership Books)

Zipfel, T. (1994) *On Target: Extending Participation to Tackle Problem Estates* (London: Priority Estates Project)

8

Community Regeneration and National Renewal in the United Kingdom

Chris Miller

Contemporary regeneration initiatives stress the need for a comprehensive strategic approach that simultaneously addresses social, environmental and economic issues. The process should involve all stakeholders and permeate all mainstream government budgets, in the planning, design, implementation, evaluation, and crucially financing, of policies. Of particular importance is the focus on engaging the 'community' in identifying what is needed and determining how these needs should be met. Thus current UK initiatives are adopting, at least at the level of rhetoric, a more holistic approach that recognizes both the multiplicity and the interconnected nature of issues confronting a growing and significant section of the population (LGA 1997; SEU 1998). Typically, these issues include unemployment or precarious and/or low waged employment, poor health, low educational attainment, inadequate public and private services, a damaged or deteriorating physical environment and 'social exclusion', though this last is more difficult to define. In addition, there has been growing acknowledgement of the increasing, and unacceptable, gap between the rich and the poor and the potential danger to social order as a consequence (Commission on Social Justice 1994; Joseph Rowntree Foundation 1995; Donnison 1998). This contrasts with what is acknowledged as the failure of earlier initiatives over the past 30 years. These have been experimental, fragmented, ad hoc, piecemeal, limited in time and scope, and often oriented toward single state-delivered services.

This chapter reviews the major initiatives in British urban regeneration over the last 30 years. It aims to set in context the regeneration policy of the Labour government returned to office in 1997 after 18 years in opposition. The current debates bring together three distinct policy strands that have dominated all such initiatives: economic revitalization, rebuilding social fabric and promoting active citizenship engaged in the process of local governance and service delivery.

Persistence of urban problems and the evolving policy reponse

The Audit Commission (1989) noted that urban problems have persisted within the UK despite economic growth. These have had a differential impact and have variously affected whole cities, areas next to prospering communities and peripheral housing estates. Britain has experienced a variety of policies to tackle such social and economic problems.

In one category there are those initiatives, introduced by central government, which have come to be seen and analyzed as 'urban policy'. Such strategies have usually had a geographical base, and focused on what have been identified, using a variety of socioeconomic data, as the most deprived urban areas. Despite considerable research, there are still many different definitions of the problem to be addressed, with the policies proposed for addressing it being variously labeled as 'anti-poverty', 'inner-city' or 'urban regeneration'.

The impact of such policies, as judged by their own objectives, has been limited. Their repetitive nature and the sense that problems appear to be constantly rediscovered would strike anyone reading government papers on urban regeneration over the past 30 years. Part of the explanation for this limited success lies in the fact that such interventions have been led by a variety of government departments reluctant to coordinate their respective activities. This may also indicate something about the symbolic nature of such strategies.

In a second category are those policies and practices found within mainstream local government provision, such as in public housing or the personal social services. These local initiatives, though small-scale, have been important in highlighting ways of working within poor neighborhoods. In addition, nonprofit organizations and community-based groups, often financially sponsored by the state, have organized to tackle social and economic problems and argued for the direct engagement of the disadvantaged in any attempt to address issues that concern them.

All initiatives have assumed that, with better management, coordination and communication, advances in social reform and improvements to the physical fabric, all underpinned by economic growth, those who had yet to prosper would ultimately benefit. In the meanwhile there would be a need for targeted compensatory policies aimed at those people and localities that were somehow on the margins of, or excluded from, social progress. Policies would provide additional resources for those unable to succeed under 'normal' conditions, to compensate for uneven economic development, and 'manage' any localized frustration at the slowness of change and the apparent 'unfairness' of market forces. Programs ignored the oft-repeated point that not all those who reside in such areas are themselves deprived nor do all the deprived so reside. Similarly, designated areas did not always make sense to local residents or the nature of problems to be tackled.

Government action has often followed either in direct response to social unrest or from a concern that, without its intervention, this might not be too far away. Race and ethnicity have also been closely associated with such unrest, although in the 1980s it was increasingly associated with alienated young males (Lawless 1979; Campbell 1993). This remains the case today, with the New Deal for Communities initiative continuing to identify those areas with a large proportion of black and ethnic minority residents as a high priority.

Yet such outbursts of social disquiet, while important in themselves, have also reflected the deeper problems in the decline and restructuring of Britain's economy and a crisis within the postwar Keynes–Beveridge welfare settlement. On one level this has been felt as a crisis of efficiency and effectiveness, where the need is to find appropriate delivery mechanisms offering the right level and quality of provision to meet rising expectations and organized pressure from a growing number of interest groups. At another, more fundamental, level it was about the whole nature of the dominant Fabian interventionist and professionalized welfare project. Increasingly, as concern grew about the potential impact of a global economy, it was also about whether the state could afford to provide such services at all.

Thus, while the need for government intervention has not been in doubt, the purpose of such action and its capacity to bring about change have been matters of contention within the policy community. A number of comprehensive evaluative studies have critically analyzed the assumptions and approaches adopted within each policy phase and to assess their overall impact and effectiveness (for example, Edwards and Batley 1978; Audit Commission 1989).

Commenting on the first 20 years of urban policy, Robson et al. (1994: 2) conclude that it is difficult to determine 'unambiguously what government has aimed to achieve...at any one time'. They do, however, identify two overarching policy objectives: the creation of employment opportunities and improving the attractiveness of such areas to both residents and employers. They suggest that, while they could identify some positive changes, overall, 'policy has not been able to make significant inroads into the socio-economic problems' with 'continuing decline in the worst areas' (p. 49). They argue for a refocusing on 'people' rather than 'places' to 'utilize the skills' and 'mobilize the support' of local residents. They highlight the need for greater coordination and a more strategic approach, and emphasize the centrality of partnerships between local authorities and the private sector. Similarly, they stress the potential of other stakeholders, especially nonprofit organizations and local communities.

Bradford and Robson (1995) note that the level of resources available is 'minuscule compared with the size of the problems . . . and the loss of mainstream money . . . has more than countered any increase in urban funds' (p. 53). Similarly, the Audit Commission (1989) was equally critical of the 'patchwork quilt' approach rather than coordinated strategic interventions.

The dominance of neoliberal market ideologies throughout the 1980s brought about the abandonment of the postwar political consensus, most notably the twin pillars of full employment and universal welfare provision, as governments asserted that they could no longer meet the electorate's growing demands. State functions and institutions, driven by an aggressive 'new managerialism', were reorganized to reflect market philosophies and practice more closely, and to redefine public expectations.

Behind this process lay a fundamental challenge to the assumption that crucial areas of social life should be a matter of societal provision. Indeed, the notion of 'society' was denied while individual, family and community responsibility were underscored. The endorsement of self-help and the assumption of a growing 'culture of dependency' created by state welfare facilitated the transfer of service provision to the nonprofit, community and informal, as well as for-profit, sectors. Where the state continued as service provider, private sector principles and practices were introduced, while overall local government faced a massive erosion of its powers and influence.

Phases of regeneration policy

Urban regeneration policy has passed through five phases in the UK. Within each phase there has been a mix of social, economic and environmental initiatives, although successive governments have varied in the extent they have emphasized each element.

Within its first, most experimental and uncoordinated, phase (1968–77), regeneration policies gave a strong emphasis to 'people' living in areas of multiple deprivation. It was a period during which the three strands – of urban regeneration, community development and public participation – came together. On the face of it these strands are echoed in the Labour government's New Deal for Communities, but in fact the policy was more contradictory with vast programs for urban renewal which entailed decanting tens of thousands of residents alongside small-scale radical community development projects challenging the free movement of capital.

A series of official reports published during the 1960s had drawn attention to urban deprivation, increasing poverty and failing services. The fruits of economic growth and full employment were failing to reach all sections of the population. This, combined with a fear of increased racial tension, generated a number of experimental programs heavily influenced by theories that pathologized the poor, and focused on their alleged deficits rather than their strengths. The poor were seen as their own worst enemies, unwilling to engage fully with the labor market or maximize those opportunities in social benefits or education. Moreover, they were suspected of passing on their bad habits to their children, who continued the process. In contrast, those engaged in policy implementation tended rather to emphasize individual or community assets blocked by events and processes beyond their control. They sought to identify the structural causes that lay behind such deprivation, challenging these through local organizations.

Of particular significance was the Urban Aid Program (UP), through which central government provided 75 per cent of the funds for approved local authority projects to tackle 'areas of special need'. Favored projects were those that were community based, emphasized service provision, or had a developmental focus to enable residents to participate in public life and build a sense of community. Despite the original emphasis given to the potential for racial conflict, program funding did not initially favor ethnic minority groups (DoE, 1980). Nevertheless, the UP continued for nearly a decade to support a multitude of community groups and non-profit organizations (Taylor and Presley 1987).

Other programs such as the Community Development Projects (CDPs) soon followed (1969–77). These were twelve local neighborhood-based experiments aimed at 'finding new ways of meeting ... needs'. As well as undertaking research, they were established to support local initiatives, bring services and communities closer together, and encourage participation.

The CDPs mounted a convincing campaign to demonstrate that at the heart of the problem lay past and current economic practices within UK and global markets (DoE 1977). A similar position was also adopted by the consultant-led three Inner Area Studies (1972–77). Rather than a failure of individuals and families, it was the absence of a local or national commitment within 'capital' that was destroying local communities, as it sought cheaper markets to maximize short-term profits, whilst persistently failing to invest long-term. The solution lay in structural reforms, with those in the CDPs arguing for state regulation of capital (CDP 1977a and b). Such a trenchant critique of government policy went alongside their support for local organizations campaigning for improved provision. This, and their work within the labor movement, led to the withdrawal of government support (Loney 1983). However, key elements of the analysis were acknowledged in the 1977 White Paper, Policy for the Inner Cities, and later by the Audit Commission (1989) who noted that, 'the particular problems of Britain's inner cities have their roots in a shift in the nature of Britain's industrial base' (p. 9).

At the same time there was a rhetorical commitment to modernizing industry and government, especially its welfare systems. This included a challenge to young, often radical, graduates to enter the public services to make the improvements which they and others were demanding (Gamble 1986). This was the first attempt to come to terms with constituencies from the new social movements and a generation unwilling to accept the assumptions of its elders (Hall 1980). Many of those so recruited saw this as an opportunity to practice the politics already tested in the extra-parliamentary arenas of student organizations, the feminist movement, campaigning and alternative service-providing organizations.

Community development workers in local government facilitated the emergence of organizations concerned with such issues as the management, renewal and redevelopment of public housing, neighborhood enhancement, legal and welfare services and community media. They also helped with the formation of campaigning, advocacy and support groups. They attempted to demonstrate to those delivering public services the value of their approach and the need for public participation and collective solutions. This fitted well with the more community-oriented approach being adopted by public agencies. However, there was often an absence of collaboration between departments and welfare professionals. Consequently, many development workers found themselves working with community organizations campaigning against the policies and practices of other departments within their employing authority.

Within the public sector itself the concept of 'radical practice' was a growing influence as practitioners sought new ways of working (Bolger et al. 1981). However, their focus on a narrow trade union militancy as an essential first step to improvements in service delivery, was not sympathetically received by service users faced with declining levels of provision and the often-indistinguishable differences in the practices of 'radical' and 'traditional' professionals (Miller 1996).

The approach of these early programs was somewhat contradictory: introduce better coordination to link services with the most disadvantaged, gather more intelligence to understand better why people were failing to take advantage of the opportunities enjoyed by the majority, provide compensatory programs to support those few that were missing out, and help manage actual or potential social unrest. While such policies created an impression of intense activity, they lacked strategic vision. Coordination between them was often poor, and the relationship between these essentially experimental initiatives and mainstream programs non-existent. The role assigned to the recipients of such policies was limited in the extreme.

Thus urban policies during those first ten years were paralleled by the growth of an increasingly critical client and user voice. At the center of their dissatisfactions were both the quantity and the quality of state-delivered services. The way in which welfare was delivered was increasingly identified as a real concern. The top-down statist approach, dominated by a professional and technocratic process, excluded service users and citizens from any role in the identification of need or the determination of how needs should be met. Further, it alienated service users and denied them ownership of provision (London to Edinburgh Weekend Return Group 1979; Hoggett and McGill 1988). The welfare state, previously supported by a broad consensus, was now attacked from the left for the way in which it perpetuated unequal gender relations, while the expansion of state sponsored community development was seen primarily as a mechanism for managing the demands and dissatisfactions of working class communities (Mayo 1977; Cockburn 1977).

Reassertion of the marketplace

Publication of the White Paper, *Policy for the Inner Cities* (DoE 1977) marked the beginning of the second phase, 1978–87, of urban policy. This 'defining document' (Burton 1997) acknowledged the scale of the problem, and the interconnectedness of issues. It advocated changing mainstream policies, and recognized the potential for 'mounting social bitterness and increasing sense of alienation' (p. 5) if no action was taken.

Crucially, it supported the extension of the Urban Programme grant to cover economic and environmental projects in a number of selected authorities.

The Labour government passed the Inner Urban Areas Act in 1978. This more than quadrupled the amount available for UP, although that amount was still small in absolute terms and did not match the budget reductions in mainstream programs. The Act introduced the practice of formalized 'partnerships' between central government and selected local authorities identified to receive additional funding for the full range of social, economic, environmental and housing projects. All other authorities continued to bid for support for social projects, now described as the 'traditional' urban program.

The Conservative government that came to power in 1979 under Margaret Thatcher retained the Act. The emphasis now, however, was on economic rather than social regeneration and led to a focus on physical regeneration and the role of private sector. Where 'people' were the target, the purpose was to maximize their employment potential, through training and job preparation skills, and helping them to be 'in readiness' when job opportunities occurred. Government stressed the need to create partnerships with the private sector, with the new non-departmental government agencies, or 'quangos', taking the lead role. Their primary task, as exemplified by the twelve time-limited flagship Urban Development Corporations (1980–92), was to create such local private sector partnerships and 'lever in' private sector funds to physical redevelopment schemes. Similarly, Enterprise Zones, free of planning controls and offering redevelopment grants and exemptions from business taxes, were established as inducements to the private sector.

In addition a small number of governmental interdepartmental City Action Teams (1985) were launched with a vague brief and a limited budget to support interagency collaboration between departments and central and local government initiatives. In 1986 the first urban Task Forces were set up, aimed at boosting economic opportunities in tightly defined geographic areas, through inter-sectoral networking, coordinating activity and the exploitation of employment opportunities.

The 1980s witnessed high levels of conflict between central and local metropolitan government. Indeed, it was not always easy to disentangle central government's stated concern for local regeneration from a desire to undermine and sideline local government. Left-wing Labour metropolitan authorities began to develop new initiatives to address local problems (Burns, Hambleton and Hoggett 1994). Supporting the principle of universal public provision did not mean having to defend a particular institutionalized way of delivering such provision. A number of authorities, exploiting technological changes, introduced decentralized services for greater physical and social access by users and local communities. Radical decentralizers offered this as a means to make services more responsive and relevant, a challenge to professional domination, and the devolution of power and extension of democracy to neighborhood level (Gregory and Smith 1986). Moreover, by drawing together local communities, the disadvantaged and socially excluded, public service trade unions and Labour Party radicals, a 'rainbow' alliance could be created as a springboard for change.

Such attempts at localism, which were alien to Labour's traditional emphasis on centralized services, were not confined to innovative methods in the delivery of mainstream provision. This 'new urban left' strategy introduced new policy concerns to the local government agenda (Boddy and Fudge 1984; Lansley et al. 1989). These included the development of the local economy through research, extending and utilizing local skills, assisting those threatened with job losses and plant closures, encouraging socially useful and environmentally friendly production and supporting cooperatives and new enterprises, especially amongst groups disadvantaged in the labor market.

Extensive support was also offered to community and nonprofit organizations, community development was expanded, local cultural activities were promoted, and citizens' rights and benefit 'takeup' campaigns developed. Of particular importance was the acknowledgement of societal diversity and the attempt, through anti-discriminatory policies and practice, to ensure that local strategies responded to the needs of groups previously excluded.

The defeat of Labour in the 1987 general election, however, following so quickly after the Conservatives' abolition of a whole tier of Labour-held local government, ushered in a new sense of 'realism' for those still in office. They withdrew into a defensive mode of protecting services and improving provision without increasing expenditure or employing more staff. The urban left had failed to create their new political base and instead adjusted rapidly to the Conservative managerialist agenda and the marginalization of local government.

Continuity and change

Immediately following Thatcher's 1987 election, she declared her intention 'to do something about those inner cities' and a government review of policy preceded the announcement of Action for Cities (1988). This introduced a third, though barely distinguishable, phase in urban policy, in which coordination and management were central. The focus continued to be on encouraging the private sector to invest in jobs and redevelopment and to create a safer and more attractive environment. Following a reorganization of the Urban Programme (1987–88), funding was restricted to the 57 designated Priority Areas. These were required to submit for approval an Inner Area Programme (IAP) that identified problems and strategies to address them. Programs from a number of government departments were rolled together in an attempt to improve coordination. New Training and Enterprise Councils (1988) were given a coordinating role in local labor market planning, delivering training and support for small businesses. They were yet another example of a quango designated as an alternative lead agency in regeneration and in a number of areas there was intense rivalry with local authorities.

Competition and collaboration

By 1990 the government had begun to give more emphasis to intersectoral partnerships and the need to engage residents in the regeneration process. City Challenge (1991) ushered in a fourth and more decisive policy phase. This introduced a competitive bidding process, initially for 15 invited UP authorities, 11 of whom were ultimately successful, to become regeneration pace-setters. City Challenge went some way to re-establishing the role of local authorities, which were asked to take a lead role in producing a strategy and to involve a range of stakeholders, including local communities, in the process. The emphasis was to be on a coordinated and collaborative approach, focused on specific geographic areas and disadvantaged groups within them, and the prize was a share of a top-sliced amount from the UP.

Only two City Challenge rounds took place before the Single Regeneration Budget (SRB) was introduced (1994). This brought together the resources from 20 different programs, although critics pointed out that the sum available would be considerably less than the combined totals from the separate programs. The SRB process invited all urban and rural areas to submit competitive bids to new regional government offices. The logic behind this open bidding system where all areas were eligible, and away from targeting funding on highly deprived areas, was to tackle areas of emerging need before their problems became too severe. However the role played by government offices of the region (GOR) questioned whether a centralized funding strategy could be reconciled with an emphasis on local participation and local partnerships.

Bids in the early rounds of the SRB were then prioritized before central government made the final decision. Success in obtaining funding from central government was not necessarily related to the level of need but rather to the 'quality' of the bid. Proposals had to be comprehensive, targeted, accessible to close monitoring, capable of giving added value, backed by partnerships and supported by the community. They had to demonstrate the existence of inter-sectoral partnerships both in the planning and the implementation of the overall strategy and its individual elements. Local authorities, TECs and the nonprofit or community sectors were all identified as potential lead agencies for such partnerships. The in-coming 1997 Labour government retained SRB although it re-established the prioritization of need in determining funding.

The longevity of the Conservative government and its marketization of the public sector had pushed the Labour Party, following its 1992 election defeat, toward a new strategy of greater collaboration with both local agencies and central government. This involved accepting the new mixed economy of welfare, in which local authorities acted as enablers rather than providers of services. As partnerships and collaboration were talked up, it was acknowledged that the success of any social intervention depended upon the involvement, or at least acquiescence, of the communities involved (Mayo and Craig 1995; Miller and Ahmad 1997). Consequently, community development, with empowerment and collaboration as its organizing principles, has been increasingly identified as a process to facilitate the new institutional arrangements and improve local neighborhoods. Under the SRB local government became more receptive to central government's intentions. The Labour-dominated Association of Metropolitan Authorities (1993) saw community development as strengthening the relevance and role of local authorities. The increasingly professionalized nonprofit sector also benefited from a higher profile, but with fewer resources offered for more outputs, organizational mergers, and the introduction of a managerialist approach within individual agencies.

Labour and the New Deal for Communities

The return in 1997 of a Labour government signaled the beginning of the fifth and latest phase in regeneration policy when it launched its flagship initiative, the New Deal for Communities, as part of its overarching social objective to reduce social exclusion.

The New Deal brings together three strands of previous policy – local partnership for delivery of program, competition as a means for allocating funding and citizen engagement in both planning and implementation

(Social Exclusion Unit, 1998). But while it preserves elements of previous policy, in particular the bidding process and the formation of partnerships, NDC does make certain changes. It has responded to those criticisms of previous policy which suggested that notions of cost and efficiency on their own were too narrow to serve as useful criteria for resource allocation. Although competitive bidding is retained, the 17 'pathfinder' districts have been selected on the basis of need. NDC represents a return to targeted funding providing some £800 million over ten years to improve relatively small areas of no more than 4,000 households, areas that in guidance from central government 'must form part of a real and recognisable neighbourhood' (DETR 1999).

New Deal for Communities also responds to the importance of rebuilding social fabric. It emphasizes the need to invest in people, to identify and support a local leadership, and to ensure within a long-term commitment that mainstream policies 'really work for the poorest neighbourhoods'. There is also a greater emphasis on participation by local residents and their organizations with firm directives on resident representation on partnership boards and prospect that well-established community groups should be in a position to take the lead in several of the pathfinder areas. The approach is described as 'comprehensive, long-term and founded on what works', an effective response to the increasing social division of the previous 20 years, designed to 'bridge the gap between the poorest neighbourhoods and the rest of Britain'. The long-term aim is defined as 'bringing neighbourhoods up to the national average' through lower long-term unemployment and worklessness, less crime, better health and higher educational qualifications.

The strategy is another example of the Labour government's 'joined-up thinking', a comprehensive approach to comprehensive problems that links together a number of policies and encourages seamless provision across departments, 'providing a backdrop that has been missing in past regeneration efforts' (p. 54). Thus the New Deal for Communities complements a range of neighborhood-directed policies such as the Sure Start initiative which provides support services for families with children under three, the new deal for the unemployed, the disabled, and single parents and the provisions on community safety under the Crime and Disorder Act 1998. These measures in turn are bound up in the changes to local government representation and management and other area-based programs such as the Action Zones on health. Moreover, NDC will be implemented in parallel with the existing Single Regeneration Budget, which is geared to areas greater in size than those envisaged under NDC.

Co-ordination is the third element within the strategy. Advisory teams were established, with membership drawn from external experts and ten central government departments, to produce a 'national strategy' to drive subsequent policies. They are focused on five themes: getting the people to work, getting the place to work, building a future for young people, improving access to local public and private services, and making the government work better. All are expected to consider issues related to race and ethnic minority issues, involve local people, and identify the need for local capacity building. Co-ordination is also an important feature of the Social Exclusion Unit. Located within the Cabinet Office, its remit is to break the 'vicious circle' caused by the 'combination of linked problems . . . ' and to encourage inter-agency, and inter-professional collaboration, identifying and disseminating 'best practice' and 'shifting the policy and practice of mainline departments' (SEU 1998).

A 'Third Way' for urban regeneration?

Central to Labour's vision is the need to alter the relationship between the state and the citizen. This is to be achieved by creating new opportunities for engagement in local political life, ensuring that the citizen is sufficiently informed to make effective interventions, and emphasizing the social obligations and responsibilities attached to the concept of citizenship. Meeting responsibilities is understood, in particular, as being productively engaged in the labor market. This is based partly on the assumption that human dignity, self-worth and a sense of societal belonging will all flow from waged labor. Only through labor market activity can citizens make a productive contribution to society, ensure their own financial self-sufficiency and reduce their dependency on the state. Yet Labour has shown little vision in relation to the nature, distribution, organization or rewards of such paid work. Indeed, it has little to say about what it considers to be current good practice, other than the introduction of an inadequate minimum wage. Most importantly, the strategy is silent on the relationships between nation states and international capital.

The Labour government is more confident on the need for strong and moral 'communities', and the requirement to re-moralize them where a shared morality is seen as absent. 'Community', which is meant to embrace family as well as voluntary effort, is to be the basis of both a moral and an economic revival, where needs are met and behavior is policed. Yet if the classical concept of the welfare state is no longer applicable, neither is Labour's view of 'community'.

If the image of a changed and dynamically changing Britain is rightly utilized to argue for new forms of welfare, the same dynamism and the forging of new relationships are ignored in respect of community (Hoggett 1997). Rather, Labour is influenced by communitarian visions of traditional, stable, homogeneous, place-based communities that are individually identifiable, and therefore able to police their members, but somehow also combine to generate one national community of common values (Etzioni 1995; Tam 1998). To achieve this element the policy introduces new moral gatekeepers, such as super-caretakers and powerful neighborhood managers, in addition to regulations concerned with anti-social behavior.

Yet the central aspect of this process is 'capacity building' and within it the role of community development agencies and those within the nonprofit sector. Developing their organizational capacity is seen as the way to ensure that communities are both receptive to the new strategy and able to play their part in it, precisely what community developers have been arguing for some time. For a more cohesive society, people should have more opportunities to influence and shape the decision-making process, their collective efforts should be valued and nourished, and their individual potential encouraged and maximized. The involvement in the planning and implementation of those directly concerned with any specific policy will surely produce better outcomes.

This opportunity, however, also poses a number of challenges for those responsible for implementing the process. Not least is that of internalizing the apparent move from being part of a somewhat marginal, even radical activity, that was often tolerated without being fully understood, to a position in which knowledge and skills are seen to be central to the regeneration process (Miller and Ahmad 1997). It also probes the dualism in government thinking: on the one hand encouraging a devolved, dispersed politics with plural centers of power, on the other wanting to control the outcomes of this new politics.

Equally, the limitations and shortcomings of earlier community initiatives are now better appreciated and have generated a call for revisions to theory and practice. Some have argued that during a period of 'profound change' there is a need, as in other areas, for 'the intellectual reconstruction' of such developmental activity (Waddington 1994). Yet Labour approaches this capacity building project with clear objectives about the kind of climate it wishes to create and some quite specific expectations about behavior and attitudes. This is another top-down initiative but it does present some opportunities, one of which is to take seriously the expressed desire to extend democracy and develop citizenship. More than any previous initiative it does take seriously the necessity for local civic engagement in both strategic planning and implementation. The first evaluations of the NDC do indicate that local residents organizations perceive a greater weight given to resident influence whilst remaining skeptical that this will survive within the lifetime of programs. Tight deadlines and the need to form partnerships quickly together with a strong central government presence in the vetting of bids through government offices of the regions build in top-down, professional bias in the implementation stage.

Capacity building should ensure that public spaces are created to enable democratic debate about all those questions concerning how needs are met, the nature of the good society and the direction to be taken to create it. Such debate is a process for generating demands and visions from the grassroots, and building new forms of local democratic organizations that contribute to mass engagement in the political process. The opportunity should be used to re-establish the value of the 'social' and its new meanings. If 'society' is to have any meaning beyond a collection of atomized individuals, this will surely highlight our interdependencies, and the importance of reciprocal relations, within and beyond the nation-state.

In so doing, we begin to question current societal relationships and the distribution of resources. To pursue this, those engaged in community development must avoid the temptation to work only within poor neighborhoods. Dialogue, networks, alliances and organizational capacity should be established that cut across neighborhood boundaries, and beyond social groups with their artificial hierarchies of disadvantage, to encompass not only other communities within the same city or nation-state, but communities in other parts of world.

Conclusion

The overriding consensus is that earlier regeneration strategies have had limited success other than at the symbolic level. Apart from during the first policy phase, the relationship between urban regeneration and the development of human or social capital, through a focus on community and community development has been tenuous. Labour's strategy for urban regeneration unites these two strands once again. Drawing on the lessons learnt from the past it also emphasizes the need for better management, coordination and intersectoral collaboration within and between programs, and the need to change the direction of mainstream departments and their budget allocations.

Despite its call for a more socially cohesive society, however, and its insistence on citizens fulfilling their responsibilities and meeting their obligations, it is reluctant to signal what such a good society might look like. Nevertheless, the emphasis given to capacity building, empowerment and citizen participation provide the opportunity to facilitate genuine local democratic debate, organizational capacity, and demands that will take us some way to answering such questions and working out how we might proceed.

References

Association of Metropolitan Authorities (1989) *Community Development – the Local Authority Role* (London: AMA)

Association of Metropolitan Authorities (1993) *Local Authorities and Community Development: Strategic Opportunities for the 1990s* (London: AMA)

Audit Commission for Local Authorities in England and Wales (1989) *Urban Regeneration and Economic Development: The Local Government Dimension* (London: HMSO)

Audit Commission for Local Authorities and the NHS in England and Wales (1991) *The Urban Regeneration Experience Observation from Local Value for Money Audit* (London: HMSO)

Body, M. and Fudge, C. (eds.) (1984) *Local Socialism* (Basingstoke: Macmillan)

Bolger, S., Corrigan, P., Docking, J. and Frost, N. (1981) *Towards Socialist Welfare Work* (Basingstoke: Macmillan)

Bradford, M. and Robson, B. (1995) An Evaluation of Urban Policy, in R. Hambleton and H. Thomas (eds.), *Urban Policy Evaluation, Challenge and Change* (London: Paul Chapman)

Burns, D., Hambleton, R. and Hoggett, P. (1994) *The Politics of Decentralisation: Revitalising Local Democracy* (Basingstoke: Macmillan)

Burton, P. (1997) 'Urban Policy and the Myth of Progress', *Policy and Politics* 25: 4 (October)

Campbell, B. (1993) *Goliath, Britain's Dangerous Places* (London: Methuen)

Cockburn, C. (1977) *The Local State: Management of Cities and People* (London: Pluto)

Commission on Social Justice (1994) *Social Justice: Strategies for National Renewal* (London: Vintage Books)

Community Development Projects (1977a) *Gilding the Ghetto* (London: Home Office)

Community Development Projects Inter-Project Editorial Team (1977b) *The Costs of Industrial Change* (London: Mary Tavistock House)

Craig, G. and Mayo, M. (1995) *Community Empowerment* (London: Zed Books)

Department of the Environment (1977) *Policy for the Inner Cities*, Cmnd 6845 (London: HMSO)

Department of the Environment (1980) *Review of the Traditional Urban Programme* (London: DoE)

Department of Environment, Transport and Regions (1998) *Index of Local Deprivation* (London: DETR)

Department of Environment, Transport and Regions (1999) *New Deals for Communities*: Phase 1 Proposals, Guidance for Applicants (London: DETR)

Donnison, D. (1998) *Agenda for a Just Society* (London: River Dram Press)

Edwards, J. and Batley, R. (1978) *The Politics of Positive Discrimination: An Evaluation of the Urban Programme 1967–77* (London: Tavistock)

Etizoni, A. (1995) *The Spirit of Community* (London: Fontana)

Furbey, R. (1999) Urban Regeneration: Reflections on a Metaphor, *Critical Social Policy* 19: 4, 419–45

Gamble, A. (1986) *Britain in Decline* (Second edition, Basingstoke: Macmillan)

Gregory, S. and Smith, J. (1986) Decentralisation Now, *Community Development Journal* 21: 2

Hall, S. (1980) Reformism and the Legislation of Consent, in National Deviancy Conference (eds.), *Permissiveness and Control* (Basingstoke: Macmillan)

Hoggett, P. (1997) Contested Communities, in P. Hoggett (ed.), *Contested Communities* (Bristol: Policy Press)

Hoggett, P. and McGill, I. (1988) Labourism: Means and Ends, *Critical Social Policy*, Issue 23 (Autumn)

Joseph Rowntree Foundation (1995) *Enquiry into Income and Wealth*, Vols. 1 and 2 (York: JRF)

Lansley, S., Goss, S. and Wolmar, C. (1989) *Councils in Conflict: The Rise and Fall of the Municipal Left* (Basingstoke: Macmillan)

Lawless, P. (1979) *Urban Deprivation and Government Initiative* (London: Faber and Faber)

Local Government Association (1997) *New Commitment to Regeneration* (London: LGA)

London to Edinburgh Weekend Return Group (1979) *In and against the State* (London: Pluto)

Loney, M. (1983) *Community against Government: The British Community Development Project 1968–78* (London: Heinemann Educational Books)

Mayo, M. (ed.) (1977) *Women in the Community* (London: Routledge and Kegan Paul)

Mayo, M. and Craig, G. (1995) Community Participation and Empowerment: The Human Face of Structural Adjustment or Tools for Democratic Transformation?, in G. Craig and M. Mayo, *Community Empowerment* (London: Zed Books)

Miller, C. (1981) Area Management: Newcastle's Priority Areas Programme, in L. Smith and D. Jones, *Deprivation, Participation and Community Action* (London: Routledge)

Miller, C. (1996) *Public Service Trade Unionism and Radical Politics* (Aldershot: Dartmouth)

Miller, C. and Ahmad, Y. (1997) Community Development at the Crossroads: A Way Forward, *Policy and Politics* 25: 3

National Audit Office (1993) *The Achievements of the Second and Third Generation Urban Development Corporations*, HC 898 (London: HMSO)

Robson, B. et al. (1994) *Assessing the Impact of Urban Policy* (London: HMSO)

Smith, L. (1981) 'Public Participation in Islington', in L. Smith and D. Jones, *Deprivation, Participation and Community Action* (London: Routledge)

Social Exclusion Unit (1998) *Bringing Britain together: A National Strategy for Neighbourhood Renewal*, Social Exclusion Unit Cm 4045 (London: HMSO)

Tam, H. (1998) *Communitarianism: A New Agenda for Politics and Citizenship* (Basingstoke: Macmillan)

Taylor, M. and Presley, F. (1987) *Community Work in the UK 1982–86* (London: Library Association Publishing and Calouste Gulbenkian Foundation)

Waddington, P. (1994) The Value Base of Community Work, in S. Jacobs and K. Popple, *Community Work in the 1990s* (Nottingham: Spokesman)

9
Urban Regeneration and Citizenship in 'Sensitive Areas' in France

Julien Damon

The French public authorities have responded to an increase in poverty and violence, and a deterioration in the fabric of urban life (housing and social relations) – all of which were particularly acute in certain areas – by implementing an ambitious public initiative of urban renewal: *'politique de la ville'*.

This policy was steadily drawn up and implemented in response to social problems concentrated particularly in a number of localities. Its target – areas often described as 'sensitive' – is vague, however. The policy has developed as a result of identifying many real and obvious problems, but also as a reaction to sensationalist media images: urban guerrillas, 'no-go' zones, ghettos, the drugs economy.

'Politique de la ville' is based on a complicated system of protagonists, procedures and principles. Because it was responsible for development in 'sensitive' areas, it received (in 1998) over 20 billion francs to finance intervention in various fields: employment, inclusion, health, culture, housing, town planning, sport, education, and so on. It addresses issues of both town planning and community development, and affects around 10 per cent of the French population, or nearly six million people.

After about 20 years in existence, the policy has developed a sophisticated legislative and statutory apparatus. It is characterized by an abundance of procedures and enacting measures with obscure acronyms, which render it as complicated to understand as to implement. Moreover, its performance is difficult to evaluate in view of the many ambitious objectives with which it was originally charged: regeneration of poor environments, reduction of segregation, mobilization of residents, economic development, integration of immigrants, prevention of delinquency.

The issues raised by the policy make possible an analysis of the development of the workings and principles of public policies in France, particularly in relation to the concept of 'exclusion'. Reducing exclusion is a recent category of public initiative, against which questions of poverty, employment, inequality, integration and citizenship are measured. The metaphor of a dual society currently much discussed (on the one side the excluded, on the other the included) provides an important principle of action (Paugam 1996). From a national perspective, the struggle against 'urban exclusion' consists of identifying geographical areas and social groups where specific processes would be necessary, legitimate and useful. This process of identification can divide people into categories, and result in initiatives targeted at specific 'communities' (geographic, social or ethnic), a notion hitherto alien to the French legal tradition. The republican state in effect used to recognize only one community, the nation, attached to a machine of wealth redistribution, the Welfare State.

Government measures in France today emphasize the practice of targeting on social and geographical grounds (particular communities and areas). The principles of equality, unity and universality, which form the basis of the French republican state, are challenged by these public interventions, and the result could be social and geographical fragmentation. Because of this potential, the *'politique de la ville'* has been the subject of numerous investigations and controversies around the transformation of the 'French-style' Welfare State and the 'French model of integration'.

At the heart of the analysis of these new policy areas are questions to do with communities and minority groups, issues which are difficult enough to define, let alone accept. Some authors defend the capacity for integration inherent in the republican model, in its role as a 'community of citizens' (Schnapper 1994). Others, by highlighting the importance of the community question, stress the need to reconsider the whole system. (Wieviorka 1996).

This chapter outlines and explains some of the main points of a fairly recent public policy area which demonstrates the way in which French government policy and intervention strategies have had to evolve in parallel with social problems. I will trace the process of incorporating these policies into national and local government practice, and then discuss the complications which can arise from targeting geographical localities. Finally, I will shed some light on the debates raised by this policy.

The history of *'politique de la ville'*

The origins of modern French urban policy are generally associated with the innovative steps taken since the 1970s to renovate the huge post-war social housing schemes built according to particular architectural models. These housing schemes, also known as *'cités'*, were constructed at the end of the war as a solution to the housing crisis. They were to facilitate the relocation of poorly housed people, the absorption of slums, and the welcoming and social advancement of immigrants (Ballain and Jacquier 1987; Barou 1992).

Since the beginnings of the 'crisis' in the 1970s, many other phenomena have arisen in the *'cités'*: 1) a serious deterioration in the state of the buildings; 2) a halt in the social advancement of estate residents; 3) an increasing concentration of social difficulties linked to the rise in unemployment; 4) a concentration of ethnic groups linked to the restricted residential options of immigrants; 5) sporadic but highly noticeable outbreaks of urban violence. Put briefly, the urban areas envisaged as providing solutions have in effect become the problems (Roché 1998). We can see here an example of what Aron (1969) called the 'the disillusionment of progress'.

Modern French urban policy is usually divided into three main stages. The first and most important priority is seen as urban re-standardization through housing upgrades. The next priority is seen as the encouragement of community development, and the last as economic regeneration. In practice, these three dimensions have always been present, and it is not so easy to work out which order they occur in. It seems more convincing to identify a process of development with some periods of slow progress and others of accelerated change, the whole marked by regular outbreaks of urban violence.

In 1973, a circular from the Ministry for Development put an end to the construction of large social housing schemes, representing a U-turn in town planning. In 1977, parallel to an overall reform of housing policy, an interministerial committee for Housing and Community Life (HVS – *Habitat et Vie Sociale*) was set up to coordinate a series of agreements concluded between local councils, social housing organizations and the state, in order to revitalize around 50 large edge-of-town housing schemes.

With the arrival of the left in power in 1981, the approach initiated by the HVS experiments was reinforced. The government ordered a series of reports establishing the operational and conceptual basis of Local Area Social Development (DSQ – *Développement Social des Quartiers*).

These reports led to systems of intervention, including the appearance of the National Commission for Local Area Social Development (CNDSQ) in 1981, after incidents which took place in the Minguettes area of Venissieux (in the Lyons region). The Commission was responsible for drawing up a contractual arrangement with the local authorities. DSQ programs were then launched. Henceforth they were to be integrated into the state/region planning agreements which constituted the framework for the integration of state and regional policies.

Three important dimensions to urban policy were thus in place in French administration at the beginning of the 1980s: job placements in response to unemployment, preventive measures to deal with breakdowns in law and order, and urban upgrading. At the same time, decentralization measures shook the traditional boundaries of responsibility between the state and regional and local government. Towns and cities, granted greater powers, became more autonomous public players, while the state began to preoccupy itself with the special problems of particular localities.

The basic structure for urban renewal had policy-guiding taskforces at central governmental level with policy-implementing contractual partners at local level. This system operated under the different left and right wing governments and by the end of the 1980s, it grew beyond its experimental status and became formally institutionalized. In October 1988, the National Council for Towns (CNV – *Conseil National des Villes*), a consultative body composed of elected representatives and experts, was created, along with the Interministerial Urban Policy (CIV – *Comité Interministériel des Villes*), whose role was to define and coordinate government action regarding urban regeneration policy, and the Interministerial Town Policy Delegation (DIV – *Délégation Interministérielle a la Ville*) which was responsible for implementing the adopted strategies. These institutions took over from those previously in place and since then have undergone only marginal reform.

Between 1989 and 1994, 400 'localities with heavy economic, social, cultural, and urban disadvantages' were classed as 'priority cases'. An action formula was set up: the urban renewal contract, which established a partnership between urban authorities and the state.

At the beginning of the 1990s, public opinion was aroused by highly publicized urban violence, in the suburbs of Lyons (Vaulx-en-Vélin) , in the northern areas of Marseilles, the Val Fourré, Sartrouville and at Mantes-la-Jolie in the Paris region. In December 1990 a ministry for urban affairs was created. Within two years, three important laws were passed. The law of 30 May 1990, known as the Besson Law, put in place the right to housing. The law of the 13 May 1991 instituted a contribution paid by the wealthier local authority areas to assist the poorer ones. The urban affairs planning law (LOV – *loi d'orientation pour la ville*) was passed in July 1991 and constituted the legal basis for urban renewal policy which must 'facilitate the integration of each locality into the urban area to which it belongs and ensure the coexistence of diverse social categories in every conurbation'.

A number of players, of varying status, became involved in urban policy. They had continually to interact and negotiate with elected representatives, residents, civil servants, businesses and associations. The aim was to bring together the financial capacities and ambitions of the state with those of local government, in the difficult context of the division of responsibilities and interests resulting from decentralization (Béhar and Estèbe 1996). Urban policy existed in a state of permanent tension between the 'statization' of local initiatives (the state taking in hand municipal policies) and the 'municipalization' of national strategies (local government taking over the financing and policy-making powers passed on by the state). The policy created an arena for conflict between local mayors and the state, but was equally a launching pad for real achievements.

Urban renewal policy was once again strengthened in 1993 with the change in government. A 'Marshall Plan' for edge-of-town estates was demanded by both the opposition and the government in the National Assembly (Parliament). The government decided upon an Urban Relaunch Plan, funded with a grant of 5.2 billion francs. The Great Urban Project (GPU – *Grand Projet Urbain*) initiative, which involved areas which had deteriorated particularly badly, was set up. The GPUs could group together several districts (*'communes'*) and introduce intensive programs spread over a five-year period. In 1994, 1300 local areas (*'quartiers'*) were identified in the urban renewal contracts, of which there were now 214. About 15 of the local areas were covered by GPU initiatives.

Five objectives were adopted for the reduction of the gap between the situation of those living in the urban-renewal localities and those living in the wider conurbations of which the localities were part: employment levels, prevention of delinquency, education, housing and public services. In the same year, 1994, a law provided professional advantages for civil servants working in 'sensitive' areas, giving priority transfers and enhanced service seniority.

Firm decisions have now been taken as to which are to be the urban renewal priority areas. The law for the reorganization and development of local government passed on 4 February 1995 (*Loi 'Pasqua'*), instituted Sensitive Urban Zones (ZUS – *Zones Urbaines Sensibles*), 'characterized by the presence of large housing schemes or of areas of substandard accommodation and by an acute imbalance between the living environment and the level of employment'. These ZUSs included Urban Revitalization Zones (ZRU – *Zones de Redynamisation Urbaine*) where the ZUSs faced particular difficulties, in terms of their regional/urban position and their economic and social characteristics. In addition provision was made for the creation of Urban Free Zones (ZFU – *Zones Franches Urbaines*) in localities at a particular disadvantage in terms of the criteria used to identify ZRUs. There are currently a total of 44 Urban Free Zones in existence in metropolitan France and in the overseas territories.

In 1996 the government introduced an 'Urban Relaunch Pact', based explicitly on the principle of 'positive geographical discrimination'. This Pact had three aims; 1) restoring business activity and employment; 2) reinforcing public stability; and 3) improving daily living conditions in the specified localities.

Following the dissolution of the National Assembly in 1997 and the election of a new left-wing government, the ministerial post devoted to urban affairs was temporarily withdrawn. The removal of this post gave rise to concerns about the future of a policy whose practices, impacts and principles were coming under increasing criticism. Even if the new left-wing government does not go back radically on what has previously been put in place, the new emphasis is now strongly on security and law and order. Throughout France, Local Security Contracts (CLS – *Contrats Locaux de Sécurité*) were set up to guarantee comprehensive policies in the prevention and control of violence. These measures were introduced among the 'law and order co-workers' (*'coproducteurs de sécurité'*) – government-appointed regional chief executives (*'préfets'*) , police officers, the business community, mayors, public prosecutors, and so on.

In response to a particularly violent winter in the 'sensitive' areas, the new government ordered a report on urban regeneration and development. Its conclusions called for actions which went beyond the logic of all the existing policies, including those in relation to zones and the new 'Urban Relaunch Pact'. A new approach to priority areas was proposed, based on the argument that there was a need to construct new levels of intervention within urban policy. Urban policy would no longer be constructed at local council level, but at the level of regional centers which would gather several towns together to form coherent urban groupings (Sueur 1998).

The government took up several elements of this report. A new minister of urban affairs (*'ministre de la ville'*) was appointed. Four action plans were decided: 1) 'guaranteeing the republican pact throughout France';

2) 'reinforcing social cohesion in towns'; 3) mobilizing all partners, primarily social financial backers and local authorities; and 4) promoting resident involvement. Financial resources are to be increased, rising to more than 30 billion francs for 1999. The total for 2003 should reach 35 billion francs.

After giving the impression of being about to abandon its urban renewal policies, the government has finished up by injecting them with increased resources. Without becoming too embroiled in complicated normative operations, the new general policy approach is an 'urban renewal' project that draws together all the players in the urban sphere.

From this historical overview we can see the explosion of new public sector practices, and the establishment of a political consensus on the need for intervention on the one hand, and a tangle of complicated procedures which localities targeted by urban renewal policy find very difficult to grasp on the other.

Localities targeted by urban renewal policy

The target of French urban renewal policy is a landscape made up of areas defined by exceptional socio-economic imbalances. It focuses on areas particularly affected by unemployment, insecurity, academic failure. Furthermore, these areas are also affected by the simultaneous rise of certain kinds of ethnic identity reassertion and protest votes (the National Front) which Taguieff (1996) calls 'islamisation/lepénisation', in reference to the growing number of Muslim organizations and the increasing membership of the National Front, led by Jean-Marie Le Pen. Should one call these areas 'sensitive', 'difficult', 'unstable, 'deteriorating', 'flash points', 'deprived', 'problematic' or even 'working-class' at the risk of stigmatizing them or denying them their unique individual identities? The semantic debates – which have their value – can go on forever, given the difficulties of trying to describe the new urban realities. One thing is true in any event: the comparison often made with American ghettos deserves to be revised.

Newspaper headlines have for a long time been littered with warnings about French 'ghettos'. Some well-argued publications have been helpful in showing how deprived areas in France are nothing like American ghettos (Wacquant 1992; Vieillard-Baron 1994). No French city has ever experienced the concentration of poverty, social ostracism and racial segregation which are unique to American cities. There is no French equivalent to the American ghetto. These reminders of the basic reality notwithstanding, Wilson (1996), from the other side of the Atlantic, raises some worrying concerns.

European cities are beginning to witness the problems of urban and social breakdown – including the rise in unemployment, the concentration of poverty and ethnic conflicts – that affect American ones. In extreme cases, tendencies to 'ghettoization' might be identified in France, but such comparisons have to be treated very carefully, as indeed do all concepts out of context (Bourdieu and Wacquant 1998). French 'deprived areas' have been so designated and labeled mainly according to their concentrations of immigrants, a phenomenon which has resulted in a certain 'ethnicizing' of urban and social questions. However, these areas are actually characterized by a great social and ethnic diversity among the people living there. Multi-ethnic, without any real community structures, they bear little resemblance to the American or British mono-ethnic ghetto (Simon 1997).

The 'deprived areas' are above all a target for government action. Judged as priority cases for intervention, they are defined according to statistical indicators which identify how far they fall below national averages. They are particularly affected by three processes: 1) a deterioration in the quality of the living environment; 2) a disproportionate rise in the levels of unemployment; and 3) a high density of immigrant populations (Rey 1996).

These areas do not, however, constitute a homogeneous mass. They differ from one to the other in size and population and by the characteristics of the wider urban areas of which they are part. There is no typical profile, rather a constellation of individual examples (Campion and Marpsat 1996).

What is more, the definition of these target localities takes place on the basis not just of objective criteria but of political criteria and local strategies. Urban renewal targeting depends as much upon agreements between central and local government about which areas to designate for specific interventions as upon socio-demographic facts. Geographical prioritization for urban renewal schemes is decided in the light of legal developments and political compromises.

The targets of urban renewal policies are in fact extremely diverse in character. Generally tenants make up the large majority in these areas, but there are also individual home-owners and co-owners. On average, the proportion of under-20 year olds is particularly high in these areas: between 20 and 50 per cent of the population. Most target areas are very cut off, but some are particularly well served by public transport. Overall, they are heavily affected by unemployment: in 1998 nearly

20 per cent of the active population in these areas were unemployed, compared with a little less than 12 per cent for the whole of France. But even in this respect situations vary considerably.

Table 9.1 brings together a series of indicators relating to the current contours of the urban renewal landscape in France.

In metropolitan France, one person in 12 – some 4.7 million people – lives in one of the 716 ZUSs (nine of which are in Paris). These areas, situated principally in the big conurbations, and more often in city centers than on city edges (except in the Paris region), contain high proportions of unemployed people, young people, immigrants and people without educational qualifications. These characteristics, nevertheless, vary considerably from region to region. Moreover, four regions between them contain more than half the country's priority area residents: Île-de-France (30 per cent of the inhabitants of metropolitan ZUSs), the Nord-Pas-de-Calais (9.2 per cent), Provence-Alpes-Côte-d'Azur (8.6 per cent) and the Rhône-Alpes region (8.5 per cent).

The areas most in the public eye, often because of the violence that has taken place there, are for the most part to be found on the periphery of large cities (Paris, Lyons, Marseilles, Lille). However, most of

Table 9.1   Individual Characteristics of Urban Renewal Zones (1998)

	ZUS	ZRU	ZFU	Conurbations with a ZUS
Proportion of households with 1 person	26.8	24.6	23.2	30.6
Proportion of households with 6 or more persons	7.5	8.8	10.5	3.1
Proportion of under-25 year olds	43.0	44.8	46.8	34.7
Proportion of foreign heads of household	15.8	15.8	18.7	8.1
Proportion heads of household in employment	50.6	52.2	54.9	33.2
Proportion of residents living in social housing	62	—	—	22
Proportion of households for which social security benefits (except pension) are more than a quarter of the income	26	29	—	14 (whole of country)
Proportion of unqualified 15–24 year-olds who have left school	36.7	38.3	39.7	27.3
Unemployment rate	18.9	20.6	21.3	11.6

Source: INSEE; Goldberger, Choffel and Le Toqueux, 1998

the target zones are to be found in the center of conurbations. Urban renewal target areas include some edge-of-town housing schemes, but equally some run down city center co-ownerships. This poses a problem for comparative approaches as, contrary to the problems of British and American 'inner cities', French deprived areas ('*quartiers*') are extremely varied from the point of view of their locations and their populations.

In any event, the public image of these areas is poor. Their inhabitants are on average less qualified, less skilled, more often from ethnic minorities, and more often unemployed, than those elsewhere. While the image of the 'youth from the edge-of-town estates' (generally an adolescent from an immigrant background) captures all the media attention and government intervention (beneficial or repressive), the reality is very diverse. The residents of 'sensitive' areas do not constitute a homogenous sub-population with easily discernible differences from the general population. Contrary to what may be reported in the more sensationalist or grimmer 'social realism' media, they do not live in a state of disorganized lawlessness, nor are they cut off from the rest of the world, or completely downtrodden (Collectif 1997).

In short, the 'sensitive' areas are not collections of problems, but lively and dynamic places. Even if insecurity and tension are sometimes higher here than elsewhere, that does not prevent the residents from day-to-day community building. The lives they live and the activities are very different from the stock clichés. Through the often unique character of their activities, their solidarity networks, the relationships they have with the authorities, and their shaping of collective life, they contribute to the continual reformulation of citizenship (Mozère, Peraldi and Rey 1999). These local displays of community life can lead to confrontations between different urban areas, but can also lead to new ways of agreeing and constructing social norms (Hatzfeld, Hatzfeld and Ringart 1998).

Studies of the way of life of people in these areas and their inventiveness (Roulleau-Berger 1993) confirm that residents do not live in closed communities (social, cultural or ethnic). They know how to use the resources and opportunities offered by their immediate locality, by the city as a whole, and by government intervention. Accounts of the lives of young people in unstable situations display their talents, hopes for the future, and a creativity capable of injecting life into these areas and establishing prosperous niche business activities.

Nonetheless, we should not swing from a negative sordid 'realism' to observing nothing but good in these areas. The creativity of people here, often referred to as 'Biz' (business), can be expressed in highly illicit activities (drugs, receiving stolen goods, and so on). It is inadvisable to gloss naively over all these activities, classing them under the general label of 'new models of citizenship'. New forms of exchange, new types of protest movement, new relationships with elected representatives and public services are emerging. But not everything that is new should be welcomed.

It is well known, for example, that in several of these areas, though they are not as isolated from the rest of the republic as is sometimes maintained, the physical safety of those who live or work there, and the civil servants whose job it is to deal with them, cannot always be guaranteed (Bui-Trong 1993). The locality, particularly for younger residents, represents a space for identification, reference and belonging, which is often violently defended (Lepoutre 1997). The police, teachers and even firemen can all bear witness to this. It is useful to highlight and value positive tendencies. However, the general picture is still worrying.

An ambivalent evaluation and some questions about targeting

The promoters, the protagonists and the observers of urban renewal all recognize that its balance sheet in terms of social development is limited (Geindre 1993; Wuhl 1996). However, its mobilization of finance and energy has not been in vain. It has clearly made possible the improvement of daily life in particular areas, while some young people have been able to seize the opportunities provided and 'find a way out'. Nevertheless, it has not succeeded in resolving or reducing all the problems which affect these areas.

In the course of time, urban renewal policy has gained a double purpose: to guarantee the regeneration of target areas and to propose new government measures which might be extended nation-wide.

In essence, urban renewal policy mobilizes very diverse resources and players who intervene together within clearly delineated areas. Policy is decided between ministers and developed by different ministries and units answerable to them. Contractually policy operates on the basis of collaboration between central and local government agencies. Based on partnership, it brings together central government agencies, locally elected representatives, social financial interests, institutions such as the National Deposit Bank ('*Caisse des Depôts et Consignations*' – the principal lender for social housing), certain service companies (private or public), European Structural Funds and local voluntary organizations.

Some central concepts forming urban renewal policy have emerged. Some such as 'social mixing' appear no more than pious hopes, since the national socio-demographic balance cannot be ordered by decree. Others offer genuine practical ideas. The notion of the 'neighborhood' (*'proximité'*), for example, has legitimized the identification of certain local areas (*'quartiers'*) as objects for government action. Through urban renewal, the state, abandoning its heavily criticized technocratic approach, wishes to become involved 'as closely as possible' in the realities of the local area (Béhar 1999). Central government no longer exists purely to lay down policy norms and control their implementation: now it also has responsibilities for regulating the regions. Urban renewal policies have not caused any major shake-ups as such, but they have permitted innovations and reflections on the future of both urban areas and the people who live in them.

By comparison with other European countries, France has gone much further in the face of urban problems than the simple regeneration of deprived areas (Jacquier 1991). Urban renewal is not merely a device for the social development of 'sensitive' areas, but a real project to remodel the institutions and ways of thinking upon which government activity is based (Béhar, Estèbe and Epstein 1998).

The focus of government policy on deprived areas has been transformed from rescuing regions in crisis, to promoting the potential of these regions. The state is no longer presenting itself solely as the guarantor of national cohesion, but also as a key player in local development, hitherto mainly the field of local players (municipal councils, voluntary organizations, businesses). In developing urban policy, the state has become the 'animating agency' (Donzelot and Estèbe 1994). Is this really a deep-seated change in urban policy, or an admission of government weakness? The answer to this question has not been fully established.

In any case, the traditional limits of French administrative activity have certainly been exceeded. The vertical approach (central government decides and puts into action) and the sectorial approach (government policies are divided up into specialist interventions) have proved obsolete. They have been abandoned in favor of transversal, decompartmentalized approaches, tackling problems in a global manner and gathering together many different protagonists.

While the role of the state is being questioned from below (decentralization) and from above (the European Union), central government is searching for an 'appropriate scale' of intervention. This search is being undertaken both at the new level of supra-communes (*'agglomérations'*) and at the level of small neighborhoods or localities within the commune (*'quartiers'*), both of which are recognized in urban renewal policy. The new modes of intervention that are being prioritized by the state (local agreements, the identification of geographical target areas and the promotion of resident participation) are a constant challenge to normal central government intervention strategies.

Through the call for, and support given to, 'resident participation', urban renewal policy has opened the way for new expressions of citizenship, without this being translated into any new legal definition of citizenship. Recognizing local differences, and even local identities, both strengthens the democratization process and presents problems for the unitary republican State. Urban renewal policy may not have shaken the foundation of French administrative procedures and legal system, but it has certainly marked a commitment toward the recognition of differences which were not previously taken into account.

It remains to be seen how far the logic of 'positive discrimination' will be taken. This new principle of French government policy is often erroneously interpreted as an importation of American affirmative action policies. Such a comparison is possible, but it must take into account both the similarities and the differences between the patterns of social development (Donzelot and Jaillet 1997).

Positive discrimination in favor of particular localities, such as that expressed in the structure of urban renewal policy in France, consists of making a detour through inequality in order to re-establish equality, by targeting specific areas and their populations (Béhar, Estèbe and Epstein 1998). This concept, only very recently vaguely confirmed in law (Melin-Soucramanien 1997; Le Pourhiet 1998; Buisson 1998), authorizes government to grant more to localities which have less in order to bring them up to the norm.

This principle is put into practice through allocating certain resources (loans, civil servants) to these localities, with a view to strengthening the government presence there, along with better legal access, education and policing. The most noteworthy positive discrimination measures were taken in the mid-1990s, with highly specific targeting (ZUSs, ZRUs, ZFUs), clearly distinguishing particular neighborhoods and localities, and therefore populations, who were to benefit from significantly greater inputs than other communities.

Over the years positive discrimination has operated as a magic slogan, opening the doors of the authorities concerned with arresting the deterioration of local areas. However, while it was constructed using a model aimed at reducing the supposed duality of urban society (on the one side deprived or 'sensitive' areas, on the other the rest of society), it has perhaps contributed more to confirming the dynamics of duality than to checking it. The positive discrimination approach, consisting of trying to fill the gap between the deprived areas and the norm, is now considered very high risk (Delevoye 1997).

Many discussions are taking place: whether the most appropriate and effective form of government intervention is to put in place specific measures or to undertake general programs; whether government services should be developed for all or targeted on the few; whether it is advisable to bring everyone up to a basic level through specific intervention on the fringes, or to rely upon the existing dynamic among people on these fringes to improve their own living standards, tapping in to national government programs (Béhar 1995).

The arguments against positive discrimination are beginning to surface. Before positive discrimination can occur, 'negative characterization' has to happen, which itself has a negative, stigmatizing effect (Castel 1995). What is more, in order to discriminate positively in favor of a population or an area, their boundaries and identifiying characteristics must be defined. This exercise is particularly dangerous in the case of deprived areas, which are deeply diverse and heterogeneous in nature. The spotlighting of closely defined areas carries the risk of imprisoning them in those definitions, and as a result, of insidiously pushing them into a ghetto situation, organised and working differently from the rest of the country (Piron 1995).

Furthermore, though there is a high concentration of poverty and job insecurity in the main urban renewal areas, these areas contain only a small proportion of the poor and insecure. Is it 'right' to focus our attention on these areas? The question is a highly complex one that is being discussed vigorously and rigorously among political scientists. Is positive discrimination effective? The answer here is a little less complicated. The tangible results of positive discrimination do not really confirm its effectiveness. Moreover, these practices can in themselves generate further problems. Positive discrimination is still discrimination. To quote Calvès (1998), it is 'paradoxical discrimination', full of ambivalence. One has to keep in mind that positive discrimination, like negative discrimination, always creates victims (we speak of 'reverse discrimination'). Because of boundaries and cut-off points, some residents find themselves excluded from measures that benefit their neighbors. The frustrations that follow can succeed in radicalizing opposition and exacerbating tensions – which deprived areas certainly do not need.

What is important is not to be 'for or against' positive discrimination – the black or white alternative on which current debate seems to focus – but more realistically to draw out the fundamental principles of an authentic universalism, at the heart of which certain benefits for people or deprived areas can be legitimately included, building on universal benefits for all and profiting from the widespread support of the whole population.

In the qualified perspective of this evaluation, and given the 'new ambition' of the urban affairs ministry, urban renewal policy now faces ten main challenges:

1. simplification of its procedures requiring a new generation of local authority agreements;
2. general reform of a state seeking to modernize itself;
3. clarifying the future of social housing and the large housing schemes some of which are well past their prime;
4. restructuring of cross-subsidizing systems between local authorities;
5. the successful implementation of community policing;
6. legal changes validating the promotion of specific localities;
7. the cooling down of debates about the ethnic dimensions of French society;
8. changes to the founding republican principles;
9. the reduction of unemployment; and
10. the progression of European integration.

Acknowledgement

The author wishes to thank Patrick Simon (INED) for his advice and suggestions on this text.

References

Aron, R. (1969) *Les désillusions du progrès. Essai sur la dialectique de la modernité* (Paris: Calmann-Levy)
Ascher, F. (1995) *Metapolis* (Paris: Odile Jacob)
Bachmann, C. and Leguennec, N. (1996) *Violences urbaines* (Paris: Albin Michel)
Ballain, R. and Jacquier, C. (1987) *Politique française en faveur des mal-loges (1945–1985)* (Paris: Ministère du Logement)
Barou, J. (1992) *La place du pauvre. Histoire et géographie sociale de l'habitat HLM* (Paris: L'Harmattan)
Begag, A. (1994) *Quartiers sensibles* (Paris: Seuil)
Béhar, D. (1995) Banlieues ghettos, quartiers populaires ou ville eclatée?, *Les Annales de la recherche urbaine* 68–69: 37–53
Béhar, D. (1999) Du terrain au territoire: la politique de la ville, *Informations sociales* 72, 26–34
Béhar, D. and Estèbe, P. (1996) Le chef de projet et le sous-préfet a la ville: entre norme et project, *Espace et sociétés*, 84–85; 37–53

172 *Julien Damon*

Béhar, D., Estebe, P. and Epstein, R. (1998) Les détours de l'égalité. Remarques sur la territorialisation des politiques sociales en France, *Revue française des affaires sociales* 52: 4, 81–94

Bourdieu, P. and Wacquant, L. (1998) Sur les ruses de la raison impérialiste, *Actes de la recherche en sciences sociales* 121–2, 109–18

Buisson, J. (1998) Principe d'égalité et discriminations positives, *Revue française de finances publiques* 63, 37–46

Bui-Trong, L. (1993) L'insécurité des quartiers sensibles: une échelle d'évaluation, *Les Cahiers de la sécurité intérieure* 14, 234–47

Calvès, G. (1998) L'affirmative action dans la jurisprudence de la cour suprême des Etats Unis, *Le Problème de la 'discrimination positive'* (Paris: LGDJ)

Campion, J.-B. and Marpsat, M (1996) La diversité des quartiers prioritaires: un défi pour la politique de la ville, *Economie et statistique* 294–5, 47–65

Castel, R. (1995) *Les Métamorphoses de la question sociale* (Paris: Fayard)

Collectif (1997) *Ces quartiers dont on parle. En marge de la ville, au coeur de la société* (La Tour d'Aigues: l'Aube)

Damamme, D. and Jobert, B. (1995) La politique de la ville ou l'injonction contradictoire en politique, *Revue française de science politique* 45: 1, 3–30

Delarue, J.-M. (1991) *Banlieues en difficultés: la rélégation* (Paris: Syros)

Delevoye, J.-P. (1997) *Cohésion sociale et territoires* (Paris: La Documentation française)

Donzelot, J. and Estebe, P. (1994) *L'Etat animateur* (Paris: Editions Esprit)

Donzelot, J. and Jaillet, M.-C. (1997) Europe, Etats-Unis: convergences et divergence des politique d'insertion, *Esprit* 232, 70–89

Dubet, F. and Lapeyronnie, D. (1992) *Les quartiers d'éxil* (Paris: Seuil)

Geindre, F. (1993) *Villes, démocratie, solidarité: le pari d'une politique* (Paris: La Documentation française)

Godard, F. and Pumain, D. (eds.) (1996) *Données Urbaines* (Paris: Anthropos)

Goldberger, F., Choffel, P. and Le Toqueux, J.-L. (1998) Les zone urbaines sensibles, *INSEE Première* 573 (avril)

Hatzfeld, H., Hatzfeld, M. and Ringart, N. (1998) *Quand la marge est créatrice. Les interstices urbains initiateurs d'emploi* (La Tour d'Aigues: l'Aube)

Jacquier, C. (1991) *Voyage dans dix quartiers européens en crise* (Paris: l'Harmattan)

Joseph, I. (1998) *La ville sans qualité* (La Tour d'Aigues: l'Aube)

Landrieu, J. et al. (1998) *La ville eclatée* (La Tour d'Aigues: l'Aube)

Le Galles, P. (1995) Politique de la ville en France et en Grande Bretagne: volontarisme et ambiguités de l'Etat, *Sociologie du travail* 2, 249–75

Le Pourhiet, A.-M. (1998) Discriminations positives ou injustices?, *Revue française de droit administratif* 14: 3, 519–25

Lepoutre, D. (1997) *Coeur de banlieue. Codes, rites et langages* (Paris: Odile Jacob)

Melin-Soucramanien, F. (1997) Les adaptations du principe d'égalité à la diversité des territoires, *Revue française de droit administratif* 13: 5, 906–25

Mozére, L., Peraldi, M. and Rey, H. (eds.) (1999) *Intelligence des banlieues* (La Tour d'Aigues: l'Aube)

Padioleau, J.-G. (1991) 'L'action publique urbaine moderniste', *Politiques et Management Public* 9: 3, 133–43

Paugam, S. (ed.) (1996) *L'exclusion. L'Etat des savoirs* (Paris: La Découverte)

Piron, O. (1995) Aujourd'hui la question de l'habitat, in F. Ascher (ed.), *Le logement en questions* (La Tour d'Aigues: l'Aube)

Rey, H. (1996) *La peur des banlieues* (Paris: Presses de Science Po)

Roché, S. (1998) *Sociologie politique de l'insecurité. Violence urbaines, inégalités et globalisation* (Paris: PUF)

Roman, J. (ed.) (1993) *Ville, exclusion et citoyenneté* (Paris: Editions Esprit)

Roulleau-Berger, L. (1993) *La Ville-Intervalle. Jeunes entre ville et banlieue* (Paris: Klincksieck)

Schweyer, F.-X. (1996) 'Vers un Etat partenaire?', in S. Paugam (ed.) *L'Exclusion. L'Etat des savoirs* (Paris: La Decouverte)

Schnapper, D. (1994) *La communauté des citoyens. Sur l'idée moderne de nation* (Paris: Gallimard)

Simon, P. (1997) L'integration et le Ghetto in E. Malet and P. Simon (eds.), *Les territoires de l'integration* (Paris: Passages/UNESCO) pp. 25–43

Sueur, J.-P. (1998) *Demain, la ville* (Paris: Las Documentation française)

Taguieff, P.-A. (1996) *La République menacée* (Paris: Textuel)

Viellard-Baron, H. (1994) *Les banlieues françaises ou le ghetto impossible* (La Tour d'Aigues: l'Aube)

Wacquant, L. (1992) Banlieues françaises et ghetto noir americain: de l'amalgame à la comparaison, *French Politics and Society* 10: 4, 81–103

Wieviorka, M. (ed.) (1996) *Une société fragmentée? Le Multiculturalisme en débat* (Paris: La Decouverte)

Wilson, W. (1996) *When Work Disappears. The World of the New Urban Poor* (New York: Knopf)

Wuhl, S. (1996) *Insertion: les politiques en crise* (Paris: PUF)

10
Community Empowerment: Rethinking Resistance in an Era of Partnership

Peter North and Irene Bruegel

Consensus at times is hegemonic. When the policy of central government proclaims community empowerment, is there any need for community struggle? Where once 'community empowerment' implied conflict and an active counter-politics, today it is part of the vocabulary of new urban governance. Doubtless the shift toward a nominally bottom-up urban policy, and the new 'institutionalist' approach of planning together while living differently (Healey 1997), reflects a concern for the inclusion of diverse groups and that it is more democratic and potentially more effective than relying on the trickling down of market gains. Our concern is that a search for consensus can rely on a process of exclusion. More specifically, a policy environment that puts a premium on what is claimed to be a strategy based on 'holistic' partnerships may also crowd out dissent. In this case limited concepts of community and empowerment are measured by improving the competitiveness of individuals in the market, not in nurturing competing voices in democratic debate.

The Third Way and partnership

The 'third sector' – community organizations – looms large in New Labour discourse. Blair argues, for instance, that '[the] left were seen as belittling voluntary activity, seeing it as a poor alternative to direct state provision, and my party at times forgot its own roots in self-help, friendly societies, co-operatives and voluntary organizations, and the insights of Robert Owen and William Morris' (Blair 1999). The think tank Demos argues that the community sector has the potential to play as pivotal role in New Labour thinking as privatization did for Margaret Thatcher (Hargreaves 1998: 65–79). The DETR working paper on 'Community-Based

Regeneration' (DETR 1998a: 2) argues that: 'Time has moved on. Communities are now increasingly keen to do it for themselves', and 'if regeneration is not owned by the community, its benefits will not endure'. For those who value community empowerment, this seems a welcome development.

However, what at first sight seems promising, on further investigation is more problematic. Some see the Blair government as meeting criticism of its neoliberal macroeconomic policies with a 'range of smaller, inexpensive interventions that are social democratic in nature' (Hutton 1998: 36). Elsewhere North (2000) argues that the support for community economic development can be seen in the same light. Community economic development, in short, is cheap and fashionable, and diverts attention away from calls for either more expensive Keynesian-style macroeconomic approaches, or major redistribution of wealth.

In this reading, the concern with social inclusion is no more than a velvet glove obscuring its overriding concern with market flexibility. The Blair administration has implemented an extended program of Welfare-to-Work with its attachment to flexible and deregulated labor markets as the engine of reform. Consequently, on top of well-publicized cuts in benefits for lone parents and for people with disabilities, the compulsory 'Restart' interview process has been extended to these groups, reflecting the view of recipients as a 'moral underclass' to be weaned off benefit dependency (Levitas 1999). As Hoggett (2001) argues, there is now little sympathy for those who will not sign up to the Blairite Utopia through paid work.

Community empowerment cannot just be dismissed as a sop to the Left. Contradictions abound around the difference between communities being empowered to seek their own solutions to their own needs and 'community' as a communitarian blend of empowerment and responsibility (Etzioni 1995). The former makes no *a priori* judgment about 'what' agendas communities generate, whilst the latter, with its emphasis on responsibility, sees community as a tool for constructing consent and disciplining the 'work-shy' as part of a wider agenda to secure the competitiveness of the UK economy. Given that communitarian values are central to Blair's own vision, 'community' is far more 'double-edged'. Consequently, while the government does stress social inclusion, it carries through the twin Thatcherite rhetorics of blaming the victim and freeing the markets. Unemployed people are still to be encouraged to take 'personal responsibility' for their situation, and to recognize the 'duties' they have to a wider society. The legacy is – in true third way style – a mixture of Left and Right, of new avenues for the vulnerable to explore, and a continued, if not extended, pressure to accept any job available, conditions that make the urban excluded feel less, not more, secure.

At the heart of the problem are questions about the relationship between community and market, or where the line between the economic and the social is to be drawn. As a free market radical rather than a communitarian, Thatcher split the market from the realms of both the family and the nation. But in stressing personal responsibility, the nation-state and law and order her legacy was limited relative to the ultimate neoliberal vision of unbridled individuals maximizing the collective good through selfish action in unconstrained markets. Blair maintains a macro-level commitment to this vision, which still collides with more communitarian – let alone 'community'-generated visions of the good life which nod more toward social solidarity and collectivism. The tension is yet to be resolved.

Still other tensions relate to institutional continuity in urban governance structures. These structures fit poorly with genuinely facilitative community involvement in regeneration – let alone the development of diverse approaches to how we wish to live. Despite successive guidance in programs that emphasizes targeting areas of need, the overall tone of post-Thatcher urban policy continues to stress competition between areas and consequently distribution according to presentational ability rather than need (Oatley 1998). But again there is a tension. Where regeneration is targeted on areas of need, a new public management commitment to short measurable time frames and traditional output measures works against a simultaneous commitment to community capacity-building, which necessarily takes more time and is harder to measure. In short, community organizations are still not given the time and resources to develop their own agendas, with the result that the more powerful continue to call the shots within partnerships.

These trends may become more marked as responsibility for regeneration is devolved to business-led Regional Development Agencies, or may be mitigated through Local Strategic Partnerships if local community organizations can gain more purchase. But given the wider overall policy environment, community empowerment can still be seen to be no more than a sop to the Left, in which the centralizing tendencies of a competitive allocation process are softened with the local color provided by community involvement.

In contrast to New Labour strategy we argue that there is a need for community resistance to initiatives imposed from above as a means of building effective and vibrant participation in revitalizing neighborhoods.

On the one hand, community organizations still have to focus on testing how much more favorable the new 'structure of political opportunities' is for gaining influence, but on the other, real local ownership of policies also implies the civil liberty to refuse to participate on the terms on offer. Often it is those outside the frame that can be seen to shake the polity sufficiently to bring real gains, if only momentarily, whether on waste, genetically modified foods, or on road building (North 1998).

We want to argue, then, in favor of being 'unreasonable' (Clavel and Krauschaar 1998), and to ask in what ways political action, outside the new structures of partnership, can open up new spaces for community organizations to succeed in their own terms. Alinsky (1971) understood the need for independence, for self-organization and for well-organized, well-honed campaigns against identifiable enemies that help communities gain a sense of their power to make a difference. We want to discuss the extent that oppositional community self-organization has a place in the era of the third way.

'Who would choose to be without a partner?'

Taylor (1995) argues that community organizations that refuse to participate in partnerships have few other places to go. Is this true? While community groups that withdraw from partnerships may lose the ability to influence the specifics of the regeneration program in question, they may thereby gain the ability to question the underlying agenda. The more effective strategy may take two contrary forms: to organize openly against the negative effects of development (for example, against road widening); or to engage in alternative lifestyles (for example living as travelers).

Against this, essentially, the argument is that community-based organizations need allies with the power and resources they do not have. The alternative is that 'community work which stays in the neighborhood rooted in local issues *as local issues* can be equated with playing into the hands of the dominant class whose interest it is to prevent the emergence of that broader view entailed in class consciousness' (Lambert 1978: 13). The argument is that while community organizations can elect to go outside mainstream governance structures, they do need to identify allies and build more powerful collective agents to avoid an allied danger of 'shut[ting] off . . . voices from access to more universal sources of power by ghettoising them with an opaque otherness' (Harvey 1992: 117). Examples of successful alliance-building includes the Anti-Fascist mobilizations of the 1930s and today (Brick Lane to Stephen

Lawrence), the Anti-Poll Tax movement (Burns 1992), or the tradition associated with Saul Alinsky (see F. Pierson, this volume). These movements, of which the miners' strike of 1984 is the most developed example, involved making links across many different types of organization. These can be characterized as partnerships – but partnerships outside, rather than inside the status quo. At the same time the politics of partnership and/or incorporation suggests that, while perhaps 'no one would want to be without a partner' (Mayo 1996), it is necessary to be choosy about *who* your partner is and *how* you implement that partnership. The implication then is that political education – understanding the nature of political power, learning to recognize interests, the skills of leadership and negotiation – is vital to the process. Here community organizations begin to generalize through struggle from the local to the global, from the particular to the universal, and begin to understand the systems of the power that keep them down.

The North Tyneside CDP provided an example of the technique in the 1970s:

> The objects of the campaign were to raise more general political demands for better housing, demands which attacked the collaboration of the Labour Government with the ruling class in cutting public expenditure, and the council's passive acceptance of this ... rather than ameliorate conditions at a local level, or try to make very local demands which often cut across or competed with demands of other community action groups in the neighbourhoods, it was necessary to generalise the frustration and the class position of local tenants and residents. (Corkey and Craig 1978: 58)

However, while it is one thing to have an understanding of constraining forces it is quite another to be able to do much about it. The urban Left of the 1970s and 1980s rarely appreciated how devastating failures of organization and community struggle could be to morale in communities that generally feel powerless. Their analysis suggested that communities did not understand the 'reality' of their situation, which would be revealed to them only by an 'outside' agency during struggle. The experience needed is of successful tactics of struggle: what works, indeed, to dismantle the constraints on action.

The new urban Left in the 1980s attempted to grapple with some of these dilemmas (Boddy and Fudge 1984; Mackintosh and Wainwright 1987; Alcock et al. 1989). A range of radical economic development approaches were developed by the Greater London Council and the other Labour-led metropolitan authorities that attempted to intervene against those structural forces, in particular against job losses in manufacturing, to promote employment that specifically benefited local communities. The municipal Left sought to promote investment in viable enterprises facing immediate difficulties who would in some ways be model employers. Alternative plans for industrial sectors were developed with trade unionists that promoted industrial democracy in what became known as 'restructuring for labour'. The Left attempted to ensure that businesses tendering for council contracts were equal opportunity employers and offered 'fair employment' and that councils purchased property to facilitate the development of plans conceived of by local residents such as Coin Street on London's South Bank. Community organizations were funded and supported in opposing developments that residents did not feel met the needs of local people – for example, in Docklands or on the South Bank. The Left was partly successful in having such strategies included in economic development programs. While some projects and initiatives from that time remain to this day, these strategies were ultimately defeated by the abolition of the Greater London Council and the metropolitan authorities by the Conservative government. Looking back, what lessons can community organizations draw from this experience?

First, the urban Left went far beyond an understanding of the forces that constrained communities to the designation of programs, backed by the resources of large local authorities, to provide an alternative to the market-led deregulation approaches undertaken by the Department of the Environment of the early 1980s and typified by the Urban Development Corporations and Enterprise Zones. The Left saw itself as piloting approaches that would inform a Left-oriented incoming Labour administration. They looked to use the local state as a vehicle for overcoming the power imbalances that meant that communities were always on the receiving end of economic resources by widening community involvement and decentralizing power.

The second lesson was that large-scale industrial strategies developed by the metropolitan authorities were built on the experiences of the sit-ins, occupations and alternative economic plans of more heady times. While appropriate for the period of heightened economic struggle that gave them birth, they did, it seemed later, prove to be inadequate as serious counter-cyclical interventions and limited as a serious response to economic restructuring. The reality was that Left Labour local authorities spent much of their time simply defending existing resources in the face of central government hostility. Their more long-term plans floundered on an overoptimistic understanding of levels of trade union and community support. Alone, the local state was never seriously expected to be able to counter destructive economic forces. As Mackintosh and Wainwright (1987: 17) put it:

> While they would mainly describe themselves as socialists of one stripe or another, they had no serious illusions about being able to 'plan' their local economies, whatever the titles of some of their fancier publications. The best that could be done was to try to understand what happening and look for points of intervention to halt decay, to redirect some types of development, and to support the regeneration of self organization among their constituents. The 'socialist' content of their work, where people thought it existed, was probably chiefly in the last point.

The urban Left, some therefore argued, were at their most effective when they acted to support and facilitate struggle from below. The local state could make a difference to local struggles by devolving power by, for example, funding community resource centers that employed local people rather than planning professionals; purchasing land for communities to put their strategies into effect, or providing alternative forms of technical advice. The urban Left could not act alone, for where there was not a groundswell of support for their actions 'the policies tended to flounder or become captured by establishment thinking' (Mackintosh and Wainwright 1987: 3). Communities also came to recognize that in a polity such as the United Kingdom where troublesome local authorities can be centrally abolished, or where community organizations themselves can be incorporated, there was no alternative to self-organization by grounded and localized community organizations (Bennington 1986). While they might get valuable support and resource from a local authority and, indeed, had a right to such support, action at the level of the local state could not substitute itself for action from below.

This raises a third but familiar problem – that of identifying 'the community'. Given the impossibility of working with all the inhabitants of a large urban area and the difficulties of moving what could be an unresponsive local bureaucracy with a tendency either to block or incorporate community organizations, the new Left tended to work through established community organizations. This could lead to well-publicized scraps over grant funding in which the weaker lost out to the stronger or more vocal.

Alternatively, 'the community' was left as no more than an ill-defined recipient of the Left's well-intentioned social policy initiatives – the local resident employed by good employer, the purchaser of socially useful production. The Left, thereby, too often substituted itself for 'the community' and planned programs that, no doubt, would benefit local people. But they too often started with organizations rather than with local people. Where policy initiatives were more explicitly localized – for example in Coin Street or Southwark's Courage Brewery site – community needs became more real and grounded. But perhaps the pre-figurative recognition of the need to involve communities in designing their own programs did not fully come into its own until the election of the Blair government in 1997.

Community-led strategies

There are, then, no short cuts. Groups within different communities have the ability to diagnose their own problems based on often complex understandings of the way their community operates, understandings of who their opponents are, and of what their goals are. But even small local communities are not homogeneous and solutions are far from clear cut. What has come to be known in the UK as 'DIY' – Do It Yourself' – culture does not start from structural analysis or necessarily even from a desire to create collectivities, but from what at times seems like an extreme individualism. They do not deal with problems of incorporation, or with the difficulty of working with the powerful as they avoid engagement with the local state.

Nevertheless the method of the urban Left still offers steps out of this impasse. By looking at potentially prefigurative examples of this era, we hope to illustrate how empowerment can become more realistic. Three endogenous community-led strategies – Local Exchange Trading Schemes (LETS), anti-roads protests and a residents' regeneration association – illustrate different tensions and perspectives on the problems and possibilities of independent action.

LETS schemes rarely seek engagement with wider partnership structures, preferring to foster an alternative economy within the city. Anti-road protesters have set out on a path of protest and direct action, linking alternative political praxis with alternative values about ecology, the car, and land use. If they engage with others it is on their own terms, in order to promote their own distinct agendas. A third example is of a residents' association that decided to maintain a distinct organization and agenda for the regeneration of a major strategic site in London, whilst engaging with wider partnerships.

We could, of course, have chosen a wide range of community protests against, for example, an incinerator or school closure. Rather, we have looked for community organizations that also pro-actively seek to create an alternative vision for a city, a movement 'for' rather than 'against'. While we do not have space here to discuss the effectiveness of these independent strategies, their very existence shows that community organizations have choices about the extent that should sign up to the dominant agenda.

Local Exchange Trading Schemes (LETS) are local networks set up to facilitate trading between members using an alternative, locally restricted form of currency. These often have a locally significant name such as the Bobbin in Manchester. Members of a LETS scheme establish a directory of goods and services on offer, contact each other for what they need and pay each other using the alternative currency. Approximately 300 such schemes were in operation in the UK in 1999, some with support from local authorities. Their success has led the government's Social Exclusion Unit to look at ways in which alternative currencies might contribute to regeneration (SEU 1998; North 2000). LETS schemes represent more than a network of people trading babysitting; rather, they reflect a hidden network of people with alternative values about the city, livelihood and work, money, and ecological sustainability (North 1999). The production of a directory itself fosters networks between people who might not otherwise have met. These can develop into rich mutual aid structures and support using a currency that makes a portfolio lifestyle, mixing part-time work, childcare, leisure, arts and culture activities more sustainable. Members use LETS to network with like-minded people, to gain access to resources, to information and knowledge, and to develop a vision of a city that meets people's needs and fosters their skills unconstrained by the availability of cash. It promotes non-traditional forms of work and care, recycling, sharing, reusing and having access to locally produced goods and services. In short, LETS represents a vision of the city as its members believe it should be. These members meet and organize to bring it about, irrespective of the views of elite groups. They do not need to pressure others to participate preferring to lead by example.

Organizations like LETS can seem marginal in impact when compared with the 'outputs' and 'outcomes' claimed by regeneration partnerships. Members trade services and expertise or lend or trade each other specific items such as tools, clothing or capital goods. What is important is that these exchanges represent a network in which local knowledge and information are passed on. That information may be that which enables previously isolated individuals to exist outside mainstream political life or consumption patterns. It enables the limited resources of those involved to be shared, making a lifestyle outside the mainstream possible. Further, LETS represents a manifestation of a possible cooperative method of organizing society in which money is used to facilitate the needs of communities rather than limit them.

LETS forms part of a larger network of mobilization which generates new projects and organizations such as food box schemes or credit unions linked to the network, or new community businesses that cater for customers in arts, organic food and complementary health. Through its directory, LETS makes a wider counter-cultural network visible to outsiders and new members (Melucci 1989) by providing an economic or trading arm to the wider green movement. At an organizational level disparate community projects link up with like-minded organizations to share limited resources, information and social capital. LETS therefore represents an alternative method of organization and project development to mainstream regeneration partnerships. Within the limits set by members' own limited access to resources, LETS enables alternative livelihoods to be lived and community building to be achieved outside formal regeneration partnerships.

A second example of independent organization is the anti-roads movement that mushroomed in the later years of the Major administration and which achieved a comprehensive rethink of roads policy. The anti-roads movement went beyond direct action or traditional protest/pressure group activity as it represented an alliance between radical ecologists and more 'conventional' protesters. It was in many ways an alliance of opposites, involving on the one side travelers, who lived their own distinct lifestyle and promoted an anti-capitalist, anti-consumption, anti-car culture, and on the other those who sought to conserve landscape and traditional small town values (North 1998). The travelers created a vision of a city where public transport and pedestrians come first, where the rights of other species are respected alongside those of humans, where nature has value in its own right and not just for the use-value of humans, and the car symbolizes a profound misunderstanding of 'risk'. This 'politics of risk' fed through into protests about animal experimentation, BSE and genetically modified foods that collectively represent a wider call for wholesome food and skepticism of mainstream science. Here, a wider movement that seeks to undermine technical, rational scientific forms of knowledge has promoted new visions and value systems that have no truck with consensus-building.

A closer form of engagement between traditional partnership structures and community organizations can be found on most partnership boards where there is more than a nod toward community involvement (Hastings et al. 1996). We will use the example of one community organization representing residents in a major redevelopment site in South London. Here, residents established their own 'Residents Regeneration Group' (RRG) as a response to plans to completely redevelop their community. This promised a comprehensive renewal of the 1960s shopping center into a major new development serving south London, providing new jobs for residents, and to address longstanding transport problems. In sum a run-down, somewhat notorious, area of public housing is to become part of the expansion of the city center south of the river. The issue the RRG had to resolve was whether to seek to become the 'official' Community Forum (as one of four sub-groups of the partnership board delivering the SRB program that sought to address community needs around the redevelopment), or whether to 'keep their powder dry' and maintain an independent existence outside the formal partnership. On one side was a concern that residents would have more influence over the process as the formal community forum. On the other, they lacked confidence in the local council's commitment to 'real' partnership and power sharing (given its previous track record), and were concerned that a close relationship with formal partnership structures should not be at the cost of curtailing their freedom of movement. The RRG therefore decided to remain independent, while also arguing that the formal community forum should have independent resources (money, workers, a building), and that the RRG should have the means to evaluate the program from the residents' perspective, and the right to publish its own report on the regeneration. An independent residents' group is to empower the community, making it a powerful stakeholder able to operate at parity with other partners. To achieve this measure of genuine power, the residents' group had to risk being considered 'unreasonable'. In this case, unusually, they were prepared to do so.

In the examples above community organizations have created their own space to act on their own visions and agendas without relying on other, perhaps more powerful partners to act on their behalf; or relying on consensus or partnership working. Their very existence points to alternatives to strategies that privilege inclusion. Communities can set their own, possibly radical agendas and thereby move the debate about regeneration on. Capacity-building needs to focus on making this available to the less powerful and to critique ways that the powerful exclude. In developing agendas for regeneration there should be space for robust, oppositional argumentation, conflict and independent action. This is an issue of both principle and pragmatism; actors have the right to disagree with others, especially as the terms of the debate often institutionally discriminate against the less powerful. More fundamentally what is regarded as 'sensible' and what is 'extreme' is open to question; pragmatically, a range of voices can forestall disruptive and damaging conflict. It took the anti-roads movement to express the beliefs of many that the transport system needed fundamental rethinking; LETS independently created a technology for empowering communities that questions conventional attitudes to money, livelihood, sustainability and in the process confronts competitiveness as the basis for urban regeneration strategies.

Community organizations need the space to develop their visions and agendas. To do this they may need to be unreasonable, to act both in and against wider partnerships, just as the old 'new' urban Left of the 1970s and early 1980s sought to act 'in and against' the state (Cockburn 1977). In the case of the residents' group, robust opposition for a time enabled less powerful actors to organize on what could later become a more level playing field. Within partnership processes, however, this independence cannot last too long. The partnership would need to be one through which consensus is actively constructed either by both sides changing their views to meet with those of their erstwhile opponents, or by transforming their former opponents into allies (Mackintosh 1992). There are, however, real limits to the extent that community organizations can transform powerful partners. The new ethos of partnership remains circumscribed by an overarching commitment to work-based welfare within a competitive capitalist economy, in which the needs of business will take pre-eminence. Within a globalizing economy the possibilities of local action on behalf of community-led organizations are as limited as they have always been. Community organizations will need to be 'realistic', but being realistic does not necessarily mean being compliant.

We would consequently argue that, irrespective of the openness of the new institutions, exclusion from a damaged mainstream is not necessarily a bad thing, if tied to a wider program of change. This can operate at three levels. First, we have to recognise that daily life itself is political, and in particular household decisions about work, livelihood and childcare. Solutions to these daily problems are not necessarily solved through access to paid work, but may better be addressed through the construction of institutions outside the mainstream such as LETS, credit unions, alternative housing projects, communal living experiments, or community development trusts. Here questions center on the extent that specific local projects offer particular technologies to change or influence specific local power circuits. National, or even global power has effects that can, at times, be confronted locally where the political opportunity structure is supportive of such a challenge. Local action can act as a mirror to society (Melucci 1989), revealing the way power operates. And power illuminated is power that can be challenged.

Finally, some communities may not sign up for partnership agreements; at times that might be the best course of action for wider social change. This process of exclusion need not be the end of the discussion; a refusal to join now may mean short-term exclusion, but vocalized opposition creates space for those who do engage with partnerships. It enables engagers to look 'reasonable' and 'constructive', thereby making it easier for engagers to move the debate closer to the more radical agendas while themselves appearing safe. Action outside the partnership can act as a demonstration of what could be, even if mainstream organizations do not as yet recognize the potential, feel is has yet to be demonstrated, or as yet do not accept the arguments it is making. They then begin to move towards more radical approaches. In a dialectical process, what seems to be an immovable ceiling is moved on and up as what is regarded as 'sensible' and what 'extreme' is recast. This process depends on 'unreasonable' people.

References

Alcock, P., Gamble, A., Gough, I., Lee, P. and Walker, A. ('The Sheffield Group') (1989) *The Social Economy and the Democratic State*, London: Lawrence and Wishart

Bennington, J. (1986) 'Local economic strategies: paradigms for a planned economy?', in *Local Economy*, 1: 1, pp. 7–44

Blair, A. (1999) Speech to the National Council of Voluntary Organizations, 21 January 1999, as reported in D. Brindle (1999), 'Blair tells cynics: its good to be a do-gooder', *Guardian*, 22 January 1999, p. 10

Boddy, M. and Fudge, C. (eds) (1984) *Local Socialism*, London: Macmillan – now Palgrave

Burns, D. (1992) *Poll Tax Rebellion*, Edinburgh: AK Press

Castells, M. (1986) *The City and the Grassroots*, London: Edward Arnold

Clavel, P. and Kraushaar, R. (1998) 'On being unreasonable progressive planning in Sheffield and Chicago', *International Planning Studies*, 3: 2, pp. 143–62

Cockburn, C. (1977) *The Local State: Managing Cities and People*, London: Pluto

Corkey, D. and Craig, G. (1978) 'CDP: Community work or class politics?', in P. Curno (ed.), *Political Issues and Community Work*, London: Routledge and Kegan Paul

Curno, P. (ed) (1978) *Political Issues and Community Work*, London: Routledge and Kegan Paul

Duncan, A. and Hobson, B. (1995) *Saturn's Children*, London: Sinclair-Stevenson

Environment, Transport and the Regions, Department of the (1998a) *Community-Based Regeneration Initiatives: A Working Paper*, London: DETR

Entzioni, A. (1995) *The Spirit of Community*, London: Fontana

Gluckstein, D. (1985) *The Western Soviets: Workers' Councils versus Parliament 1915–20*, London: Bookmark

Hargreaves, I. (1998) 'A Step beyond Morris Dancing: The Third Sector Revival', in I. Hargreaves and I. Christie (eds), *Tomorrow's Politics: the Third Way and Beyond*, London: Demos

Harvey, D. (1992) *The Condition of Postmodernity*, Oxford: Blackwell

Hastings, A., McArthur, A. and McGreggor, A. (1996) *Less than Equal? Community Organizations and Regeneration Partnerships*, Bristol: Policy Press

Healey, P. (1997) *Collaborative Planning: Shaping Places in Fragmented Societies*, London: Macmillan – now Palgrave

Hoggett, P. (2001) 'Agency, Rationality and Social Policy', *Journal of Social Policy*, 30: 1, pp. 37–56

Hutton, W. (1998) 'The State We Should Be In', *Marxism Today*, October

Kelsey, J. (1995) *The New Zealand Experiment: A World Model for Structural Adjustment?*, Auckland: University of Auckland Press

Lambert, J. (1978) 'Political Values and Community Work Practice', in P. Curno (ed.), *Political Issues and Community Work*, London: Routledge and Kegan Paul

Levitas, R. (1999) *Social Inclusion and New Labour*, London: n.p.

Mackintosh, M. (1992) 'Partnership: Issues of Policy and Negotiation', *Local Economy*, 7: 3, pp. 210–25

Mackintosh, M. and Wainwright, H. (eds) (1987) *A Taste of Power: The Politics of Local Economics*, London: Verso

Melucci, A. (1989) *Nomads of the Present*, London: Hutchinson Radius

Miller, C. (1999) 'Partners in Regeneration: Constructing a Local Regime for Urban Management', *Policy and Politics*, 27: 3

Mouffe, C. (1998) 'The Radical Centre; A Politics without Adversary', in *Soundings*, pp. 11–23

Mumbey, J. and Craig, G. (1978) 'Joint Union–Resident Action', in P. Curno (ed.), *Political Issues and Community Work*, London: Routledge and Kegan Paul

North, P. (1998) 'Save our Solsbury!: The Anatomy of an Anti-roads Protest', *Environmental Politics*, 7: 3, pp. 1–25

North, P. (1999) 'Explorations in Heterotopia: LETS and the Micropolitics of Money and Livelihood', *Environment and Planning D: Society and Space*, 17: 1, pp. 69–86

North, P.(2000) 'Is There Space for Organization from Below within the UK Government's Action Zones?: A Test of "Collaborative Planning"', 37: 8, pp. 1261–78

Oatley, N. (1998) 'Managing Decline: Institutional Fixes and Urban Policy in England (or New Labour: New Pragmatism)', paper presented at conference 'Cities and the Millennium', University of East London, December 1998

Routledge, P. and Simmons, J. (1995) 'Embodying Spirits of Resistance', *Environment and Planning D: Society and Space*, 13, pp. 471–98

Social Exclusion Unit (1998) *Bringing Britain Together: A National Strategy for Neighbourhood Renewal*, London: SEU

Smith, J. (1978) 'Hard lines and Soft Options: A Criticism of Some Left Attitudes to Community Work', in P. Curno (ed.), *Political Issues and Community Work*, London: Routledge and Kegan Paul

Taylor, M. (1995) *Unleashing the Potential: Bringing Residents to the Centre of Regeneration*, York: Joseph Rowntree Foundation

11

Communitarianism and Gender in the New Urban Policy

Joan Smith

This chapter examines the link between the regeneration policy of the British Labour government, elected in 1997, and its wider social policy objectives. In exploring that link I focus on the array of measures designed to reinforce social order. In particular I consider how the government's perception of the conduct of both young men as sources of disorder and of young women who become single mothers and thus undermine the regulatory power of the family has shaped its view of regeneration. Although the broad policy objectives are couched in the discourse of social exclusion, particular policies are drawn from communitarian explanations for community disintegration. Fundamentally these explanations attribute urban social devastation to a range of maladies to be found in the 'private sphere' – family breakdown, lone mothers unable to exert discipline, the moral failures of working-class parents to raise children with 'community values' in mind.

The chapter considers the tension between social exclusion and communitarian approaches to rebuilding communities. It then turns to discuss the concept of social capital which is widely invoked as a progressive alternative to communitarian driven policy. I argue that in both the US and the UK community building approaches based on social capital and social networks, while more sophisticated than anything communitarianism has spawned, nevertheless allow the central issue of gross income inequality and the necessity of redistributive measures to be avoided. Finally, I offer a perspective that recognizes that community rebuilding is a gendered experience, one that relies on the 'elastic supply of women's labour'. Central to this approach is the issue of who runs a specific program and what standpoints are taken. Much of the writing on this approach has grown from the experience of women organizing in the developing countries as well as from principles derived from feminist organizing in the developed world; together they powerfully confront the communitarian logic of current regeneration policy toward poor urban neighborhoods.

Area regeneration and New Labour policy

Labour government policy as outlined in 'New Deal for Communities' (SEU 1998) aimed to turn round Britain's most deprived neighbourhoods by finding out what worked in 17 'pathfinder' areas. The program was launched with a report from the government's own Social Exclusion Unit which presented a detailed summary of the social and economic deterioration in 44 area 'blackspots' (SEU 1998). The Social Exclusion report, drawing heavily on John Hills' (1993) and Anne Power's research (1997), analyzed the impact on neighborhoods of the Conservative drive to reverse the redistributional elements of tax and welfare policy, of disinvestment in public housing and the loss of manufacturing industry. Public housing estates, which had once housed mixed-income families, became a residual service housing families on benefits with extensive child poverty.

Following the Social Exclusion Unit's report the Labour government proposed a policy for regenerating disadvantaged neighborhoods that departed in several respects from the cycle of policies outlined by Miller elsewhere in this volume. First, they were comprehensive. One of the central planks of 'New Deal for Communities' was that the 'pathfinder' areas would receive long-term funding for holistic solutions that involve neighborhood safety and economic development as well as improvements in health and social services. Funding from other programs, such as Sure Start, was also triggered to produce a fully integrated program. Further, funding has been targeted to specific areas identified as being in most need, replacing the open competition for funding under the older urban programs such as City Challenge and the Single Regeneration Budget.

However, area regeneration policies do not take place in a policy vacuum. First, the majority of inhabitants in many targeted areas are welfare dependent. But, in line with New Labour's commitment to welfare to work programs, neither the SEU report nor Labour's policy agenda proposed a universal reversal of the decline in the value of welfare benefits that took place over the previous 18 years. There is no suggestion that benefits, which were disengaged from rising with average wage rates, should be reattached to that escalator. Instead, welfare and improved benefit rates are linked to work and workforce development more directly than ever before.

New benefits are targeted at specific groups of the socially excluded, living in low-income households and in particular areas or neighbourhoods. In particular the government has targeted young people who are not in education, training or employment (or 'NEET') and created a new initiative which revives benefits for some young people aged 16 years to 18 years (all of whom had their right to Income Support removed in 1988) living in low-income households, who stay on in education. This gives an income similar to a youth training wage for young people from the poorest families. They have also targeted lone mothers, and the Working Tax Credit and allowance for those paying child care costs provides a package of benefits available for low-paid working mothers higher than for lone mothers unable to work. In line with New Labour beliefs that communities may legitimately exert their sense of moral values in relation to deviant behavior, area regeneration policies were also introduced simultaneously with certain extraordinary powers regulating crime and disorder, new tenancies and tenant behavior, and the behavior of children and neighborhood nuisance.

At the heart of the Labour government's agenda therefore is a contradiction in vision. One strand of government policy, emanating from the Social Exclusion Unit, is preoccupied with the loss of social cohesion and social exclusion. However, the policies that address the problems highlighted by the SEU analysis derive from the alternative discourse of communitarianism. The theories behind each of these perspectives and the policies they give rise to are, however, fundamentally incompatible.

The language of social exclusion and communitarian policy

The concept of social exclusion originally derived from French political and academic discourse of the 1970s when the phrase *les exclus* came to refer to people with learning or physical health problems and to the 10 percent excluded from French insurance schemes through a lack of occupational insurance contributions. It has become so integrated into French Republican thought that all French political parties are publicly committed to policies promoting 'insertion' and 'reinsertion' and the benefit payment to those over 25 years has been called 'Revenue Minimum d'Insertion'. The commitment to social inclusion has underwritten, even among the French right, a political justification of state intervention quite unlike the market liberalization policies of the US and UK during the past two decades. It is this difference which underlies the debate between Jospin of France on the one hand and Clinton,

Blair, Schroeder on the other at the summit to discuss the third way or the new way for welfare in the year 2000 (*Observer*, 21 November 1999).

The concept of social exclusion grew in importance in Europe generally from 1989. During the presidency of Jacques Delors, the idea of combatting social exclusion across the European Union, particularly among specified social groups (young people, battered women, ethnic minorities), was written into a series of EU public programs and the European Social Charter. From there it moved into Labour Party policy and led to the creation of the Social Exclusion Unit attached to the Cabinet Office as soon as Labour came to power.

The most radical interpretations of social exclusion have been developed by analysts working in the International Labour Office and other international agencies. They have used the concept to rethink the process of both impoverishment and marginalization. Wolfe argues that, 'Exclusion is an active concept like exploitation. Someone or something bars out or drives out someone or something else, which reacts as best it can' (Wolfe 1995). Although inequality and exclusion overlap they are not the same. Silver, also working at the ILO, has argued: 'Indeed, if poverty is usually alleviated by social welfare policies, exclusion, it is said, must be addressed by insertion, integration, the rights and entitlements of citizenship, and participation in social life. Redistributive policies may still be necessary, but the term "exclusion" calls for a rethinking of the terms of social solidarity' (Silver 1995).

Communitarian thinking takes quite a different approach to 'social solidarity' and to the rights and entitlements of citizenship. It makes a strong critique of the right to privacy especially in the 'zone of intimacy' – the family and interpersonal relationships. What has concerned proponents such as Michael Sandel (1982) and Mary Ann Glendon (1991) is that doctrines of privacy were being pressed into service to defend decisional autonomy, to create areas of personal behaviour that government had no right to invade or restrict in any way. This they objected to strongly on the grounds that it presupposed an atomistic concept of the self, an individual 'unencumbered' by social or personal obligation. Sandel in particular argues that all persons are 'situated' and that their identities are shaped through community-mediated processes of socialization.

Further, communitarians argue that because we are dealing with concrete, situated selves and not individuals in the abstract, the development of self is closely tied to social preconditions, namely the shared values and membership in solidary communities in which norms and traditions are transmitted with legitimacy. Thus, even in the hands of communitarians' most sophisticated proponents such as Glendon and Sandel, 'the community' has the right to institutionalize its values and norms. In doing so they restrict the issue of norms, values and 'the social good' to a single overarching conception, as if there is a collective identity upon which all agree.

In lesser hands, like Etzioni's, the communitarian argument loses specificity and a simplistic majoritarian definition of community values prevails. The concern 'to protect the integrity of those dimensions of individual identities and conceptions of the good that differ from majoritarian interpretations of collective identity' is completely missing. They 'suppress the problem posed by the *difference* and potential conflict between individual and group identity' (Cohen 1997: 151). The 'Responsive Community Platform', drafted by Amitai Etzioni, Mary Ann Glendon and William Galston in November 1991, emphasized a citizen's responsibilities toward family, society and community rather than their social rights (Etzioni 1993). It placed an emphasis on the family stability and family morality that meshed with Blair's Christian socialism, and promoted both education and community safety that meshed with new Labour's concern for social order.

Community regeneration, welfare reform and paternalist policy

While in opposition Blair regularly and explicitly returned to communitarian themes. He argued for example, 'At the heart of everything New Labour stands for is the theme of rights and responsibilities. For every right we enjoy we owe responsibilities. That is the most basic family value of all. You can take, but you give too'. Labour had to develop tough policies on disorder because of the suffering of people on council estates. Their 'lives are made hell by teenage tearaways, vandals, drug-dealers, muggers, graffiti artists and the culture of despair that has been spawned by the break-down in the decent values on which Britain was built' (Blair 1996). In government, Blair has consistently called upon communitarian values in order to support his policies (Heron and Dwyer 1999).

> The breakdown of family and community bonds is intimately linked to the breakdown in law and order. Both family and community rely on notions of mutual respect and duty. It is in the family that we first learn to negotiate boundaries of acceptable conduct and to recognise that we owe responsibilities to others as well as to ourselves. (Speech to the Family Breakdown and Criminal Activity Conference, 24 May 1994, reproduced in Blair 1996)

There is, then, a fundamental argument between the concept of social exclusion, which sees rebuilding social solidarity through public resources, and communitarianism, which emphasizes enforcing a shared morality and nurturing social responsibility under the watchful eye of the justice and welfare systems. Of the two visions, social exclusion and communitarianism, the latter trumps the former by compelling particular behaviors through statute, regardless of individual need. Within social legislation after 1997, alongside the increased funding for measures designed to help communities regenerate themselves were new measures to exclude identified persons from those communities, to control the behavior of young people and to target a range of increasingly compulsory programs. Statutory controls were aimed at those in the community whom the government believed to be undermining the work and family ethic of those communities.

New Labour's law and order agenda follows closely on from the family responsibility and crime and order agenda in the United States, rather than earlier Labour policy toward offending and disadvantage or other European approaches. So too does the approach to single mothers. As Ruth Fincher has argued, in the US, 'teenage African American men and women have been rendered in analysis the "problem" inhabitants of inner cities, from a focus in the young women's case on out-of-wedlock births and in the young men's case on their involvement in violent and criminal behavior' (Fincher 1998).

In particular the Crime and Disorder Act flowed directly from New Labour visions of a safe community in which increased powers of social control are necessary in dangerous areas and over dangerous young people. The Act allows local authorities to impose local curfews, to remove young children from the street at night and to return truanting children to school. Further, it creates new controls over persons (principally young men) through the serving of anti-social behavior orders which can lead to an injunction against spitting in the street, street harassment or behavior designed to intimidate. Such offences, if ignored, can lead to six-month prison sentences or for repeated offences, five years (Crawford 1997).

New Labour polices have also led to legislation that has reversed those aspects of the welfare state which have supported lone mothers in the past, including the abolition of lone parent additional benefit payment for new claimants. They have made more onerous the conditions under which women must cooperate with the Child Support Agency, increasing the benefit stop (the proportion of payment held back from young mothers who do not cooperate with the agency). Under the New Deal for

Employment the government has also increased the pressure on mothers on benefit to retrain and find employment. The settlements will, when fully enacted, change the face of welfare for lone mothers in the UK, as they have done in the US (Handler, 1997).

In the UK therefore, as in the US, the work ethic has come to under-write welfare policies, pushing out the family ethic which once provided support for mothers with children. MacGregor has characterized these new welfare settlements in the UK and US as 'paternalist', contrasting them with the neoliberal regimes of the 1980s in both countries and the welfare regime which existed in the UK prior to that (MacGregor 1999). Paternalist welfare states aim at a meritocratic society with full employment and their systems heavily favor welfare-to-work regimes based on the obligations of citizens and a strictly residual safety net for those unable to work. In MacGregor's analysis these are regimes of social inclusion and social intrusion, preferable to the disintegration and social exclusion suffered under neoliberal welfare states but a far cry from the aims of social cohesion and social integration that characterized trad-itional welfare states. They are also a far cry from the regimes envisaged under social exclusion theory – where inclusion is not allied to social control but to broadened citizenship rights.

The false promise of social capital

The question therefore remains – what alternatives are there to pater-nalist, communitarian policies in rebuilding communities? In the US both urban sociologists and activists, following the earlier work of Coleman and Putnam, have begun to invoke the concept of social capital as a pathway out of the impasse created by the withdrawal of federal fund-ing from welfare and urban programs. Putnam has summarized the idea of social capital as following:

> By analogy to physical capital and human capital, social capital refers to the norms and networks of civil society that lubricate co-operative action among both citizens and their institutions. Without adequate supplies of social capital – that is, without civic engagement, health community institutions, norms of mutual reciprocity and trust – social institutions falter. (Putnam 1998)

Particular local studies have been used to demonstrate that for young black people the most important way out of poverty is through a network of out-of-area contacts who include whites and people in work (de Souza Briggs 1998). Early indications from some studies have also suggested that mixed housing developments may be more conducive for people from disadvantaged areas gaining access to education, training or employment. Such studies have led to a further distinction between social support (help with getting by) and social leverage (help with getting ahead) as well as discussions of the different role of social glue (solidarity within the community) and social bridges. In the UK, Perri 6 has begun the discussion of social networks and routes out of poverty and the means through which the unemployed find jobs (Perri 6 1997).

There are good reasons, however, to be sceptical of Putnam's romanticized notion of community. First, it is open to question whether membership of a range of small, voluntary associations (bowling clubs, bird-watching) leads to generalized social trust, democracy and functioning communities (Levi 1996). Second is the apparent reduction of concepts of community and civic life to the level of idealized family (Putzel 1997). Third is the way debates on social capital and civic life focus attention away from the economic effects on these neighbourhoods of job loss through globalization and income loss through welfare reduction (Foley and Edwards 1997). Finally, simplified discussions of social capital also draw attention away from the level of social conflict within communities.

Thus the utility of the idea of social capital, whether on a theoretical or practical level, is still under debate. Gittell and Vidal (1998), despite their critique, argue that it has real value in helping 'to frame and better understanding community development practice', particularly when looking at the role of intermediary organizations. They found that a concentration on the 'bridging' process allowed programs to overcome special interests as well as to provide external resources that facilitates the process.

On the other hand, one aspect of social capital parallels communitarian objectives, namely that the poorest communities are being asked to find the wherewithal to lift themselves out of their social degradation. While it provides some recognition of economic and structural forces, which it accepts are beyond the capacity of residents to change, the focus of social capital is resolutely away from redistributive justice and redistributive action by government. Halperin's effective riposte to neighborhood revitalization efforts is applicable here: 'The idea that poor neighborhoods contain the resources and capacities for their own regeneration can be, and often has been, used to promote self-help without the requisite external supports and linkages. . . .' (1995: 222)

There is also a large difference between measuring the potential mobility of people to find employment and therefore, often, to leave an area, and the measurement of increased social capital in an area. Only a minority of women setting up micro-businesses in an area in the US said that they had become more involved with the community or with their families. This is not surprising as these enterprises were individual initiatives not community business initiatives. In the UK the initiatives that have been most common in communities of distress are related to credit. Many of the areas have been abandoned by credit agencies and women have learned business skills in their attempt to turn their communities from debt-ridden to self-crediting (see North and Bruegel, this volume). But their work falls more clearly in the realm of traditional women's organizing – within the community, for the community, the family and themselves. Increasingly, western non-government organizations and women community organizers are learning some of these lessons from those in developing countries.

Gender and community rebuilding

Organizations in the UK have also sought to introduce the model of community activism which has grown in the developing world into the UK. Following their work in India and South Africa, Oxfam and Homeless International flew in community activists against homelessness from those countries for a 'Groundswell' conference (*Guardian* 18 September 1998). Audrey Bronstein of Oxfam and Ruth McLeod of Homeless International both argue that women are the most active and effective organizers within their community and their statement was supported by the two male organizers from India and South Africa. The purpose of this visit was to generate a gendered perspective on organizing communities within UK homeless agencies. Many organizations, from Oxfam to the UN, have learned to place their funds and their trust in the outcome of women-driven community organizing, and writers in the developed world have increasingly sought to borrow the insights which have been gained.

In relation to community organizing in developing countries the debate has moved beyond outreach work to involve women, to sophisticated models of gender planning. Moser has attempted to deconstruct the different approach of women and men to the task of 'community management', their different relationship to the consumption needs of their community, and the difficulties they have to overcome at both the personal and structural level. She writes:

'Community Managing' then, is defined as the work undertaken at the community level, around the allocation, provisioning and managing of items of collective consumption. A wide diversity of consumption needs for the reproduction of labour power have been increasingly socialized at the level of the community.... Thus, for women the point of residence includes not only the home but also extends into the surrounding areas. Social relationships include not only household members but also neighbours. Mobilization and organization at the community level is a natural extension of their domestic work. (Moser 1993)

Moser goes on to argue that men also work at the level of the community but, because they begin from different roles, their role in the community also differs. Whereas women are involved in the community as an extension of their role in the domestic arena and therefore see themselves as community managers, men see themselves as community politicians. 'In low-income communities throughout the world there is a consistent trend for political organizations to be run by men with mainly male members, and for collective consumption groups to be in the hands of women.'

From his study of community organizing in Newcastle upon Tyne, McCulloch would also agree with Moser's analysis. McCulloch not only draws attention to the involvement of women in community organizing but asks particular questions about which women are active in the community and what differentiates their attitude to community organizing from that of men (McCulloch 1997). He makes three points. First, the women fall into two particular age groups; those who are mothering and are aged late twenties through to early forties, and older women aged 55 years and up. Second they are committed to the area through ties of family and friendship and less likely to leave the area as many male activists did. (Women were aware of the career aspirations of many male community organizers and would occasionally express disdain for men who made a career out of community organizing and/or moved out of the area, while they continued to work within their neighborhood). Third, women's volunteer work is undervalued and although women were the majority of the active volunteers only one of them was given a paid post of three that were available; there were six paid posts in all, and only one went to an active volunteering woman.

McCulloch gives us an important reminder that official acceptance of women's role in organizing 'collective consumption' is also another way of harnessing women's labor to the economic agenda of the government, as well as the needs of the community. The most popular approach among policy-makers, both national and international, is that which identifies women's productive labor and economic participation as a pathway to ensuring their equitable treatment in society (referred to by Moser as the 'efficiency approach'. Moser argues that in developing societies, 'the efficiency approach relies heavily on the elasticity of women's labour in both their reproductive and community managing roles. It only meets practical gender needs at the cost of longer working hours and increased unpaid work' (Moser 1993). What is true for women in developing countries is also true for women in the US and UK. Developing countries can meet their growth targets in a period of declining social services, and developed societies can reduce their welfare spending by relying on all three roles of women (mother/consumption needs of the household, worker/producer, and community manager/consumption needs of the community). Such an approach to community rebuilding is built upon the elasticity of women's time. The issue then becomes who is in control of women's time – government-sponsored initiatives or women-led organizations.

As theories of social capital and social network construction abound, it is important to remind women that it is their everyday work that creates the realm of community between the public and the private, and that this work should be defended against welfare-cutting agendas.

> While the empirical importance of women's social reproduction work inside the home has been established, only recently has women's social-reproduction labor in the community, often essential for survival in lower-income communities, been recognised as a type of resistance or political activity ... (Feldman, Stall and Wright, 1999)

Women organizing: principles and practices

The distinction between the private or domestic sphere and the public or political sphere has long been under attack from feminists. It underpins a range of ideologies that assign men and women to different spheres of social life. Invoking the public/private distinction often assigns women to what is viewed as the more trivial private sphere or is used to screen off acts of abuse or domination. Pateman (1989) outlines the consequences in one of the more sophisticated appraisals of the public/private distinction. The private/public distinction, says Weintraub (1997), excludes women, on the basis of their 'naturally' private character, 'from both of the spheres in which men have increasingly claimed equality and agency . . . as independent actors in civil society [which now includes the family] and as citizens in the political community'.

In North America opposition to a purely 'public action' approach to community organizing has been more readily theorized by women who have themselves been community activists. Callaghan's review of her 30 years' experience of community organizing in Canada leads her to develop a particular model of feminist organizing. She argues that women active in their community have, in the past, been constructed as either 'devoted volunteers', working in the field of care and/or for small-scale changes, or as paid 'radical organizers' working for change and large-scale feminist concerns. This stereotyping of women's community activities into carers or activists reflect outsider views of community organizing which fail to see feminists experimenting with egalitarian organizational structures, the integration of private and public realms and a creative integration of collaboration and confrontation (Callaghan 1997).

Stall and Stoecker (1998) contrast the role of paid community organizers who live outside the community with that of women who organize within their own community. They argue that there is a significant difference between an organizing model that work with churches and formal institutions, such as that of the IAF, and a women's centred model that moves outward from the household and 'parallels differences between the community experiences of men and women'. For Stall and Stoecker the origins of women's community building lie both in the homeplace creation of African-American women and the organized activities of Black Women's clubs, and the 'municipal housekeeping' activities of white women at the turn of the century including the settlement house movement. They argue that these activities from the nineteenth century through to the civil rights and feminist movements of the 1960s allowed women to transform both public and private agendas, including their own health care, parenting practices, cultural practices and career paths.

What is different about a woman-centered model of community organization? First, it begins with organizing community itself – 'building expanded private sphere relationships and empowering indivduals through those relationships' (Stall and Stoecker 1998), dissolving the boundaries between public and private life and between the household and civil society. Second, its principal aim is empowerment, whilst the goal of the Alinsky model and others is to gain political influence in the public sphere. Stall and Stoecker, more than Callaghan, are also concerned with the 'paradox of empowerment' at the heart of the women-centered model of organizing community, that is the need to

organize at both the personal and the structural level. Third, empowerment leads to the naming of the issues that must be solved in order to
overcome gender and race boundaries. Callaghan sees this process as
being part of the women organizing model – the power to name which
issues are important. In the past feminist community organizing has led
to the 'naming' of sexual assault and domestic violence, making a once
private matter public.

Most importantly Naples has drawn attention to the way 'Women of
colour often find themselves on the borders of multiple communities –
each claiming their allegiance and each with different definitions of
what political actions are correct and which demonstrate betrayal'
(Naples 1998). Community boundaries are more fluid than politicians
wish; they shift as new political and economic pressures arise and are
often built through struggles for social justice and economic security as
well as through small-scale changes that make such struggles possible
(child care, creating community centres, etc). However, as Naples also
points out, current community organizing by women is now less oriented
toward political organizing and more oriented toward community household survival.

Naples argues that a woman's own experience translates into a 'standpoint' (or wide, socialized understanding) by means of different routes,
including through their collective experience, their individual experience and through other women's politicised understandings. Moreover,
'standpoints' are both embodied and constructed in community. Of
necessity, such standpoints are gendered, embodying women's experiences of community organizing. In many ways Naples' discussion of the
building of 'standpoints' parallels discussions on the ways that leadership is generated in other fields. In principle understanding standpoints
should enable women to reject the solutions born of the communitarian
perspective, to appropriate as their own enabling solutions born of their
and their community's needs.

Conclusion

The emphasis in the original social exclusion report outlining the New
Deal for Communities was one of turning around estates which had
been left to sink under free market social policies. It identified five areas
for rebuilding: getting people to work, filling empty local authority
houses (or demolishing them where necessary), controlling neighbor
nuisance through local wardens and 'super-caretakers' as well as through

eviction, regenerating missing facilities on local estates including cheap shopping and financial services, and providing a range of special services for children and young people through the school system. The government's own indicators for evaluating its New Deal for Communities program changed the original emphasis on social exclusion to a communitarian one by looking for four indicators – tackling worklessness, improving health, tackling crime and raising educational achievement (www.detr.1998).

As Crawford has argued, in the past 20 years there has been an increasing shift in emphasis in government policy from a focus on criminal individuals to a focus on criminal places, or 'dangerous places' with family breakdown and lack of parental control major determinants of the crisis. Because particular areas are visibly unpleasant places to live, is it possible to enact, in the name of community well-being, a series of measures which have undermined individual civil rights across the UK, and to construct an understanding that civil liberties run counter to public and community safety (Crawford 1997). The redistributive strand of New Labour policy has yielded to a communitarian discourse and passed measures on crime, social disorder and lone parents that comprehensively displaces a wealth redistributive program.

'New Deal for Communities' was, in area terms, the equivalent of residual, welfare targeting. All NDC resources are spent in specific areas on programs that have successfully bid for the money. Pockets of deprivation elsewhere, even next door, remain unfunded. Some communities that successfully exclude the worst drug offenders and families of the most violent young men, are located near sources of new employment opportunities, and manage to harness their own resources to provide services for their communities, will regenerate. Their models of working will provide important landmarks. Other communities, however, will be ones in which one or all of these processes fail to happen and those living there will then be expected to shoulder the responsibility for that failure, alongside all the other failures of their lives.

Women find themselves as the scapegoats of this Third Way – as mothers out of control of young people, as single parent mothers, as benefit claimants. The burden of care will continue to fall disproportionately on their shoulders as state help is targeted at those in work because their employers pay sufficiently low wages that working tax credits must be used to finance the working poor. Previous achievements of women's organizing, such as the establishment of domestic violence units within the police and the recognition of domestic violence as a cause of priority need for rehousing, risk being eroded through the conflation of good families with good communities and the 'virtuous' circle of social capital growth.

Only by learning from the examples of women's organizing practice in both the developing and developed world will community-based organizations build on the 'elasticity of women's time' without either overpowering women with their demands or stealing from them their abilities and commitment. Principles derived from the past 30 years of women-led organizations will allow communities to regenerate in ways which empower all the members of those communities.

References

Blair, A. (1996) *New Britain: My Vision of a Young Country* (London: Fourth Estate)
Callaghan, M. (1997) Feminist Community Organizing in Canada: Postcards from the Edge, in B. Wharf and M. Claque, *Community Organizing: Canadian Experiences* (Toronto and Oxford: Oxford University Press)
Cohen, J. (1997) Rethinking Privacy: Autonomy, Identity and the Abortion Controversy, in J. Weintraub and K. Kumar, *Public and Private Thought in Practice Perspectives on a Grand Dichotomy* (Chicago: University of Chicago Press)
Crawford, X. (1997) *Local Governance of Crime: Appeals to Community Partnership* (Oxford: Oxford University Press)
de Souza Briggs, X. (1998) Brown Kids in White Suburbs: Housing Mobility and the Many Faces of Social Capital, *Housing Policy Debate* 9 :1, 177–221
de Souza Briggs, X. and Mueller, E.J., with Sullivan, M.L. (1997) *From Neighborhood to Community: Evidence on the Social Effects of Community Development* (New York: Community Development Research Center)
Dominelli, L. (1995) Women in the Community: Feminist Principles and Organising in Community Work, *Community Development Journal* 30: 2 (April)
Duncan, S. and Edwards, R. (1997) Single Mothers in Britain: Unsupported Workers or Mothers, in S. Duncan and R. Edwards, *Single Mothers in an International Context* (London: UCL Press)
Etzioni, A. (1993) *The Spirit of Community: The Reinvention of American Society* (New York: Touchstone)
Feldman R. and Stall, S. (1999) The Politics of Space Appropriation: A Case study of Women's Struggles for Homeplace in Chicago Public Housing, Conference Proceedings, *Shelter, Women and Development*, 282–5.
Fincher, R. and Jacobs, J. (eds.) (1998) *Cities of Difference* (New York: The Guilford Press)
Fincher, R. (1998) In the Right Place. At the Right Time in R. Fincher and J. Jacobs (eds.), *Cities of Difference* (New York: The Oxford Press)
Foley, M. and Edwards, B. (1997) Escape from Politics? Social Theory and the Social Capital Debate, *American Behavioural Scientist* 40: 5
Gittell, R. and Vidal, A. (1998) *Community Organising. Building Social Capital as a Development Strategy* (New York and London: Sage)
Glendon M.A. (1991) *Rights Talk* (New York: Free Press)
Halperin, R. (1995) *Rebuilding the Inner City A History of Neighborhood Initiatives to Address Poverty in the United States* (New York: Columbia University Press)

Handler, J. (1997) 'Welfare Reform in the United States', *Osgoode Hall Law Journal* 35: 2, 289-307

Heron, E. and Dwyer, P. (1999) Doing the Right Thing: Labour's Attempt to Forge a New Welfare Deal between the Individual and the State, in *Social Policy and Administration* 33: 1 (March)

Hills, J. (1993) *The Future of the Welfare State* (York: Joseph Rowntree Foundation)

Howe, X. (1998) 'Gender, Race and Community Activism. Competing Strategies in the Struggle for Public Education', in N. Naples (ed.), *Community Activism and Feminist Politics: Organizing across Race, Class and Gender* (London: Routledge & Kegan Paul)

Lang, R.E. and Hornburg, S.P. (1998) 'What is Social Capital and Why is it Important to Public Policy?', in *Housing Policy Debate* 9(1) (Washington: Fannie Mae Foundation)

Levi, P. (1996) Social and Unsocial Policy: A review Essay of Robert Putnam's *Making Democracy Work, Politics and Society* 24: 1, 45-56

MacGregor, S. (1999) 'Welfare, Neo-Liberalism and New Paternalism: Three Ways for Social Policy in Late Capitalist Societies', *Capital and Class*

May, N. (1997) *Challenging Assumptions. Gender Issues in Urban Regeneration* (York: Joseph Rowntree Foundation)

Mayo, M. (1994) *Communities and Caring* (London: MacMillan)

McCulloch, A. (1997) You've Fucked up the Estate and Now You're Carrying a Briefcase, in P. Hoggett (ed.), *Contested Communities* (Bristol: Policy Press)

Moser, C. (1993) *Gender Planning and Development. Theory, Practice and Training* (London and New York: Routledge)

Naples N. (ed.) (1998) *Community Activism and Feminist Politics: Organizing across Race, Class and Gender* (London: Routledge & Kegan Paul)

Newman, X. and Schare, X. (1997) *Housing Policy Debate*, (4) (Washington: Fannie Mae Foundation)

Nussbaum, M. and Glover, J. (1995) *Women, Culture and Development* (Oxford: Oxford University Press)

Pateman, C. (1989) Feminist Critiques of the Public/Private Dichotomy, in *The Disorder of Women: Democracy, Feminism and Political Theory* (Stanford, California: Stanford University Press)

Perri 6, (1997) *Escaping Poverty: From Safety Nets to Networks of Opportunity* (London: Demos)

Power, A. (1997) *Estates on the Edge: The Social Consequences of Housing in Northen Europe* (London: Macmillan)

Putnam, R.D. (1998) Foreword to Special Issue: Social Capital: Its Importance to Housing and Community Development, *Housing Policy Debate* 9(1) (Washington: Fannie Mae Foundation)

Putnam, R.D. (1993) 'The Prosperous Community: Social Capital and Public Life', *The American Prospect* 13 (Spring)

Putzel, J. (1997) Accounting for the 'Dark Side' of Social Capital: Reading Robert Putnam on Democracy, *Journal of International Development* 9: 7

Sandel, M. (1982) *Liberalism and the Limits of Justice* (Cambridge University Press)

Silver, H. (1995) *Social Exclusion and Social Solidarity*, International Institute for Labour Studies Discussion Paper 69 (Geneva: ILO)

Social Exclusion Union (1998) *Bringing Britain Together: A National Strategy for Neighbourhood Renewal*, Cm 4045 (London: HMSO)

Social Exclusion Unit (1999a) *Bridging the Gap: New Opportunities for 16–18 year olds not in Education, Employment or Training*, Cm 4405 (London: HMSO)

Social Exclusion Unit (1999b) *Teenage Pregnancy*, Cm 4342 (London: HMSO)

Stall, S. and Stoecker, R. (1998) 'Community Organizing or Organizing Community? Gender and the Crafts of Empowerment', *Gender and Society* 12(6) (December): 729–56

Weintraub, J. (1997) 'The Public/Private Distinction', in J. Weintraub and K. Kumar, *Public and Private in Thought and Practice. Perspectives on a Grand Dichotomy* (Chicago: Chicago University Press)

Wolfe, M. (1995) 'Globalization and Social Exclusion: Some Paradoxes', in G. Rodgers, C. Gore and J. Figueirido, *Social Exclusion: Rhetoric, Reality, Responses* (Geneva: International Institute for Labour Studies, ILO)

12
Rebuilding Communities: Common Problems and Approaches

John Pierson

Poverty in the poorest urban neighborhoods is uniquely destructive because it works through a corrosive synergy, unleashing a combination of forces that undermines what is in its path whether local institutions, norms of behavior or the well-being of families and individuals. The segregated, physically devastated environment has few jobs to offer, receives poor services and politically disenfranchises and demobilizes the people.

Despite a range of remedies over the past 30 years, it is fair to say that until recently public policy has done little to roll back this huge social fracture. The picture is now changing, however. Exploring initiatives on both sides of the Atlantic reveals a number of affinities in the predicaments faced. They provide, for those committed to eradicating the worst forms of this poverty, a fund of lessons for rebuilding local communities.

Three themes arising from this experience dominate community building in the new millenium. First is the extent to which regeneration programs will have to harness the power of the market and particularly the labor market. This question is caught up in the debate over the primacy of a 'social' or 'economic' model (Porter 1995). Second is the realization that popular inclusion in programs is a prerequisite to their success. Third is the necessity of reviving our notion of local politics through strategies designed to strengthen the public sphere. Each of these, important as it is on its own, cannot underpin neighborhood renewal without the others.

The chapter explores each of these in turn and in doing so seeks to draw out certain contemporary lessons. In these discussions we consider specific initiatives and approaches that capture the dilemmas facing those who take up community-building tasks.

The labor market and the 'economic model'

The arrival of welfare-to-work policies significantly changes the scope and context of community building. The objective of welfare reform in both the UK and the US is to diminish social exclusion by accelerating the upward social mobility of the poor and compelling greater levels of participation in the labor market. A range of policies flows from this focus on the labor market as the fulcrum of social policy. Among these are vouchers for further choice in housing, education and social services and the concept of individual development accounts – tax exempt accounts used to complete college or vocational training or to buy a home, start a business, supplement a pension – with individual contributions matched by external source. Their purpose is to encourage holding assets and promote geographical mobility.

Welfare to work significantly affects neighborhood revitalization strategies as historically conceived. The question is: how far is community building a function of the strength, or weakness, of the labor market?

Competitive advantages of the inner city

In an important article, Michael Porter of Harvard Business School (Porter 1995) argues that past regeneration efforts have been guided by a 'social model' built around meeting the needs of individuals. Aid to inner cities came in the form of relief programs such as income assistance, housing subsidies and food subsidies – all of which address highly visible and real social needs. Their objective was to lift people out of poverty by redistributing wealth. However the social model failed to address the significant underinvestment in skills and workforce development, either as a result of a plain lack of funding or misdirected programs. He offers a strategy that sees community building as a function of overcoming economic problems, using certain strengths in the marketplace. Inner city areas will succeed to the extent they welcome new investment and provide entrepreneurs with autonomy.

Recognizing and utilizing the competitive advantages of inner-city areas will provide a mainspring for development: 'True empowerment will come only through increased economic opportunity; a statist approach will guarantee continued decline of inner cities just as it hobbled economies of developing countries.' Urban centers, he argues, are now ready to move beyond the stage of community development corporations. CDCs have their strengths but have too often rested on limited and garbled communication between entrepreneurs and advocates for inner cities.

Porter looks for clusters of companies with the critical mass in skills, information, relationships and infrastructure in a given field. Through his research he has found four main advantages which the inner city enjoys:

1. *Strategic locations* – inner cities sit near congested high-rent areas, major business centers, transportation and communications nodes. They offer proximity to potentially powerful local markets.
2. *Inner city markets* – remain poorly served, especially in retailing, financial services and personal services compared with saturated markets elsewhere. Although average inner city incomes are relatively low, high population density translates into an immense market with substantial purchasing power and can be a leading indicator of future trends such as music, food, fashion.
3. *Integration with regional clusters* – ability to access competitive clusters and to compete for downstream products and services; but networks and relationships with surrounding companies woefully underdeveloped
4. *Human resources* – most inner-city residents are industrious and eager to work.

There are disadvantages. The costs of land and building are high as a result of restrictive zoning, building codes and permits. Construction is more regulated than elsewhere and builds in uncertainty and waiting. There is a poor transportation infrastructure.

What is interesting is that Porter's policy does not simply repeat free-market nostrums (as for example did the UK's enterprise zone policy of the 1980s). Government action is required to redirect corporate philanthropy from charitable social services to improving business-to-business relationships especially in job training and management assistance. Inner cities should be first in line for government assistance – infrastructure, crime prevention, environmental clean-up, land development. The recent economic renaissance in Harlem has followed this approach closely. The 'economic model' can be allied with objectives of social justice and based on a partnership between government and civil society. The city of Philadelphia, for example, has also demonstrated this in its sophisticated ten-year plan for recovery which blends historical sensitivity, passionate attention to people's welfare with a commitment to reviving collective bargaining *and* utilizing its workforce's competitive advantages (Office of City Controller of Philadelphia 1999).

Job development and network poverty

Improving connections and creating new effective intermediaries between poor communities and living wage jobs must be a natural focus of community building organizations (Harrison and Weiss 1998). That there are powerful examples of such intermediaries to report such as QUEST and CET, both of which had their origins in Hispanic communities in California and Texas, is a measure of the intensity of the experimentation underway. Certain job development schemes offer an instructive example of how broad coalitions based on the recognition of different interests and embedded in the community can effect radical change. Both schemes serve as models for how a focus on power can create stronger partnerships but because job development itself is now central to community development.

The contemporary labor market has become extremely formidable for those from poor urban neighborhoods. They are characterized by too few higher paying jobs, lower wages and heightened insecurity. Decreasing unemployment has not necessarily reduced poverty. Indeed many new jobs and replacement vacancies are low skilled, as defined by the US Bureau of Labor as 'jobs that can be learned quickly and that generally do not require post-secondary education'. A number of observers have pointed to a 'skills mismatch'. The largest pools of the unemployed – young black inner city males in the US and white male working-class youth in Britain – are perceived by gatekeepers as disruptive, aggressive and unwilling to adapt to social and business norms (Wilson 1996; Power and Tunstall 1997; Power and Mumford 1999; Turok and Edge 1999).

This mismatch has arisen in part because of the increased requirement for 'soft skills' – skills that relate to motivation, teamwork and problem-solving reflecting the move toward services and retail, team production processes, and emphasis of quality of service (Giloth 1998: 5). The emerging service economy itself does not provide orderly advancement (as did the earlier manufacturing economy) because of the gulf between high-wage, high-skill jobs at one end and low-wage, low-skill work at the other. Some economists argue that skills in the technical sense are less critical to employability than attitude, and that the notion of 'soft skills' is simply a way of denoting the willingness to learn and to accept the disciplinary requirements of most workplaces.

The jobs market has become difficult to negotiate; job descriptions are more fluid and firms, focusing on 'core competencies', have hived off entry-level jobs to other organizations. It is becoming increasingly clear that low-income, excluded individuals – no matter how highly motivated – cannot on their own reconstruct and negotiate a city's map of social and business connections (Harrison and Weiss 1998). This is no longer a transaction where individuals acquire skills and then join a job queue where they are individually assessed.

The networks to which job seekers and prospective employers belong fail to intersect. What networks can transmit is some form of trust and commitment. Network poverty is centrally a deficit in the means of securing trust and is strongly associated with a culture of fatalism, in which people have little trust either in the reliability of systems or of other persons. 'Isolation is but one form of network poverty, but in cultural terms it appears to be quite similar to the other kinds – in entrenched enclaves, for example' (Perri 6 1997).

While there is a heavy emphasis on training schemes in New Labour (and formerly in the Clinton administration) their record has been patchy at best. In both the UK and the US training systems have not made a significant impact on the employability of low-income urban residents principally because they are isolated from employers and are not connected to clear paths to employment (Osterman 1999: 133). School-based schemes and stand-alone programs have not generally been productive while employer-centered training produces the greatest payoffs but mainly exist for college graduates and not for low-skilled workers. Osterman (1999) argues that for the most part job development programs are 'content-free', that is they attempt to improve the administrative structure of job training without much attention to what the components of that structure actually deliver. 'The implicit assumption is that if the system is simplified, performance information generated, and a market for training programs created (with the invisible hand residing in the one-stop center) then the issue of content will work itself out.' Previous history, however, does not lend confidence to that outcome (Osterman 1999: 140). Britain's time-consuming reform of vocational training from the late 1980s onwards offers an illustrative example of the difficulties of matching intent with accomplishment.

Because of this complexity training and job placement must be mediated by collective institutions if they are to be fully effective. 'The individual who seeks skills and jobs must be supported by the greater economic and political power of intermediary agents – organisations that can break paths, open doors, insist on quality services, and negotiate collectively with employers and governments' (Weiss and Harrison 1998: 38–9). The labor market intermediary is an organization that matches an employer with a job opening and a person who wants that job. It exists to create an advantage for applicants whether through information or networks (Osterman 1999: 133). In areas of concentrated poverty they offer integrated services, more intensive and person-centered support for the unemployed and at the same time able to provide businesses with closer support than city-wide organisations. The 'intermediate labor market' offers long-term unemployed temporary work experience at a reasonable wage in the course of providing socially useful services combined with vocational training and personal development.

Most importantly successful job search assistance programs can change the structure of local labor markets. To do so they need to provide information that certain kinds of social networks would have delivered had they existed. They emphasize where to look for jobs, work readiness, how to prepare a CV, and how to handle interviews rather than training in a specific skill. Good programs teach the behavioral attributes necessary together with the norms regarding what is and what is not acceptable in work discipline. They combine close personal support while advocating the worth of their trainees, provide informal recruiting and follow-up counseling.

Establishing an effective workforce development program for a locality underpins the necessity of focusing on interests of the parties involved, including community residents, and creating organizations with authority and the power to negotiate. Programs require reciprocity with local employers with settings defined by, and applicants selected by, employers. The emphasis is not so much on skills in a technical sense as on perceived attitudes and socialization. There are never enough jobs, but the connectedness and reputation of the training organization and its embeddedness in the community powerfully affects its influence in finding work for its candidates. Equally community organizations are interested in work available locally which pay a living wage.

The Center for Employment Training (CET) in San Jose, California, provides one effective model for matching disadvantaged populations with job opportunities. A number of evaluations have established that CET trainees are placed into jobs at higher rates, remain in those jobs longer and over time enjoy substantial gains in earnings than other programs. It achieves this for constituents who in the main are unemployed farm workers, lone mothers on welfare, out of school youth, ex-offenders and people whose second language is English. Because of this documented success the Department of Labour is funding the replication of CET's formula – 'bringing to scale' – in other urban areas in an initiative of great interest.

Weiss and Harrison note two qualitative characteristics that account for CET's success. First, it has 'institutionalized the employer ethos' and interfaces with trusted training networks of companies. Firms became important stakeholders. Training facilities resemble the workplace, while supervisors and trainers, who come from local companies, handle any liaison difficulties. Industrial Advisory Boards and Technical Advisory Committees take the lead in curriculum development and fund raising. There is continuous and immediate contact with the corporate world; the established trust is crucial to success.

> CET works on both the supply and demand sides of the labour market; its approach to the latter explicitly recognises the importance of inserting itself into precisely those networks that companies already value. CET provides screening, reliability, follow-up counselling, and high quality labour. (Harrison and Weiss 1998)

Second, CET's connection to a social movement is central to its success. It is embedded in the history and struggles of west coast Hispanic communities with its genesis in the farmworkers' union and Hispanic politics and culture.

Participation and popular inclusion

The second theme is the growing awareness that most successful efforts to revitalize poor urban neighborhoods are either begun by local residents and their community institutions, or are based on collaboration with local citizens and receive popular legitimacy. It has now become possible to see this fact in a clearer light. Lisbeth Shore, in her authoritative survey of American anti-poverty programs, concludes that it is impossible to escape the fact that community building is based on the belief that inner-city residents and institutions can and must be primary actors in efforts to solve the problems of their neighborhoods (Shore 1997).

Virtually all the principal community development programs require some level of resident participation, from City Challenge, the single regeneration budget (SRB) and New Deal for Communities (NDC) in the UK to Empowerment Zones in the US and the *'politique de ville'* in France (HUD 1997; SEU 1998; DETR 1999). But participation is inseparable from considerations of power. In both the UK and the US residents' participation in urban revitalization programs has too often remained formal and unrealized while service agencies or local political interests capture community development activity for their own ends. There is no magic formula simply because the critical role of power is recognized however. Rather the reverse: *only* through politics – understood in its broadest definition – can matters of power and interests be harnessed to create effective, broad-based programs.

Yet the significance of this 'shift to the people' raises many questions over the degree of influence local residents have in program planning and implementation. Nor have researchers and evaluators necessarily provided sufficient clarification.

Stoutland (1999) asks whether it is possible for revitalization programs to be controlled by their communities. Funders, whether nonprofit or governmental organizations, will not cede power to the degree that they lose control of the project they are paying for. They will want to retain the 'golden share', so to speak. If this is so, won't local residents and organizations face the dilemma of sacrificing control over decision making in order to ensure financial survival?

She further asks how we can determine the extent to which an initiative is community controlled. The standard indicator of community control over an initiative is the number of residents on the partnership board. Those whose boards primarily consist of residents are held as an example of resident control but this ignores other processes in which power and influence may be wielded. Outside this one criterion however, little further work has been done in trying to develop further indicators of resident control (Stoutland, 1999).

Indeed, a great many studies demonstrate the difficulty in converting aspirations on resident participation found in guidelines or even in formal arrangements for representation into resident influence. The obstacles to participation and the discouragement faced by residents are enormous. Stoecker (1997) gives several reasons why residents find it difficult to participate in community development corporations that are valid for initiatives generally. Partnership boards can give only broad guidance because of the technical nature of the projects. Board membership is neither glamorous nor exciting. Indeed it is often tedious, time-consuming and difficult work for people with little margin of personal resource. His findings strongly echo Gittell's study of participation in an earlier generation of program as well as broader studies (Gittell, 1980; Verba et al. 1995).

The great number of tasks and sheer range of objectives of comprehensive programs also present difficulties for residents. To reduce crime, improve education, provide training, raise health standards, create jobs – all are typically present in program objectives and are all extremely difficult to achieve (HUD 1997; DETR 1999). As a number of observers have pointed out, such objectives run directly counter to the macro-trends in the economy and to the direction of government policy which has sought to remove constraints on the functioning of the markets. These would be enormous responsibilities for the most powerful agencies of central government; now they have in effect been delegated by central government to local actors without providing commensurate powers and resources (Halperin 1995; Turok 1999).

It is not surprising, for example, that several reports on the effectiveness of participatory partnerships within programs under the single regeneration budget (SRB) in the UK have found that they were simply marriages of convenience set up to achieve other objectives such as auxiliary funding for local statutory services. Partnerships were often dominated by strategic local agencies (such as Training and Enterprise Councils or local authorities in the UK) but were using concepts of participation and partnership to secure legitimacy and improve funding, but which disguised the imbalance of power between parties. In her examination of four Scottish Urban Partnerships Hastings found a tangle of organizations and interests each hoping to re-educate the other. Theories underpinning partnership such as synergy and mutual transformation, proved to be too broad to explain what was happening on the ground. In the main the partnerships she investigated were built solely around the coordination of expenditure and not on the innovative, creative interplay of the different cultures and objectives of the partners (Hastings 1996). Others have found that the distraction of creating partnership structures, whether collaboratives in the US or partnership boards in the UK became an end in itself (Taylor 1995; Chaskin and Peters 1997).

With the introduction of Empowerment Zone/Enterprise Community initiative in 1993 the Clinton administration aimed to invest in both people and place and to create locally initiated strategies that bring together local agencies, business and neighborhood organizations. The principles endorsed in the EZ/EC program restated the original ideals of community development in the 1960s: The strategic planning process should give voice to local residents' own vision for change, provide economic opportunity through private sector jobs and training and, sustain community development through comprehensive coordination through community-based partnerships with all sectors represented. To achieve these it relied on 2.5 billion dollars in tax incentives for hiring local people and planning boards to ensure the representation of all sectors of the community including poor residents and government agencies.

Given the opportunities to participate local citizens did so with considerable energy at the grassroots. The lessons drawn from the implementation of the EZ program confirm the difficulties that lie in wait for programs that attempt to base partnerships on consensus without making explicit the interests or the relative share of power. Gittell and colleagues have studied the EZ/EC implementation in Chicago, Atlanta and New York. In Atlanta, despite statutory requirements giving community groups a distinct role in implementation, their effectiveness in high poverty neighborhoods 'was limited by a lack of resources, the necessity of working with the established elites to leverage influence, and their exclusion from the informal structures of power' (Gittell et al. 1998).

This was also true of New York. Ironically in Chicago, a city where local community development organizations have historically had great strength and influence in city-wide coalitions, that very strength produced prolonged struggles over the governance of the EZ program. Although implementation had begun in the city with a promising start, with unprecedented levels of cooperation between the neighborhoods and City Hall, patronage politics of the city finally won out.

The experience of implementation provides another indication of how established patterns of political power will not only limit the independence and growth of community development organizations but throw up effective local political barriers to their capacities *even in the middle of implementing processes designed to enhance those capacities.* Weir (1999) also concluded that empowerment zones do little to create civic involvement. 'The limited achievement of empowerment zones in community building and development reflects the central flaw in the program's animating premise: that consensual decision making among groups with vastly unequal power can transform and empower poor communities.' (1999: 168).

In relation to central city areas of multiple and intense deprivation it becomes increasingly more difficult to make resident participation credible. There is simply too little margin of resource at the disposal of local residents to support grassroots and organizational activity at the level necessary to make for effective participation (Halperin 1995). The irreducible role of government as 'the broker of last resort' becomes more, not less critical as a result.

Although resident participation is a requirement in HOPE VI, the program to rescue public housing projects in the US, standards for measuring it were left vague both in legislation and in HUD's guidelines which called only for 'meaningful opportunities for participation' (HUD 1998). But since any plans deeply affect residents, either through displacement or upheaval the participative initiatives under HOPE VI have entailed numerous battles, local votes, resident veto of plans, litigation, resignations of public housing authority directors, the formation and reformation of resident committees. Participation of residents could proceed fitfully at best against the background of partial implementation and demolition. As Salama has observed: 'Resident participation becomes a strange concept when virtually no residents remain to participate. Although a meaningful give-and-take is preferred, one cannot legislate sincerity and good faith on both sides' (Salama 1999: 131).

There is, then, persistent tension between sustaining a grassroots base that seeks to exert influence within an initiative and securing financial resources from outside funders. Once significant resources are obtained perhaps relying on participatory channels, there is a danger that other objectives are set aside for fear of alienating funding allies. Weir (1999) proposes that one way to diminish these conflicts is through coalition building with a focus on inherently less contested assets such as building networks and job links which do not necessarily carry threats to those with political power to defend. Equally the use of intermediaries, such as the Local Initiative Support Corporation (see chapter 4) to raise the profile of community development among funders and to open channels between funders and projects is an effective way of minimizing such tensions.

Participation contains its own dynamic. A consultation process, done well, can lead to further pressure for more active engagement by local residents. Done badly it can lead to manipulation and simply reinforce passivity and cynicism (Gaventa 1999). Despite the risks inherent in the concept of social capital it is evident that where groups have a history of trust and of working together through effective networks the capacity for participation is enhanced. Gaventa draws an important lesson for policy: 'Mandates for participation from "above" must be linked with pre-existing capacities for participation "from below". If there has not been a prior history of local action and organizational development, there will be fewer building blocks for larger-scale participation to occur' (1999: 35). The Industrial Areas Foundation in the US and the Citizens Organising Foundation in the UK make the same point – without power, without 'standing' or influence – there can be no program success.

Politics and power

The ambiguities around participation cannot be resolved as long as the specific interests of agencies and groups remain unarticulated hiding an extreme imbalance of power. Partnership promotes a discourse that constructs relations without reference to the balance of power within those relationships. Those who take the discourse at face value and call for greater 'empowerment' through partnership only further extend the ambiguity for this essentially is an impossible task. An inquiry into participation and an articulation of interests by degrees leads to questions of political mobilization and creation of countervailing power.

In examining the difficulties and dilemmas around resident participation in community development the notion of 'countervailing power' provides a different way of understanding participation from that of the ambiguous language of partnership, and empowerment. The creation of countervailing power through a mobilized grassroots organization does not necessarily undermine formal attempts at 'partnership' but is more explicit in its understanding of interests and self-interests involved when organizations or groups begin negotiating effective, durable arrangements.

So it is important to think clearly about power and how it is deployed both within specific urban regimes and revitalization programs themselves. There are clear signs that this is happening as rejuvenated citizen politics emerges to fill the gaps opening up in political authority across state, region, and locality. It is revealing to watch this development particularly in the United Kingdom where central authority has been so strong and the people perceived more as 'subjects' than citizens. The Citizen Organising Foundation for example, has attained credibility and effectiveness in east London, Merseyside, Sheffield, the Black Country, northeast Wales and Bristol. Each local organization has established an independent base within faith congregations and worked diligently to bring civic institutions such as schools into their broad-based organizing efforts. They strive for independence from government funding by raising monies from charitable trusts and religious organizations. While they have adapted their methods and strategies from the work of the Industrial Areas Foundation in the United States COF organizations have successfully adapted this approach to British conditions. They draw in particular on the inspiration and traditions of the struggle for social justice in the trade union movement and dissenting religious communities.

At one level COF organizations prosecute an intense struggle with the problems and deprivations that confront their local communities such as the withdrawal of banking services, fighting the presence of toxic waste, the outflow of capital from neighborhoods. They initiate 'actions' that bring people into direct contact with politicians and organizations that shape their lives. They also act in concert as in their campaign for 'financial citizenship' in which representatives from 100 community organizations converged on Canary Wharf in 1998 to lobby and open a dialogue with the Financial Services Authority about the absence of banking and insurance facilities in run-down inner-city areas. COF-trained leaders made clear how, on the one hand, disadvantaged neighborhoods suffer from the withdrawal of straightforward banking and insurance services and, on the other, are vulnerable to dubious financial products from salesmen from mainstream institutions as well as loan sharks (Observer 1998; COF 2000).

The concerns of COF organizations are not just about locality but also have the aim of strengthening the 'public sphere' – the public arena for debate – and to re-establish a fuller conception of politics as fundamental to the development of full citizenship and the revival of local democracy. Citizens are not born but made. COF aims to 'reweave the fabric of UK society' by reinventing the art of politics at the neighborhood level, by developing the tools of leadership, compromise, negotiation, public discourse and power. This dual interest in the local issue *and* civil society sets COF apart. Those mediating institutions that were once the largest and most successful in providing civil society with its energy and capacity – schools, workplace organizations, trade unions – are precisely those that have been most undercut by the turn toward aggressive market policies. In particular COF organizations rely on the energy and commitment embodied in faith congregations. They draw on the trust, social networks and norms of reciprocity which faith communities bring to the building of 'power-organisations' (Wood 1997: 601). They further contribute significantly 'in projecting that power into the public arena to reshape the life conditions and structural pressures'. COF politics then is an explicit attempt at reversing civic enfeeblement.

Throughout the process COF organizers work both toward mobilizing sufficient local momentum to win the issue *and* to position the organization to accumulate power for the long term. This involves selecting higher level issues to engage with and adopting more complex alliances and collaborative relationships in order to influence the outcome on major issues. It is extremely important to understand that organizers do not undertake this work themselves but have developed a local, diverse leadership, confident and trained in negotiation and well briefed in terms of the issue and in expert opinion on that issue. For COF as with the IAF in the US politics is a fundamental component of social development. Conflict is part of politics and to a degree is a constitutive element of the organising process. 'It provides the drama that sustains members' interest, the whetstone on which leaders' skill and political acumen are sharpened, and the antidote to efforts by economic or political elites to manipulate the organisation.' (Wood 1997: 602)

Though it is noted for its combative 'actions' against selected targets conflict represents only one aspect of their approach. COF also aims to construct broad coalitions across class and ethnic lines. In this conflict and negotiation, self-interest and building shared interests go hand in hand. Effective political collaboration and constructing coalitions require the open expression of discrete, even opposing interests. The politics of coalition, of collaboration or partnership cannot take place without it. As Wood (1998: 602) has put it, 'Community organising as a way of projecting social capital-based power into the public arena offers precisely a way into more democratic politics. [This is] the hard work of politics, not the illusion of a conflict-free civil society.'

The approach and style of COF, as with the IAF in the US has had its measure of criticism, in particular from those who argue that it does not challenge capitalism or the power elites sufficiently (Henderson and Salmon 1995: 22, 30; Marquez 1993). In pursuing broad coalitions, by invoking universals such as 'community', 'civil society' and the public sphere it fails to respond to the interests and necessity of identity, particularly those social identities – based on gender and race – that are formed through oppression. These critics argue that the emphasis on 'winnable issues' means that the broad-base organization cannot respond to the particular needs or demands of minority groups. 'Organising largely ignores the ideological and structural nature of inequalities in our society, and ... spends much of its time taking up real, but secondary issues.' It equates justice with getting a bit more of the 'cake' for 'me/my community' and does not demand real change (Henderson and Salmon 1995).

Such criticism is to misconstrue the activities of the COF and the nature of local politics that it seeks to revive. The COF and the IAF place their greatest emphasis on revivifying the public arena, the *agora*, and see politics and the building of effective local independent political power as indispensable. They share with the politics of recognition the notion that diversity – of peoples, interests, cultures – characterizes the public sphere. But so do alliances. Precisely because of its diversity and clash of interests, engagement with these interests and building bridges between them is necessary to get things done.

The perspective of COF and the IAF throws a new light on constructions of partnership where an ambience of 'cozyness' prevails. Conduct in partnerships is often based on a private, non-political, agency-based culture that draws its models of leadership from the corporate world and bureaucratic state, both of whose interests are served by this illusion that partnership entails the feeling that 'we're all in this together'. This avoids accountability for action and certainly evades the question of whose interests are and are not being met. Those with amassed power are more than willing to exploit the unease over conflict or tension within a diverse coalition. In partnerships there is a strong presumption of agreement; it becomes the unwritten rule. Once that is in place 'action' – concrete local steps toward recognizing interests and rebalancing the distribution of power – becomes difficult. Talking becomes the action.

The perspective of COF and other grassroots organizations like it embraces the realization that resolving urban social and economic problems *only* happens if sufficient local political power can be amassed by independent grassroots organizations. It encourages the recognition that program development occurs as much when groups acknowledge their interests and are prepared to assert them through a political (but not necessarily a party-political) process. Building countervailing power means 'confronting decision makers . . . with pressures that push them in a particular direction. Presumably they face other sets of pressures pointing toward a different outcome. The decisions that actually result represent some compromise between these competing pressures.' (Osterman 1999: 163). The concept of reaching widely shared goals as well as creating a more inclusive political regime through building organizational independence and political influence *outside* formal partnership arrangements may seem strange. Yet such organizations may have a greater impact as much because they compel stakeholders to examine true interests within a long-term framework than because they are deceived by arrangements which promotes false unity.

References

Bingham, R.D. and Mier, R. (eds.) (1993) *Theories of Local Economic Development: Perspectives From Across the Disciplines* (Newbury Park, Califonia; London and New Delhi: Sage Publications Inc.)

Byrd, M. (1999) Urbanism, Metropolitan Development, and Identity Politics: Social Psychological Considerations of Left-Wing Mainline Organizing in Metropolitan Nashville, *Journal for the Scientific Study of Religion* 38: 1, 146–59

Chaskin, R. and Peters, C. (1997) *Governance in Empowerment Zone Communities* (Chicago: The Chapin Center for Children)

Citizen Organising Foundation Institute (n.d.), *A Banking Audit for Financial Citizenship*

de Souza Briggs, X. (1998) Brownkids in White Suburbs: Housing Mobility and the Many Faces of Social Capital, *Housing Policy Debate*, 9: 1, 177–221

de Souza Briggs, X. and Mueller, E.J. with Sullivan, M.L. (1997) *From Neighbourhood to Community: Evidence on the Social Effects of Community Development* (New York: Community Development Research Center)

DETR (1999) *New Deals for Communities: Phase Proposals Guidance for Applicants* (London: DETR)

Ferguson, R.F. and Dickens, W.T. (1999) *Urban Problems and Community Development* (Washington, DC: Brookings Institution Press)

Gaventá, J. (1999) Participation, Poverty and Social Exclusion in North and South, *Institute of Labour Studies* 111, 24–38

Giloth, R.P. (1998) *Jobs & Economic Development: Strategies and Practice* (Newbury Park, Califonia; London and New Delhi: Sage Publications Inc.)

Gittell, M. (1980) *Limits to Citizen Participation: The Decline of Community Organizations* (Newbury Park: Sage)

Halperin, R. (1995) *Rebuilding the Inner City* (New York: Columbia University Press)

Harrison, B. and Weiss, M. (1998) *Workforce Development Networks: Community-Based Organizations and Regional Alliances* (Newbury Park, Califonia; London and New Delhi: Sage Publications Inc.)

Hastings, A. (1996) Unravelling the Process of 'Partnership' in Urban Regeneration Policy, Urban Studies 33: 2, 253–68

HUD (1997) *The State of Our Cities* (Washington: US Department of Housing and Urban Development)

Katznelson, I. (1992) *Marxism and the City* (Oxford: Clarendon Press)

Marquez, B. (1993) The Industrial Areas Foundation and the Mexican-American Community in Texas: The Politics of Issue Mobilization, *Contributions in Political Science* 333, 127–146

Murnane, R.J. and Levy, F. (1996) *Teaching the New Basic Skills: Principles for Educating Children to Thrive in a Changing Economy* (New York, London, Toronto, Sydney, Singapore: Martin Kessler Books, The Free Press)

Observer (1998) Direct Action: The New Politics, 15 November

Osterman, P. (1999) *Securing Prosperity – The American Labor Market: How It Has Changed and What to Do about It* (Princeton, New Jersey: Princeton University Press)

Parkinson, M. (1998) *Combating Social Exclusion: Lessons from Area-based Programmes in Europe* (Bristol: The Policy Press)

Perri, G. (1997) *Escaping Poverty: From Safety Nets to Networks of Opportunity* (London: Demos)

Plummer, J. and Zipfel, T. (1998) *Regeneration and Employment: A New Agenda for TECs, Communities and Partnerships* (Bristol: The Policy Press)

Porter, M. (1995) The Competitive Advantage of the Inner City, *Harvard Business Review*

Power, A. (1997) *Estates on the Edge: The Social Consequences of a Mass Housing in Northern Europe* (London: Macmillan, and New York: St. Martin's Press Inc.)

Power, A. and Mumford, K. (1999) *The Slow Death of Great Cities? Urban Abandonment or Urban Renaissance* (York: York Publishing Services)

Power, A. and Tunstall, R. (1997) *Dangerous Disorder: Riots and Violent Disturbances in Thirteen Areas of Britain, 1991–92* (York: York Publishing Services)

Salama, J.J. (1999) The Redevelopment of Distressed Public Housing: Early Results from HOPE VI Projects in Atlanta, Chicago and San Antonio, *Housing Policy Debate* 10(1): 95–142

Shore, L. (1997) *Common Purpose: Strengthening Families and Neighborhoods To Rebuild America* (New York: Anchor Books)

Social Exclusion Unit (1998) *Bringing Britain Together: A National Strategy for Neighbourhood Renewal*, Cmnd 4045 (London: HMSO)

Stoeker, R. (1997) The CDC Model of Urban Redevelopment, *Journal of Urban Affairs* 19: 1, 1–22

Stokes, P. and Knight, B. (1997) *Working Paper No. 2: Organising A Civil Society* (Birmingham: Foundation for Civil Society)

Stoutland, S. (1999) Community Development Corporations, in R. Ferguson and W. Hickens, *Urban Problems and Community Development* (Washington, DC: Brookings Institution)

Taylor, M. (1995) *Unleashing the Potential: Bringing Residents to the Centre of Regeneration* (York: Joseph Rowntree Foundation)

Turok, I. (1999) Employment in British Cities, *Radical Statistics* 71, 3–9

Turok, I. and Edge, N. (1999) *The Jobs Gap in Britain's Cities: Employment Loss and Labour Market Consequences* (Bristol: Policy Press)

Verba, S., K. Schlozman and H. Brady (1995) *Voice and Equality: Civic Voluntarism in American Politics* (Cambridge, Mass: Harvard University Press)

Warren, M.R. (1998) 'Community Building and Political Power: A Community Organizing Approach to Democratic Renewal', *American Behavioural Scientist* 42: 1, 78–92

Weir, M. (1999) Power, Money, and Politics, in R. Ferguson and W. Dickens, *Urban Problems and Community Development* (Washington, DC: Brookings Institution)

Wilson, J. (1996) *When Work Disappears: The World of the New Urban Poor* (New York: Knopf)

Wilson, R.H. (ed.) (1997) *Public Policy and Community: Activism and Governance in Texas* (Austin, Texas: University of Texas Press)

Wood, R.L. (1994) Faith in Action: Religious Resources for Political Success in Three Congregations, *Sociology of Religion* 55: 4, 397–417

Wood, R.L. (1997) 'Social Capital and Political Culture: God Meets Politics in the Inner City', *American Behavioral Scientist* 40: 5, 595–605

Index

29398